BEST, PELE,
AND A HALF-TIME
BOVRIL

BEST, PELE,
AND A HALF-TIME
BOVRIL

A NOSTALGIC LOOK AT THE 1970s –
FOOTBALL'S LAST GREAT DECADE

ANDREW SMART

JOHN BLAKE

This edition published in 2014

ISBN: 978 1 78219 886 4

British Library Cataloguing-in-Publication Data:

A catalogue record for this book is available from the British Library.

Design by www.envydesign.co.uk

Printed and bound in Great Britain by CPI Group (UK) Ltd

1 3 5 7 9 10 8 6 4 2

This is for J-J, the one and only.

'Choose the job you love, and you'll never have to work a day in your life.'
Confucius

CONTENTS

FOREWORD

I don't think anyone would argue that over the past 30-odd years professional football has changed out of all recognition.

Off the field it has become a corporate world of big business, high finance, tycoons and agents.

And even when the players step across that white line it is different.

Character is certainly not a word I would use about today's footballers. They all seem to be clones, the majority quite boring.

I played with people like Stan Bowles and Charlie George – real characters. Before my time there was Rodney Marsh and Frank Worthington, players that people would pay good money to turn up and watch. How many are there today? For my money, the last real character was Gazza.

And you could say the same about the referees. We had Clive Thomas, Roger Kirkpatrick – refs you could have a bit of banter with, refs who gave as good as they got and who you respected for it.

BEST, PELE AND A HALF-TIME BOVRIL

It's all changed. Money rules everything at the expense of tradition and a real love of the game.

Andy Smart reminds us of the days when football had a real sense of value and fans could easily identify with the teams and players they supported. The great names like Best, Pele and my old team mate, John Robertson. Great games like the day Hereford shocked Newcastle in the FA Cup. And great managers like that pair I played for – Clough and Taylor.

For those reasons and those memories, I certainly have no problem with Andy's argument that the 1970s was football's last great decade.

Garry Birtles – twice winner of the European Cup with Nottingham Forest; Manchester United and England

INTRODUCTION

HERE WE GO, HERE WE GO

When a brittle north-westerly wind is blowing down off the Cheviots, there can be few bleaker outposts of the Football League than Brunton Park, Carlisle.

I remember it well.

A glacial February afternoon in 1979. Down on the pitch in front of a sparse and well-muffled crowd of diehards, Carlisle United were entertaining Mansfield Town in the old Division Two. (I use the word *entertaining* in its social context, not as a critique of the match.) From my freezing, hard, wooden seat in the press box, I attempted to deliver a coherent report via a faint telephone line to the *Football Post* in Nottingham. I gazed up at the frosty green hillside in the middle distance, arched behind what is now catchily named the Pioneer Foods Stand, and tried to count the sheep.

It was at romantic venues such as Brunton Park in Carlisle, Edgeley Park in Stockport, Feethams in Darlington and

Plainmoor in Torquay where I spent most Saturday afternoons during the late 1970s. At Spotland – the once-rickety home of Rochdale – I recall a game of near-stultifying tedium. At last, the final minute; Mansfield's stout defensive performance had given them the better of things for much of the previous 89. My bellowed dictation reflected this superiority with, perhaps, a little bias for the benefit of our local readership.

With the referee about to bring a blessed end to the stalemate, the Stags stupidly gave away a penalty and I had to report, faithfully and accurately, that the official's decision was wholly justified. Sitting in Spotland's open press box, with spectator seating all around, I felt a light tap on my shoulder. I glanced around to be confronted by the gurning face of a veteran 'Dale supporter. 'Eh, lad,' he said in a broad Lancashire tone from beneath a grease-stained cap, its peak sharp enough to slice bread. 'That's first true word thee 'ave spoken all t'match.' At that precise moment in my young and stuttering career I wondered if my journalistic heroes, Ian Wooldridge or Hugh McIlvanney, had ever had such a richly invigorating experience on a visit to Old Trafford or the San Siro.

These isolated memories underpin my *raison d'être* for this book. I missed much of the live action of the 1970s. While Liverpool were winning titles and European Cups – while the 'real' football was unfolding at Highbury and at Old Trafford ... while my own club, Nottingham Forest, was pre-eminent under Brian Clough – I was trawling around the backwaters of the Victoria Ground, Hartlepool, and Gay Meadow in Shrewsbury.

I have to confess, I was in my element. I had been hooked on football from Day One, 26 October 1957. I was 10 years old and my father took me to the City Ground to watch Forest play Blackpool. To be honest, I don't remember too much about the match. We stood on the terraces but not together. As was the quaint tradition in those days, I was passed down to the front and did not see my father again until the final whistle blew. If truth be told, he was not a great fan but I was intoxicated by the atmosphere of a 41,000 crowd: a monochrome, flat-capped mass of bodies out of which rose a thick pall of steam and tumultuous roars. The ball was dark brown; it was also thickly stitched. The players' boots were laced to just below the knee. The shorts were baggy and flapping.

I recall one incident from that match, which Forest lost 2-1. They had an abrasive, impudent little inside forward named Johnny Quigley. Right in front of me he got the ball and took on the first Blackpool player who came in with a quick challenge. He just happened to be Stanley Matthews – Footballer of the Year; Legend; Hero. Quigley nut-megged him. Matthews was not best pleased but the crowd loved it.

Over the next 20 years Forest had their fleeting moments: an FA Cup win in 1959, when FA Cup wins meant something; Division One runners-up in 1967. But no one in their right mind would dare to have predicted that Forest, along with many other sides now viewed as bit-part extras, would play a leading role in football's last great decade.

Perhaps my album of the 1970s is coloured with self-interest. For me, it was *the* decade. Not a particularly great period of world history: the first real oil crisis squeezing the pips out of world economies; Britain gripped by industrial turmoil; the three-day week and power cuts; the Troubles in Northern Ireland; tension in the Middle East. The permissive 1960s had passed. The times they were a-changing.

Football was no different. The 1960s had seen the end of the maximum wage, bringing the most profound changes the game would see until the Bosman ruling. As the 1970s dawned the first million-pound transfer fee was still nine years away. But 'player power' was fast approaching. Big business was taking over too; balance sheets were soon to become more important than team sheets.

The 1970s saw the last throes of the working-man's game. It was football's last democratic decade when clubs from the sticks could dream of a championship, the FA Cup, even European glory. From Everton in 1970 to Liverpool in 1979, *six* different clubs won the Division One title: Liverpool four times; Derby County two; Everton, Arsenal, Nottingham Forest, Leeds United. The chances of a Derby, Forest or Leeds doing that now are unimaginable. Since 1980, the big four – Manchester United, Liverpool, Chelsea and Arsenal – have won the title 29 times out of a possible 34.

So we can be forgiven for looking back nostalgically at the 1970s. It was a different time, a different era; a different world. And despite the hysteria whipped up by the media in trying to persuade armchair fans that the Premier League race has never been more exciting, try telling that to fans of Wigan, Norwich, Aston Villa, Everton, Fulham, Sunderland and the rest of the Premiership cannon fodder whose fans cannot begin to dream about challenging for the title because it will never happen.

Football in the 1970s was played on a Saturday afternoon and kicked off at 3pm. Players ran around but never rolled around. The only person you saw wearing multi-coloured boots was Elton John, and gloves were the exclusive possession of goalkeepers.

It seemed like every club, no matter how unfashionable, had a player worth paying to see. Chelsea had Alan Hudson, QPR had Stan Bowles, there was Tony Currie at Sheffield United, Frank Worthington at Leicester, Mick Channon at Southampton,

Charlie George at Arsenal. And there was a chap called Best at Manchester United. It was also the era of pioneering black players such as Cyrille Regis, Garth Crooks, Viv Anderson and Brendan Batson, who combated systemic racism from the terraces. Batson told of playing for West Brom at West Ham. Bananas were hurled from the crowd as the team warmed up; Batson ate one. Regis shoved another down his shorts and the two players volleyed others back into the crowd.

English clubs dominated European competitions, with Liverpool the Goliath of the game. This was the age of the Anfield dynasty created by Bill Shankly and embellished by Bob Paisley, and a coterie of stars such as Kevin Keegan, John Toshack and Ray Clemence. Four years out of five Liverpool won the Division One title, plus two European Cups, breaking the Bayern Munich stranglehold on the trophy. Incredibly, their run of success at home and on the continent was halted not by Manchester United, Arsenal or Chelsea but by humble, newly promoted Forest under the less-than-humble Brian Clough. He had already won the title with Derby in the early 1970s and might have brought the European Cup to the old Baseball Ground, had they not been the victims of several dubious decisions in a semi-final against Juventus. More than 30 years on, such achievements by modest provincial clubs seem all the more remarkable because of the way football has changed. A bit like climbing Everest in flip-flops.

We will never see the like again, that is for sure. Ask John McGovern, who was Clough's captain and lynchpin in both his Derby championship side and the all-conquering Forest team that scrambled out of the old Second Division, won the First Division title the next season and then won the old-style, infinitely more entertaining, European Cup twice on the bounce.

It will never happen again, no team will repeat what we did. It is just not possible. Things have changed too much in the game now. A team like Forest could not just go from the Championship and then challenge realistically in Europe. I don't even think a promoted team could challenge for the title in their first season – it just can't happen. The gap between the top teams in the Premiership and everyone else is just so big. Could you see any of the teams at the top of the Championship at the minute going into the Premiership and challenging for the title next season? Their priority now is just to survive, to avoid being relegated.

The balance began to tip unfavourably towards the heavyweights during the 1970s. Powerful figures at powerful clubs were waking up to the potential of television and the first mutterings of a European league were heard. Alan Hardaker, the formidable Football League secretary in the early 1970s, predicted there could also be a British league featuring the top teams from the home countries. It never happened but you could follow his train of thought.

Leicester City chairman Len Shipman, a wily administrator who was also president of the Football League, was perhaps the first to sense the effect these changes would have as the decade unfolded. He said that football was 'facing its own industrial revolution ... as clubs, players and public adjust to new status and new ideas and concepts'. He spelled out the challenges that football in the 1970s had to face and overcome:

1 'We have to build a new relationship between

clubs and supporters.' *Well, it might be argued that long-suffering fans are still waiting for that and it seems further away now than ever.*

2 'We have to encourage a new relationship between clubs and players, encouraging the latter to realise their full earning potential.' *No argument there. With their extraordinary contracts and 'image rights', the players now have more earning potential than a Wall Street banker.*

3 'The present League edifice has to be moulded to take shape within the emerging structure of the new society.' *What would Shipman think if he could see the Football League today, cast adrift by the Premier League overlords who, in June 2012, negotiated a television deal for £3.018 billion?*

Shipman concluded with a dire warning: 'The roots of football in this country are almost certain to founder for want of nourishment if the smaller club is not to be allowed to live. The League could disintegrate at the very time it is enjoying its greatest success. Wise counsel, based on wider considerations than self-interest must prevail.'

Sorry, Mr Shipman, but no one was listening.

Those prophetic words underscored the dark side of the 1970s. Attendances plummeted like News Corp shares, tumbling through the years to their lowest level since the Second World War. Perhaps the biggest single cause was hooliganism. The yob culture invaded the terraces, and hooliganism – which came to be known as 'the English disease' – brought tribal violence to football, sending terrified mums, dads and children scurrying for cover. Many of them never returned to football.

Novelist Martin Amis captured the consequence of hooliganism as succinctly as anyone, writing, 'Every British male, at some time or other, goes to his last football match. It may very well be his first football match.'

The attendance slump was also blamed on football overkill. Too many competitions – remember the Anglo Scottish Cup, the Simod Cup and the Watney Cup? Too many matches, too much TV coverage. Yet weighed against today's satellite soccer-fest, European Champions League, non-stop qualifying and competition to win the European Championship or the World Cup, and booming attendances, that argument is less powerful.

A more telling factor might be that football was becoming boring. It was the legacy of Ramsey's wingless wonders of 1966. There was a select group of mavericks that people would pay good money to watch but there were also a lot of faceless teams filled with muscle-strapped midfield players who enjoyed nothing better than stifling the life out of a game. Even Liverpool, for all their achievements, were sometimes graceless in the ascendency; past masters at killing a game off with endless exchanges along their cultured back four.

But we should do nothing to detract from Liverpool's domination, which heralded a golden decade for British sides in European football. Liverpool won the European Cup in 1977 and 1978, Forest in 1979 and again in 1980. Manchester City (1970), Chelsea (1971) and Rangers (1972) all won the now defunct Cup Winners Cup. Arsenal (1970) and Leeds (1971) won the Fairs Cup. Then it became the UEFA Cup, which was won by Tottenham Hotspur (1972) and Liverpool (1973 and 1976).

Paradoxically, while English clubs were enjoying all this unfettered success the international segment of our game was, to put it simply but accurately, downright dire. At the dawn of the decade World Cup winner Alf Ramsey was preparing his defence of the trophy in the hostile climate of Mexico with a squad most observers believed was better than the class of 1966. But it would all end in tears. A fatal mistake by Ramsey denied England a path to the final and a second meeting with Brazil. Whether England would have withstood Brazil's samba soccer any better than Italy is debatable but the nation had dreamed of the chance.

Through the 1970s England would slip into the international wilderness as successive managers failed to shape some golden talent into a winning team. Somehow teams featuring Colin Bell, Martin Chivers, Alan Ball, Malcolm Macdonald, Kevin Keegan, Francis Lee and Emlyn Hughes became a national embarrassment, unable to make the finals at two successive World Cups. Alf Ramsey was sacked and one-time grocer Joe Mercer did an instantly forgettable caretaker's job for seven matches – the highlight being a share of the Home Championship with Scotland. Then Don Revie slipped away in the night to pick up a sack of Arabian gold and all the time the people's choice sat and waited for the call that never came. 'They were scared of me,' alleged Clough. And, as with most of his opinions, he was right.

This then is my recall of the 1970s – a personal recollection of the victors and villains, memories of an era when the pursuit of glory was a realistic goal nurtured by all teams, an era that gave us George Best and Clyde Best, Denis Law and Cloughie's Law, Bobby Charlton and bobby dazzlers.

Where football is concerned, it really was better in my day.

CHAPTER ONE

EN-GER-LAND!

Dressed soberly and neatly in a neutral two-piece suit, Sir Alf Ramsey stood before the FA's executive committee like a naughty schoolboy called before the headmaster. Or, to use his own rather more biting analogy, like a man on trial.

Sitting before him was a row of silent, morose faces, anonymous for the most part, the one notable exception being the insufferably boorish Professor Sir Harold Warris Thompson PhD (Oxon). Sir Alf might have guessed what was coming. He had never got on well with Thompson, who belonged to the old school — the one in which gentlemen like himself believed players like Ramsey should use the tradesmen's entrance and at all times know their place.

Essex-born Ramsey was certainly from the players' world and had little time for anyone outside that cocoon, whether press or administrators. Raised in the distinctly ordinary town of Dagenham (he had served as a squaddie in the Army), he played his best football with Spurs and England, and had been a damned good manager with Ipswich Town. But he was prickly at best, insular and enigmatic; hugely sensitive to criticism and guarded in his speech, a handicap mainly due to his unattractive, clipped voice – the result of misguided elocution lessons intended to rid him of an unappealing north London accent.

Thompson, ex-public school, snobbish and patronising, looked down on the one-time errand boy with disdain. 'He always referred to me, even to my face, as Ramsey, which I found insulting,' Sir Alf once said. That sort of attitude never sat well with Sir Alf, whose background was certainly less privileged than Thompson's but did not stop him from being a highly intelligent, thoughtful and considerate individual who knew what constituted fair and proper behaviour, and was never slow to point out the shortcomings in others. He had done so with Thompson.

There was an incident during a 1972 England tour when the man from the FA breezed into the England dressing room swathed in a fug of smoke from the large cigar he was ostentatiously boasting. It was not right and Alf, on behalf of his players, asked Thompson to stub it out. A minor rebuff perhaps but the overbearing official took it as a personal slight, an insult he never forgot. So, when it came to that day in 1974 when Ramsey was to meet his fate, he would have looked into Sir Harold's eyes and gleaned not a vestige of sympathy or indecision. Thompson was, said an FA official, a bullying autocrat – 'He was a bastard. He treated the staff like shit.'

The decision to sack Sir Alf Ramsey was inevitable, predictable; unanimous. None of those faceless committee men would ever vote against Thompson: Ramsey's fate was sealed. And they did not allow him to go with a shred of dignity – no appeasing phrases like 'by mutual consent' or 'offered his resignation'. The FA, through their mouthpiece Ted Croker, let it be known that Sir Alf had been summarily dismissed, 'a termination clause' in his contract having been invoked. Thompson had had his revenge. What a shabby way to end the career of the only manager who, at the time of writing, has ever won an international competition with England.

In his masterly 2006 biography *Sir Alf*, Leo McKinstry delivered a damning verdict on the Ramsey affair when he wrote, 'England's most successful manager would have had a legacy fit for a hero had it not been for the malevolence of the FA chief Harold Thompson.' Well, at least Ramsey got his knighthood after the glory of 1966. How that must have irked Thompson.

But it had all started to go wrong for Ramsey in the 1970 World Cup in Mexico. He was attempting to defend the trophy in the most hostile of environments – Mexico at the height of summer, suffocating heat at altitude. Ramsey, who had usurped most of the authority of the amateurs who ran the FA since being appointed to replace Walter Winterbottom in 1964, did not repeat his bravura when he had predicted, repeatedly, that England would win the World Cup on home soil, but he left nothing to chance in his preparations for Mexico. And most commentators then and now believe the squad he took to Central America was stronger, more flexible, versatile and experienced than the heroes of 1966. Alan Mullery, the Spurs midfielder who would oust Nobby Stiles from Ramsey's first team, reflected, 'We all felt, including Alf, that we were probably the strongest squad England had ever had in their whole history – stronger even than in 1966. We were convinced we could win it.'

Ramsey brought modern thinking to management. He was,

for instance, among the first to realise the value of correct diet allied to peak fitness, something not lost on Stiles for one. 'Alf's preparations for Mexico were incredible,' remembered Stiles. 'They'd be reckoned obsolete by today's standards but in those days they were revolutionary. No stone was left unturned. He even took HP Sauce to Mexico. I'll always remember that – HP Sauce on the tables.'

The most obvious obstacles to retaining the Jules Rimet Trophy were the conditions, the cultural divide ... and Brazil. The South Americans had also assembled a squad of formidable talent, built around Pele, who was nearing the peak of his awesome powers, and had rightly been installed as pre-tournament favourites, with England not far behind. A year earlier on a preparation tour to Mexico, England had narrowly lost to Brazil in Rio – their only defeat in a run of 19 games – and many punters had got the two sides pencilled in for the World Cup final. That tour certainly gave England and Ramsey an insight into what problems they would face with the stifling heat, exacerbated by altitude, and everything was done to mitigate its effect. But they weren't so successful when it came to embracing the Latin culture.

The 'gringos' from England were not hugely popular in that part of the world. Much of the animosity stemmed from the notorious 1966 World Cup quarter-final against Argentina at Wembley, which had descended into near anarchy when German referee Rudolf Kreitlin's hyper-officious performance resulted in the sending-off of Argentina's captain Antonio Rattin. Ramsey then compounded the fracas into an international incident by forcibly trying to stop England players from swapping shirts with their beaten opponents. In his post-match interviews, Ramsey branded the Argentinian players 'animals' – a remark he was forced by the FA to withdraw – but they do not like such insults down South America way ... and they do not forget. It did not get any better on that 1969 tour when Ramsey's bristliness seriously hacked off the local media – hardly the most advisable piece of diplomacy.

It blew up in their faces shortly before the tournament began, on 18 May 1970, to be precise, in the city of Bogotá, Colombia. England captain Bobby Moore and his team mate Bobby Charlton – an instantly recognisable figure wherever he went in the world – were on a shopping expedition for a present for Charlton's wife in the swish Tequendama Hotel's jewellery shop Fuego Verde (or Green Fire) owned by Señor Danilo Rojas. After they left the premises Señor Rojas and his assistant Carla Padilla called the police and made an allegation that they had seen Moore put a £600 bracelet in his pocket.

A week later, on their return to Bogotá after warm-up games in Quito, Ecuador, England players were greeted by the sight of tough-looking Colombian police officers marching on to the team aircraft and placing their captain under arrest. There was much wailing and gnashing of teeth in the England camp. Ramsey said, 'When this affair blew up the players regarded it as a sick joke. I'm sure none of them thought for a moment that it was serious.'

Moore was held under house arrest for three days before being released on certain conditions, to enable him to play in the World Cup finals. What was not so widely known at the time was the part Prime Minister Harold Wilson played in the affair, secret documents revealing years later that he had pressured British embassy staff in Colombia to keep Moore out of jail and ensure he was free to represent his country. For his part, Moore conducted himself with the same calmness and dignity that categorised his career, his only comment on the affair coming when he was released, telling waiting newsmen with remarkable sang-froid, 'I am happy to be a free man.'

When the England party finally landed in Mexico for the tournament, the world's press were waiting ... and what did they see as the squad descended from the aircraft? West Bromwich Albion striker Jeff Astle being helped down the steps, apparently the worse for wear. It was a Gazza moment and the hawks were soon picking at the fresh meat of a juicy story. The official line from the England team doctor was that Astle, who had a strong aversion to flying, had suffered serious air sickness caused by turbulence. But the local newshounds were not going to accept that and wrote the headlines as they saw them, describing the England side as a bunch of 'thieves and drunks'. Astle was dismayed by the furore and his wife Laraine gave this withering reaction: 'I suppose next they'll shove a couple of girls into one of the boys' bedrooms.'

By then England wanted nothing more than to get on with the football and leave all the controversy behind them. They had been drawn in Group 3 along with Romania, Czechoslovakia and Brazil. Inevitably, it earned the tediously predictable 'Group of Death' tag from the media. Ramsey, perhaps by accident, perhaps by design, engendered a siege mentality in the camp, giving most journalists short shrift, doing his best to protect his players and ensure their concentration was deflected no further.

On 2 June 1970 at 4pm, the world champions were ready to begin defence of their crown in Estadio Jalisco, Guadalajara against an uncompromising but limited Romania. Ramsey chose this line-up: Gordon Banks, Keith Newton, Terry Cooper, Brian Labone, Bobby Moore, Alan Mullery, Alan Ball, Bobby Charlton, Francis Lee, Geoff Hurst and Martin Peters. Substitutes: Tommy Wright and Peter Osgood.

England, in all-white, soon discovered that Romania were skilled in the black arts as first Cooper and then Mullery were scythed down, cynically, professionally, enraging the considerable English contingent of fans watching from the sun-baked terraces behind strands of ugly barbed wire, but delighting the thousands of sombrero-waving Mexicans who were fervently in the Romanian camp for the afternoon. They clearly liked Romania's brutal 10-man style of defence, pitched at such a violent level that would be wholly unacceptable to referees today. After one shin-high tackle by Mihai Mocanu, which left Francis Lee writhing in agony, the 'tough' Belgian referee Vital Laroux demonstrated his authority. The way he waved away Romanian protestations after awarding a free kick to England was truly frightening!

Still, patient England finally got their reward in the 65th minute when Ball floated a pass to Lee. A backward header found Hurst on the left of the six-yard box with much to do but he beat his marker with a quick turn before firing right-footed across the body of keeper Sterica Adamache into the far corner. Even though it did not go down well with the 'Guanatos' from Guadalajara, the result confirmed England's standing as one of the teams to beat.

England then had five days to prepare for the next challenge, against pre-tournament favourites Brazil, Ramsey drilling into his players the importance of possession in the blistering midday heat. The management did everything they could to get the team ready but they had no control over the early hours' invasion of Brazilian fans, bolstered by a bunch of locals who filled the street outside England's city-centre hotel with such a cacophony of noise that sleep was nigh on impossible.

England shrugged it off, matching Brazil's patience and comfort on the ball. It was high-quality stuff, pass for pass, but such was the respect out there, little happened in and around the penalty box. That well-known duo Peters and Lee missed a couple of reasonable chances, Mullery dumped Pele on the seat of his pants with a bit of Division One crudity and, on 59 minutes from a chance created by Tostao and Pele, Jairzinho drove the ball past Banks to clinch a 1-0 win.

There was one other incident that has been mentioned a couple of times since. Midway through the first half Brazil captain Carlos Alberto found Jairzinho on the right. The winger brushed past Terry Cooper, who seemed a single breath away from chopping him down, but fair play to the Leeds man, he sportingly allowed him to pass and sling over the cross that Pele headed downwards for Gordon Banks to produce the save perpetually described as the best ever. It was also after the England–Brazil clash that Pele described Bobby Moore as the best defender he had ever played against.

England had lost an epic match by the slenderest of margins and there was plenty of money on a repeat encounter in the final. Both teams progressed easily to the quarter-finals, Brazil scoring eight goals in their three group matches compared to England's two, the second coming in another 1-0 win, this time over the Czechs, courtesy of Allan Clarke's debut penalty.

England's quarter-final took them even nearer to the sky, to Estadio Nou Camp in León – a mere 6,000 feet above sea level – where they would face the West Germans, who had played all their group matches there and were more acclimatised to the thinner air at such high altitude. It would be one telling factor in a game that hinged on specifics. Before the kick-off Gordon Banks went down with a mystery bug and, despite the inevitable conspiracy theories which still abound in some quarters, the blame was put on a rogue bottle of local beer. It meant a surprise opportunity for Chelsea's talented keeper Peter 'The Cat' Bonetti.

England appeared in their 1966 red tops – 'like a crimson flame' enthused ITV commentator Hugh Johns – and for the best part of an hour they looked capable of burning off the German challenge. Mullery got the first goal, on 31 minutes, from Keith Newton's clever pass to the near post, Mullery getting across his man to drive the ball home. On 49 minutes Hurst weighted the perfect pass into the path of Newton's charge down the right. The Everton man's cross fell nicely for Peters at the far post and he finished with aplomb to leave England two up and cruising towards the semi-final.

The events of the next hour haunt England fans, and old players, to this day. On 68 minutes Franz Beckenbauer dropped a shoulder to Mullery and fired in a low 20-yarder. It was an average, nothing shot but somehow it got beneath Bonetti's dive and the Germans were visibly charged with new belief. At that point the tiring Bobby Charlton was substituted. It was the end of his international career. The move, replacing him with the energetic Colin Bell, seemed obvious yet, the Germans would say later, the removal of Charlton's threat released Beckenbauer from his defensive guard. The Germans stepped up a gear.

Even more controversial was Ramsey's decision to withdraw another hero of 1966, Martin Peters, sending on Norman Hunter and instantly further weakening England's midfield. Within eight minutes Germany were level – the veteran Uwe Seeler looping a header over Bonetti, stranded yards from his line. It went to extra time.

Four years on from Wembley, the same score, the same scenario. With 22 players hauling battle-weary legs across the baked León turf beneath a merciless sun, the next goal was always going to be the winner. Jurgen Grabowski turned Cooper left, then right. His cross to the far post was headed back by Johannes Loehr and there was the arch-poacher Gerd 'Der Bomber' Muller – or 'Gertie Muller' as Hugh Johns insisted on calling him – acrobatically volleying waist-high for 3-2. There were plenty of empty words in the aftermath but the truth was that England had messed up. From Bonetti's nightmares to Ramsey's substitutions, they had blown it big time.

From that low point, England would endure four successive hapless managers and 12 depressing years before they would see the World Cup finals again. And for Ramsey the vultures were circling; his time was fast running out. Over the next couple of seasons he slowly shed his heroes of 1966 and as they said their international farewells he seemed to lose his way or, more accurately, he got left behind tactically. The 'wingless' revolution he had started had been evolved by other nations, other managers, and Ramsey had not moved with the times. England were beaten 3-1 at Wembley by West Germany again; Geoff Hurst was substituted, thus ending his international days.

The 1974 World Cup qualifying campaign was Ramsey's last tilt at repeating the glory of 1966 but it was an empty gesture, bereft of the poise and conviction that had triumphed years before. He hit rock bottom in the Wembley qualifier against Poland, who had already beaten England 2-0 on home soil. Ramsey had a fine clutch of players to call on: Shilton, Madeley, Hughes, Bell, McFarland, Hunter, Currie, Channon, Chivers, Clarke. It should have been enough but Ramsey's luck had run out. They blitzed the Poles, the shot ratio something like 20 to 1, but a goalkeeper named Jan Tomaszewski – known forever more as a 'clown', thanks to Brian Clough's dismissive insult – had one of those nights.

The only shot that beat him was an Allan Clarke penalty but by then Poland had scored a comic goal of her own. Hunter, of all people, missed a tackle on the touchline, allowing Jan Domarski to get possession and his low shot went under the body of Peter Shilton. England were out of the World Cup and, it would soon come to pass, Alf Ramsey was out of a job.

Among the stars England relied on that night was Sheffield United's playmaker Tony Currie, a talented midfield operator who would surely have graced the Munich finals and, perhaps, established himself as a world-class footballer had England got it right. After the team's demise he attempted to deflect attention away from the obvious villains: Ramsey, Hunter and Shilton.

> Perhaps we were all that bit over-eager and failed to put away chances we would have scored in club games. In the first half I hit one over the bar and then early in the second I thought I had cracked it when Allan Clarke gave me the ball just to the left of the goal. But I let it run just a fraction too far and my shot went wide. I suppose I might get ten chances like that and put nine of them away but, let's face it, the Poles not only defended brilliantly but everything seemed to go for them.

Tomaszewski went on to greater things, two penalty saves helping Poland to third place in the World Cup to prove he was a decent goalkeeper, and then a career as a journalist and controversial commentator on Polish football, proving he was also an intelligent chap to boot. Years later he reflected on the Clough label, commenting, 'I wasn't offended when he called me a clown. His comments were the perfect motivation for me. I met him in a TV studio in England a few years later. He was friendly, though he didn't exactly apologise for what he had said. At the time he knew that Alf Ramsey would leave if England didn't qualify. He wanted his job.'

Smart bloke.

The tabloids went for Ramsey's throat, waging a virulent campaign to oust the only England manager who had ever won anything. They had never warmed to him and had only been prepared to put up with his brusqueness while he was winning. Never Ramsey's friends, they readily became his worst enemies. The FA, and particularly Sir Harold Thompson, had wanted rid anyway; now they had their excuse. Sir Alf survived for two more games, including a 1-0 loss to Italy at Wembley. It was the Italians' first victory in England, the winning goal scored by a certain Fabio Capello.

The decision to dismiss Sir Alf Ramsey – after 113 games, which produced 69 wins and 27 draws – was taken on St Valentine's Day, 1974. He could hardly have been more shocked if Al Capone had led the massacre. Football had seen the best and almost the last of Ramsey who, apart from a brief, undistinguished spell at Birmingham, slipped quietly into retirement. No interviews, no autobiographies. His life ended in an Alzheimer's fog on 28 April 1999 and he was laid to rest, privately, in Ipswich. A few days later the town also hosted his memorial service, forcing any FA members who cared to attend to travel up from London; few did. Ramsey had never forgiven the FA over his sacking and at least he had had the last say.

The FA for their part couldn't have handled it more badly ... especially as they had no one lined up to take his place. Less than impressed by candidates like Gordon Jago (QPR), Gordon Milne (Coventry) and Jimmy Bloomfield (Leicester), they turned to 60-year-old Joe Mercer, a jovial old boy who enjoyed a laugh with the players and had a great rapport with the media – the complete opposite of Ramsey. But he made it clear he was only a stand-in and so the FA continued to hunt down a new boss. To be fair, 'uncle Joe' did alright in his seven games, losing just once, and the FA might have avoided a lot of heartache had they persuaded him to take it on long term.

But a telephone call out of the blue seemed to be the answer to a prayer. It was from Don Revie, manager of a Leeds United side that had been in and around the top of the game for the best part of a decade. The FA had probably thought him untouchable, so enmeshed as he was in everything that was Leeds United, but Revie admitted later, 'I made the first move. They did not contact me. I fancied being England manager.'

At this point someone at Lancaster Gate should have taken a deep breath and had the courage to say 'hold on a minute, this guy comes with some baggage'. But, of course, no one did. Despite warnings from people like Football League secretary Alan Hardaker, who wrote, 'Revie as England manager is a classic case of poacher turning gamekeeper,' no one heeded the rumours and innuendo that followed Revie around. The whispers of illegal payments to players – even bribery – were everywhere but, once again, no one who mattered was listening.

So, on 4 July 1974 Don Revie walked out of his Elland Road home for the dysfunctional 'family' that is England. Revie had thrived on an intimacy with the players in his charge. He knew which players to console, which players to push; he knew all about their personal problems, never forgot a birthday and was very much a father figure to those he had raised to become the mighty Leeds. But England was, and still is, a very different proposition for a manager: you can't get close to people you see only occasionally.

Revie's style of management was spot on at club level – the dossiers, the tactics, the detail – but it didn't sit well with international players. 'Players aren't really that intelligent,' was the astute comment of Mick Channon. 'They didn't need all that, they just want to play football.' Revie quickly alienated established stars like Kevin Keegan, Stan Bowles and Kevin Beattie, three players who at one time or another all walked out of the England camp in protest at his methods.

To be fair, Revie enjoyed something of a honeymoon start to his England career, winning his first game, against the Czechs, by 3-0 and remaining unbeaten through 10 matches. His England team inflicted a sweet defeat on West Germany, their first loss since winning the World Cup in 1974; Malcolm Macdonald did his record-breaking feat of scoring all five goals against Cyprus; and Scotland were hammered 5-1 at Wembley. But there was a thread running through all those games that was undermining Revie's confidence – not once was he able to name the same team two games in a row.

The perennial battle with club managers for the release of players for international duty was gnawing at his nerves. It wasn't like this at Leeds, that team picked itself. For England, he gave international caps to an unlikely list of players including Steve Whitworth, Colin Viljoen, Dave Thomas, Ian Gillard, Phil Boyle, Mike Doyle, Jeff Blockley and, from the old Third Division, Peter Taylor. Revie chopped and changed with bewildering regularity. Players were picked, dropped and then recalled. Mick Channon and Alan Ball – the man Revie had made his first captain – were among them. The fiery little World Cup winner never forgave him.

And the honeymoon came to a sharp conclusion. First, England failed to qualify for the European championships, dumped by Portugal and the eventual winners, Czechoslovakia. Then came the qualifying groups for the 1978 World Cup in Argentina with England less than impressive. Against Finland at Wembley the style of a 2-1 win brought chants of 'rubbish' cascading from the stands. Revie, shoulders hunched, squirmed in his seat. England had to win their games against Italy, home and away, if they were to get a ticket to South America.

Revie did everything he could to prepare his side ... according to the Revie manual. In *The Official FA History*, published in 1997, Niall Edworthy revealed that Revie had the Italians watched seven times in the run-up to the crucial qualifier in Rome. His dossiers were thicker than a Jeffrey Archer novel, detailed and analytical, but like a foreign language to his players, who were confused, bothered and bewildered by the weight of evidence.

Revie selected this team: Clemence, Clement, Mills, Greenhoff, McFarland, Hughes, Keegan, Channon, Bowles, Cherry and Brooking. And for half an hour they withstood the cohesive and energetic attacks of a young Italian side built around seven players from Juventus, until a deflected free kick by Giancarlo Antognoni gave the home side the lead. Such was the complexity of England's qualifying group that season that a 1-0 defeat wouldn't have been disastrous. If they could beat Italy by two goals or more at Wembley, they could still do it. But that slender hope died 12 minutes from time when Roberto Bettega ended a wonderfully fluid move with a flying header. The return leg was a year away but England would have plenty to contemplate, knowing they would have to stick five or six past the Italians to stand a chance of going through.

What they needed was a period of consolidation to rebuild confidence; what they got was utter tripe. Holland played them off the park at Wembley, winning 2-0, followed by a scratchy 2-1 win in Belfast over Northern Ireland. Then they lost successive Home Championship matches at Wembley to Wales and Scotland, the latter an iniquitous afternoon, which culminated in tartan-clad fans swamping the Wembley pitch, ripping down the goal frames and tearing up great chunks of turf to take back to Glasgow. Revie had had enough and what came next would blacken his name forever.

England were due to fly off for a summer tour to South America when Revie announced that he would not be accompanying the party. His story was that he intended to flit around the continent, assessing opposition for the forthcoming European Championships. Nothing could have been further from the truth. Revie, doing his best to conceal his identity, boarded a plane for Dubai to talk money and contracts with the men who ran the game in the United Arab Emirates.

On 12 July 1977, the nation woke up to headlines in the *Daily Mail* announcing his resignation, a sensational exclusive which, so the legend has it, earned him £30,000 – a sum dwarfed by the huge crock of Arab gold he had been promised. 'Nearly everyone in the country seems to want me out and I am giving them what they want,' Revie's *Daily Mail* story quoted. 'I know people will accuse me of running away and it sickens me I cannot finish the job.'

Well, he was right there. The press shredded his reputation beneath banners that called him a traitor and a cheat. The FA turned to the law, slapping a 10-year ban on Revie having any active role in English football. Revie then challenged that in the High Court and Judge Cantley ruled the suspension was unlawful but it was a pyrrhic victory for Revie. Judge Cantley told him, 'You published and presented to the public a sensational and notorious example of disloyalty, breach of duty, discourtesy and selfishness. Your conduct brought English professional football, at a high level, into disrepute.'

Revie scuttled back to the United Arab Emirates and over the next seven years or so did much to establish football at an acceptable professional level in that part of the world. He eventually came back to England and had a brief association with QPR before withdrawing from the game, still a comparatively young man. He was only 61 when he died in 1989 from motor neurone disease.

England began the search for a new manager and, had they chosen to go to the country, Brian Clough would have won a landslide victory. Cloughie was always the people's choice – they liked what he had to say, the way his teams played football, the fact that he knew how to build and lead a winning team. As his son Nigel once observed, 'He would say things about his bosses or the FA that the man in the street wanted to say.' If only England, having sunk just about as low as at any time in the history of international football, could have had a bit of that magic, the glories of 1966 might have been revisited. But did he ever stand a chance of landing the top job? Never in a million years.

Fans maintain to this day that he was the best manager England never had and, in some respects, they are probably right. Given the chance, Clough might have been able to order top-class Division One stars to stand up straight, get their hair cut, hands out of pockets, tell them they were too ugly, too slow, too fat ... even hand out a punch or two if they did not do what he said. But then again, maybe the Kevin Keegans, Emlyn Hughes and Mick Channons of this world would not have stood for it.

And, like it or not, there is more to managing England than sending out 11 men to follow a set of tactics designed to win a football match. The job also calls for diplomacy, respect and responsibility. But Clough did not do diplomacy; he spoke his mind and the fans loved him for it but you could not have an England manager capable of coming up with such insults as: 'Football hooligans – well, there are ninety-two club chairmen for a start.'

His reputation preceded him and the men at the FA had long memories. They would have remembered some of his more outlandish statements, especially when they were on the receiving end. In 1972 he offered this pearl of wisdom: 'An ICI foreman was almost certainly once on the shop floor, a bus inspector once drove a bus. But how many FA officials and club directors have ever been footballers?' Brian Clough for England manager? Never in a million years.

Ex-public schoolboy Sir Harold Thompson, the much-despised chairman of the FA, used to look down on Alf Ramsey because of his working-class upbringing and Ramsey was a man who, in the main, kept his opinions to himself. Thompson v Clough? It would have been fascinating to watch but it would never have worked. Never in a million years.

The FA did go through the charade of interviewing Clough, and other no-win candidates like Lawrie McMenemy, but the decision had already been taken: the new England manager was to be Ron Greenwood, a 55-year-old good-natured, inoffensive character. Nicknamed 'Reverend Ron' by the players at West Ham, he spoke in a kind of grinding monotone, with words you fancy were tactically chosen to avoid offending anyone.

In a documentary on the life of Brian Clough, former FA press officer Glen Kirton said, 'The decision had already been made that Ron Greenwood was the preferred candidate. There wasn't a vote. Sir Harold Thompson would have said, "I want to appoint Ron Greenwood," and they would have agreed. The decision was made beforehand. Ron Greenwood was not on the candidate list.'

'Good guy, safe but boring,' was Clough's reaction, before adding the razor-sharp barb he could never resist: 'If the post of England manager had been filled on the basis of outstanding achievement, Ron Greenwood would not have had a smell.'

There goes Old Big 'Ead again, shooting from the lip without checking his bullets. It has to be conceded that Greenwood never won a league title when he was manager of West Ham, but when it came to knock-out competitions, he did not have a bad record, . winning the FA Cup in 1964, followed by the European Cup Winners Cup the year after, and in a style that was universally admired. Decent credentials to be England manager, whose perennial remit is to try to win a cup competition. It is not necessary to go 42 league games unbeaten, as Clough's Forest once did; just survive enough games to make the finals of the World Cup or European Championships.

When you look at it from Thompson's angle, he made a pretty shrewd choice. Greenwood knew his place, would mind his 'p's and q's' and, if his England side was a mirror of the West Ham teams he built, playing that cultured passing style that even Clough must have grudgingly admired, so much the better. And there was a bit of a mess to sort out following Revie's abrupt end to a demoralising reign. Someone had to go about rebuilding England's international reputation, which had been so badly besmirched. Would Clough have been the right man for that particular job? I wonder. Perhaps not at that time; perhaps his time should have come in 1982 when

Greenwood's stint was over. By then he had won his European Cups, had nothing left to prove or achieve at club level and, arguably, had matured from the sort of character who once told an FA council member to 'Fuck off' during his brief stint as England youth manager. Those long memories again. Clough, once again, was passed over.

But this chapter is about playing out the 1970s and it is fair to say that Greenwood, technically a gifted coach who is credited with the emergence of West Ham's England triumvirate of Moore, Hurst and Peters, made a reasonable fist of perhaps the toughest job in football. There are few countries around the globe where so much is demanded of the national side yet so little help is forthcoming from the very people who bang on about how important it is that England do well. Like Ramsey and Revie before him, Greenwood had to juggle his pack according to who was available.

Greenwood was asked to breathe life into England's fading hopes of qualifying for the 1978 World Cup in Argentina but made his managerial debut in a friendly at Wembley against the Swiss. Back in the late 1970s the Swiss weren't much higher up the ranking ladder than Luxembourg or Liechtenstein but they more than matched their hosts on that desperate September night. Greenwood ripped up the Ramsey manual and reverted to a style he understood, making best use of wide men to feed his strikers. To that end, he brought back Liverpool's Ian Callaghan – more than 10 years after his last cap. And he had Trevor Francis of Birmingham, Kevin Keegan and Mick Channon up front as well. They were lucky to draw 0-0.

Next came a World Cup qualifier against the aforesaid Luxembourg. Greenwood made four changes, hoping that England could cash in with a flood of goals and keep their hopes of being in Argentina afloat. A 2-0 win over another of Europe's whipping boys was not nearly good enough. But Greenwood stuck to his guns for the next match, the final qualifier against Italy at Wembley. Four more changes, again all up front, saw Steve Coppell of Manchester United and Manchester City's Peter Barnes brought in on the wings. It was a rare night of glory for England with a 2-0 win over the powerful Italians, goals from Keegan and Trevor Brooking meaning that Italy had to beat Luxembourg in their closing group match. Of course they did the business and England missed out again.

But Greenwood was re-establishing England's credentials on the international stage. He had a settled back four, with Phil Neal, Mick Mills, Dave Watson and Emlyn Hughes, and a wealth of creative talent to call on. Greenwood also made a little bit of history when, in November 1978, he selected .Viv Anderson of Nottingham Forest for the friendly game against Czechoslovakia – the first black footballer to be capped for the country. England won 1-0 and Anderson, known affectionately as 'Spider', did well, both defensively and for the part he played in Coppell's winning goal. Greenwood stated, 'Yellow, purple or black – if they're good enough, I'll pick them.' But it would be seven months and five internationals before Anderson got his second cap.

It was also around this time that Greenwood got into his ridiculous dilemma of trying to sort out who was the country's best goalkeeper: Ray Clemence or Peter Shilton. It displayed an indecisiveness that would always colour opinion of his time in charge. Between May 1978 and November 1979 England played 17 internationals. Clemence won 11 caps, Shilton 6, with neither man playing more than two games in succession. Shilton wrote in his autobiography, 'Ray and I were both disappointed not to be the regular first choice and neither of us was happy with the arrangement but we accepted it and got on with the job. But it was not encouraging to know that, should I play a blinder, I still wouldn't be selected for the next game.' Greenwood's record in that time was 13 wins, three draws and a single loss, which, statistically at least, looked impressive, but what a nonsense he created.

Still, at least he returned England to the latter stages of a major international competition but their tawdry performance in the 1980 European Championship is best forgotten. The first match, against Belgium, was notable only for the intervention of Italian riot police to break up terrace mayhem. Ray 'Butch' Wilkins scored for England in a 1-1 draw. England then lost to Italy and a Marco Tardelli goal before defeating Spain 2-1, with goals from Trevor Brooking and Tony Woodcock, watched by less than 15,000 people. It wasn't enough; they didn't qualify for the knock-out stages.

When it came to the crunch, England were no further forward than the day they sacked Alf Ramsey.

CHAPTER TWO

WEMBLEY
WIZARDS

O nce upon a time, before football sold its soul to television, and Manchester United were told it was OK to opt out for a jaunt to South America, the FA Cup was the most magical competition in the world.

It is not pushing things too far to say that, for many players, it was the pinnacle of their career, coveted above and beyond the old First Division championship. It was the stuff of legends that survive to this day: the Matthews Final; Jackie Milburn's Wembley exploits of the early 1950s, which brought Newcastle United their last significant domestic honours; the bravery of Bert Trautmann, post-Munich Manchester United; and some of the most romantic, incredible stories of the mighty being vanquished by the underdog.

But in this 21st-century era where cash is God and European qualification all that is worth fighting for, it has been devalued out of all recognition. The big boys treat it with something bordering on contempt, fielding weakened sides to save their best players for the more important weekly battle for points because that's where the money is. The pity is that the big boys can get away with it. So rich have they become that they can afford understudies who are better than most first-team players at other clubs. Which is why, pretty much like the Premiership, the FA Cup has become the exclusive property of the top four.

Before Portsmouth capitalised on an unprecedented run of good fortune to snatch the 2008 trophy, 16 of the previous 17 finals had been won by Manchester United, Liverpool, Arsenal or Chelsea. And since 2008? Chelsea twice and the new billionaires on the block, Manchester City. Wigan triumphed in 2013 only by the largesse of a seemingly disinterested Manchester City who, it should be noted, named only two English players in the starting XI.

During the 1970s there were *nine* different winners of the 10 finals. Ipswich, Sunderland, Southampton and West Ham were among them. Supporters of every team in the top two divisions nurtured realistic dreams of Wembley glory, bewitched by the promise of a walk down Wembley Way, wearing a daft hat and a rosette the size of a frying pan.

And they knew their place in the Wembley final had been earned the hard way. No manager would dare to betray the fans by deliberately fielding a weakened side, no matter what the opposition. Leeds had all their stars on show when they got turned over at Colchester, Coventry had most of their cup holders when they went down to Sutton United, West Ham had their World Cup trio in the team that lost at Mansfield, Newcastle's best could not handle Hereford in that oft-repeated third rounder at Edgar Street. That was what the FA Cup was all about.

Nowadays the odd giant-killing act still happens and, for the minnows, it is something to remember. But if a top side does get turned over, it is little more than a temporary embarrassment, often watched by a handful of diehards and soon forgotten when Barcelona or Bayern beckon.

And even the magic of a trip to Wembley has all but disappeared, for the FA have stripped the final of its unique status by holding the semi-finals in NW10 as well. No matter if it was United to play Liverpool, Newcastle against Sunderland, the fans would have to fork out for the trip south – thereby helping Wembley pay its bills. Once it was the Holy Grail, few players ever getting the chance to play in the famous stadium. Now, it welcomes not just the runners-up but those not even good enough to get there, and where's the glory in that? Who remembers losing semi-finalists?

This is how it used to be, as explained by Tony Book, who picked up the famous old trophy for Manchester City in 1969 – 'Playing in the semi-final is almost as nerve-wracking as the final itself. You know you're just one step away. It must be the biggest disappointment in the world not to win in the semi-final. If you lose in the final, you've at least been to Wembley.'

Anyone who has been lucky enough to attend an FA Cup final, especially at the cranky old Wembley, will have memories that will last a lifetime. The walk up Wembley Way, the souvenir sellers, the ticket touts, endless queues, steps running with steaming urine, 'Abide With Me', sunburn, the ecstasy and the agony.

And for the armchair fans up and down the country, Cup Final Saturday used to take on a ritualistic stature. Get the pots done, pack the wife off to the shops and settle down with beer and sarnies for five hours of unique entertainment.

The BBC mixed their build-up with a staple diet of horse

racing, boxing and, by way of light relief, *It's A Knockout* with Stuart Hall and Eddie 'Up and Under' Waring on the microphones. But ITV had an ace of its own: Second World War hero Kent Walton with the words and the masters of the mat providing the action – a special FA Cup final helping of professional wrestling. It was part of the FA Cup Final ritual. From around 11am you took your seat in front of the TV to watch the build-up: the team hotels, meeting the players, reviews of previous rounds, travelling on the team bus. But for about an hour, just after lunch, football took a break as Dickie Davies grinned a welcome to *World of Sport* cup-final-day wrestling.

That would be the cue for the mid-Atlantic tones of Kent Walton, a tail-end charlie rear gunner during the war, to begin waxing lyrical about the entertainment on offer. Usually, Jackie 'Mr TV' Pallo would top the bill, often against his archrival Mick McManus, whose appearance could be guaranteed to provoke a chorus of boos. Mick would work up the crowd with his backhanded wrestling style, getting away with what he could, what the referee would allow. 'I was always full of energy,' he once reminisced. 'That's the way I wrestled and, if the referee wasn't looking, I would give them the old elbow.'

The crowd would respond with their jeers and cheers, creating a unique atmosphere in which normally meek grannies would arm themselves with a sharp umbrella and do their best to render the villains of the ring some serious injury. In fact, feisty 67-year-old grandmother Blanch Lecross, of Bristol, was threatened with a life ban after continued attacks on wrestlers, leaping from her ringside seat to punch them when they fought dirty and, on one occasion, stubbing her cigarette out on a grappler's backside.

If the Jackie-and-Mick show was top of the bill, there were other great names of the sport who became legends from those

Saturday afternoon shows that began in the mid-1950s, with live broadcasts from places like Brent Town Hall.

Names like Leon Arras who, if memory serves, was actually the late actor Brian Glover; 'Cry Baby' Jim Breaks; toothless Les Kellett; Johnny Kwango; Steve Logan, who was Mick McManus's regular partner for those breathtaking tag matches; Bert Royal; Alan Dennison; the mysterious masked man of the mat, Kendo Nagasaki; battling babes Mitzi Mueller and Klondyke Kate; world champ George Kidd; Bomber Pat Roach, who found fame on TV in *Auf Weidersehen, Pet*; Tony St Clair; and who could ever forget the Mongolian Mauler? We all had a particular favourite. Mine was a full-blooded member of the Canadian Kahnawake tribe, who would climb into the ring complete with feathered headdress, Mohawk haircut and blood-curdling yells. Born in 1935, Billy Two Rivers came to England in 1959 and became an immediate TV favourite with his colourful appearance and that war dance whenever he lost his temper.

Mat fans will have noticed by now that two names are missing from the list of wrestling's all-stars – Big Daddy and Giant Haystacks, two of the most popular grapplers that ever delivered a forearm smash or applied a Boston crab. Sadly, these two larger-than-life figures are no longer with us but fight fans recall their legendary clashes in the ring, which, at the sport's peak, would be watched by 10 million television viewers. In fact, it is recorded that after a concert at the Royal Albert Hall, Frank Sinatra watched Giant Haystacks in action and then declared that British wrestlers were the best in the world.

Giant Haystacks contracted cancer in 1997 and, after a year-long battle, he died on Sunday, 29 November 1998. His fiercest opponent was the fighter with the gentlest name, Shirley Crabtree, alias Big Daddy. A bit like the character from Johnny

Cash's hit 'A Boy Named Sue', Crabtree learned his trade defending his name against jeering chums at school in Halifax. He became a professional wrestler in 1952 and was instantly recognisable with his spangled top hat and Union Jack costume. Weighing in at 25 stone, he would produce his speciality move to great applause, dropping on his opponents with the full weight of his somewhat over-endowed stomach – a trick he called 'the belly-splash' move! Big Daddy died in Halifax General Hospital in 1997 after suffering a stroke. He was 67. There is a lovely story about Crabtree when he was running a Yorkshire nightclub and once asked an agent, 'How much does she go out for then, that Tamla Motown?'

No, FA Cup final day has never been the same without the wrestling.

The decade opened with one of the most exciting, memorable, violent and ultimately compelling finals in history. Chelsea, the swaggering boys from the King's Road with their fancy velvet flares, sexy aura of 1970s cool and insufferably catchy 'Blue Is The Colour' team song, against the cloth-capped 'ard men from Leeds, a team that was tough to beat and equally tough to like. Leeds were chasing a league, cup and European Cup treble; they would end up with nowt.

The date of the final was 11 April 1970, scheduled weeks earlier than usual to accommodate World Cup holders England, who were off to Mexico to prepare for the defence of their trophy. That meant the game was played soon after the Horse of the Year Show had turned Wembley's usually lush green sward into a hoof-pummelled, manure-stained mud heap that should have defied any attempts to produce a spectacle. John Hollins, the Chelsea midfielder, later said, 'It was appalling. Whenever you tackled someone, you took up three or four feet of turf. After each tackle you had to pull the grass back into place like a carpet. It poured with rain during the match, which made the ground even heavier. Nowadays, the referee would have called it off.'

Yet, despite the conditions, and much to the credit of both teams, the final was a pulsating affair, partly because Chelsea's enforcers, like Ron 'Chopper' Harris, David Webb and their muscular, rangy centre-forward Peter Osgood, were determined not to yield to the sluggers from the North: the Bremners, Giles and Charltons of their particular world. The game was a manager's nightmare, open and end to end, but Leeds were undoubtedly the better side. With Eddie Gray giving a virtuoso performance against the hapless Webb on the left, no one was surprised when Leeds went in front, Jack Charlton scoring with a soft, trickling header, assisted by the mud. But then Leeds keeper Gary Sprake lived up to his calamitous reputation by allowing Peter Houseman's tentative shot to roll beneath his body. Charlton briefly, fiercely berated his goalkeeper – not a particularly edifying moment, it has to be said.

Leeds went in front after the break, a more appreciable goal scored by Mick Jones from a rebound off the post. So why didn't Leeds, the ultra-professionals led by Don Revie, the most tactically-obsessed manager of his era, then shut up shop? Good question. That much-vaunted Leeds defence of Paul Madeley, Terry Cooper, Norman Hunter and Jack Charlton somehow lost the plot. They had to take collective responsibility for allowing Ian Hutchinson, Chelsea's ebullient number 10, who succumbed to illness at the age of 54, to ghost in and equalise. Extra time on that cloying surface failed to find a winner. The sides would replay at Old Trafford after the first drawn final in Wembley history.

Before they met again Leeds lost a European Cup semi-final to Celtic and the league title took a sharp left turn and headed down the East Lancs Road to Goodison Park. All they had left was the cup but Leeds United's season was about to crash and burn.

The replay was watched by an estimated domestic television audience of 32 million – 31.5 million of them probably praying for a Chelsea victory – and the Blues from Stamford Bridge were determined to deliver, no matter what it took.

Once again, they were largely outplayed by Leeds but they were on level terms in the boxing match. In an exercise conducted for *The Times* in 2008, respected referee David Elleray sat in front of a TV screen and, nearly 40 years after the event, assessed the replay and that night's official, Eric Jennings. Elleray declared that he would have handed out six red cards and 20 yellows! But that would be now and 1970 was a different time, with different values. Jennings let a lot of things go and, in so doing, played his part in creating an unforgettable night of unbridled passion and endeavour.

John Hollins remembered the charged atmosphere – how could he forget? Chelsea had never won the FA Cup before! 'People were standing up to each other, head to head, as they do nowadays except they were hitting each other. The ref would say, "Play on, keep going." He played great advantage. If he had stopped it, there would have been an incident. The incident didn't happen because he simply played on.'

There are a couple of notable clips worthy of access on YouTube. Osgood rattles into Jack Charlton close to the touchline. Charlton responds by giving the Chelsea man a quick kick. 'Play on,' says the referee. Circa 2011 and the result would be hysterical headlines. And Chelsea full-back Eddie McCready ends a Leeds attack by flying through the air, feet first, to take out Bremner, head high.

'That surely had to be dangerous play,' commented Brian

Moore with a singular lack of the over-emotive response you might expect from a Tyldesley or a Green. Dangerous play? It was aerial assault, a kamikaze attack that left Bremner ruefully rubbing his head. Didier Drogba would have demanded a transplant.

Leeds took the lead with the sort of goal that has become the trademark of the modern-day Manchester United, breaking up an attack on the edge of their own penalty area, sweeping forward past despairing Chelsea tackles, and then Jones bursts into the area and thunders his shot past Peter Bonetti who, incidentally, was still limping from an earlier coming together with the Leeds attack.

Apparently, the second half foul count was something like Chelsea 35, Leeds 11. Did it contribute to the reversal of fortunes? It must have done, I suppose. The Leeds defence was nowhere when the gifted Alan Hudson flighted a cross from deep onto the head of the onrushing Osgood. 1-1.

I have to confess, I was one of the 31.5m television viewers willing Chelsea to find a winner and I can still see Hutchinson wiping the ball on his muddied shirt and then hurling a trademark long throw into the box. And there, at the far post, bullying his way above his tormentor Gray was the lantern-jawed David Webb to head the winner. Desperate Dan had won the day.

The 1971 final was another historic occasion but for different reasons. Arsenal clinched only the second league and cup double of the 20th century ... and that achievement is worthy of an entire chapter to come.

So, on to 1972: the centenary final. Leeds were back, still a major force in domestic and European football, but once again they had missed out on the First Division title, due in great part to a controversial Elland Road defeat at the hands of West Brom (more of that later as well). Arsenal were the cup holders.

'Marching On Together' sang the Leeds faithful for the first time, as their heroes crashed against the well-drilled Arsenal defence like breakers on a California beach. It wasn't a memorable match – Leeds edged the attacking honours but not by much. Even the winning goal, beautifully steered into the far corner of Bob Wilson's goal by Allan Clarke's head, didn't ignite or excite. It was almost slow-motion delivery. Still, given the healing powers of time, I can't help feeling it was the least that Leeds deserved after so many heartbreaking disappointments.

And they were back again in 1973 but this was a day when the wonderful, magical, anything-is-possible romance of the FA Cup illuminated the nation and even had hard-faced housewives in street-corner launderettes talking about the moment. For many, it was the apogee of the Leeds story. All the near misses, all the crap and opprobrium, it all fell in a steaming heap on that May afternoon in 1973 when Second Division Sunderland defied football logic to answer a nation's prayers.

It would be an understatement to say Leeds did not do themselves justice: their performance suggested that the antipathy towards their style of play over the spread of several seasons had finally become a burden too heavy to bear. Bremner, in particular, perhaps needled by Sunderland boss Bob Stokoe's pre-match remarks, which were clearly designed to influence referee Ken Burns, was not the inspirational, driven figure so often seen providing the heartbeat to Leeds' rhythm.

There were portents before the kick-off, if you like to search for such things. No Second Division team had won the FA Cup since 1931, so the shock was overdue. Conversely, no side from the North East of England had ever lost an FA Cup final at Wembley. That one surprised me too.

The game hinged on two moments that continue to live in the

memory. After 31 minutes in which Sunderland had chased and harried a noticeably restrained Leeds, burly Vic Halom knocked down a corner in the Leeds box and Ian Porterfield swung a waist-high boot at the ball and drove it past David Harvey. As discarded newspapers blew through the empty streets of the depressed northeast town, there was nothing but joy behind closed doors. In the pubs, clubs and living rooms of Sunderland, delirium took over.

Everyone knew Leeds would get their chance to equalise. It came after half-time. Paul Reaney's deep cross was met by Trevor Cherry, diving bravely. Sunderland keeper Jim Montgomery parried the header to Lorimer. The Leeds man shot – it hit the bar. Only afterwards, with the benefit of television slo-mo, did it become clear that Montgomery had tipped it to safety, the second half of a double wonder save.

He would never go so far as to admit defeat but Bremner later confided that he felt from that moment on it would not be Leeds' day. And so it came to pass. At the final whistle Revie stood transfixed, shattered, desolate. Bob Stokoe, his comb-over hidden beneath a natty trilby, and dressed in a flasher's rain mac covering a bizarre red tracksuit, skipped and gamboled his way across the sodden Wembley turf, making a beeline for Montgomery. Truly remarkable, Brian!

Liverpool and Newcastle came to Wembley in 1974 but, in truth, it was a poor, one-sided affair that the Merseysiders won with something to spare. It is perhaps best remembered for the duel between the two managers, Bill Shankly and Joe Harvey. I remember the BBC holding an innovative split-screen interview with Shanks and a visibly nervous Harvey before the game. In that instantly recognisable gruff Ayrshire voice, Shankly talked up Liverpool. Dogmatic, unshakeable, he was totally confident.

Harvey, an ex-sergeant major renowned for his touchline bellow, was thrown out of his normally purposeful stride; he didn't know how to respond. He looked rattled, incapable of handling Shankly's domineering attitude. Liverpool were already ahead of the game. As the BBC wound up the interview, Shankly could be seen removing the microphone from around his neck and clearly heard remarking, 'Jesus Christ, Joe Harvey is beaten already and the bloody game hasn't even started!'

Asked about it years later, Shankly said, 'Then I heard David Coleman laughing and I realised what I had said had gone over. I hadn't meant it to because we had finished our talk.' Did Shankly really believe the mikes had been turned off or was this another slice of Bill's intuitive psychology?

Perhaps Harvey wanted it too much. As a player 20 years earlier, he had won the cup in Milburn's team and it was his greatest ambition to add it to the St James's Park trophy room as manager. But the harsh truth was there for all to see – his team weren't good enough. Although they had Malcolm 'Supermac' Macdonald, John Tudor, Terry McDermott and Frank Clark among their ranks, they just never got going, never came to terms with Liverpool's strength and movement. Simply put, they were outplayed by a Kevin Keegan-inspired Liverpool.

The Merseysiders had missed out on the league title but still they mounted a formidable presence with Ray Clemence in goal behind a back four that included Tommy Smith, Alec Lindsay and Phil Thompson. Emlyn Hughes was there, Steve Heighway, the talented Scot, Peter Cormack, diminutive but big-hearted duo Ian Callaghan and Brian Hall, and Keegan's strike partner, John Toshack. The first half was goalless but there was a sense of inevitability about the eventual outcome, such was the ease with which Liverpool were moving through the game.

Keegan scored first after the break, then Steve Heighway struck before Liverpool rounded off a routine victory with a quite sublime goal. It involved a dozen passes – one by Tommy Smith delicately made off the outside of his boot before he ran on for the return to play in a low cross the falling Keegan couldn't fail to convert. It was at this point that the camera panned across to the benches. Shankly, his jaw thrust forward, was giving some unfathomable instructions to his team by waving his hands from side to side. Nearby sat Joe Harvey, expressionless, his arms resting immobile on his knees – there was nothing he could say or do. At the final whistle Shankly gleefully hugged his boot-room staff, while Harvey, looking uncannily like Richard M. Nixon with that dark and distinctive widow's peak, stared dejectedly at the ground. Within a year, both of them had left football for good.

The 1975 FA Cup final was a classic example of everything that was good about the competition. Modest Division One side West Ham United faced Fulham from the Second Division. Two sides that were never likely to challenge for a league title but, on their day, had proved good enough to get through six successive ties to earn a place at Wembley.

West Ham, managed by the ever-thoughtful Ron Greenwood, were the overwhelming and natural favourites: they had Trevor Brooking, Frank Lampard Snr and the rampaging Billy Bonds in their 11. Fulham, managed by Alec Stock, an affable gent who spoke in tones more suited to Henley, had a smattering of ageing stars like Alan Mullery and, in one of those delightful coincidences the football fates seem to love, a certain Bobby Moore who would be forever linked with the Hammers.

West Ham legend Moore had decided to finish his career at Craven Cottage 18 months earlier, moving across London for

£25,000. In his first season with Fulham he helped them defeat West Ham in a League Cup tie. But there the romance ended. Although most eyes at Wembley were on Moore, who would be making his last appearance on the ground he had graced so many times as England captain, it was speedy West Ham striker Alan Taylor, a £40,000 capture from Rochdale, who stole the headlines by scoring twice, with a couple of assists from Fulham keeper Peter Mellor, to give his side victory. Quite a feat that, as he had scored twice to beat Arsenal in the quarter-finals and twice to get past Ipswich at the semi-final stage.

In 1976 another bunch of Second Division no-hopers added to the Wembley mystique by defeating mighty Manchester United. Southampton were given little more than a dog's chance. National newspapers decided that United were the biggest certainties of the century and bookies were offering odds of 7-1 against a Saints victory. It was too good a punt for a horse-racing fanatic like Saints striker Mick Channon to ignore. He even rang manager Lawrie McMenemy on the morning of the match. 'Can you believe it?' he told the giant Geordie. 'It's a two-horse race and they are giving us seven to one!'

The danger was not lost on United boss Tommy Docherty, who would later reflect, '...the fact that most people had us as certainties suckered us into not being on our mettle as we should have been. As a result, the merest hint of complacency took a substantial edge off our game on the day.'

Wembley was steaming under a hot May sun. The heat trapped inside the stadium sucked the breath from burning lungs. Southampton started the match at such a pace that they were gasping for air before the first half had finished. Yet United, for all their star presence in the shape of Martin Buchan, Steve Coppell, Brian Greenhoff, Gerry Daly, Stuart Pearson, Sammy

McIlroy, Lou Macari – every one an international – couldn't get past the Southampton goalkeeper Ian Turner or break the shield thrown up by the likes of Nick Holmes, Jim Steele and swarthy captain Peter Rodrigues.

This was to be their day, an occasion for the journeymen to step up to the plate and make a name for themselves. For one man in particular it was to provide the defining moment of his career. When Southampton quit their spiritual home at the Dell a few seasons ago for the ultra-modern St Mary's, they decided to name four entertaining suites after four giants from the club's history. Matt Le Tissier, Mick Channon and Terry Paine were all shoe-ins ... but the fourth? No, not Lawrie McMenemy, the ex-Guardsman who guided that Southampton side to glory; nor Ted Bates, his assistant that day, who served the club as coach, manager, director and president for an incredible 66 years. That accolade went to Bobby Stokes, a talented enough player though not one you would place among the game's greats.

But, of course, he presented the modest south-coast club with the single most important triumph in their history when he ran past a bemused Martin Buchan onto Scottish midfielder Jim McCalliog's career pass and beat Alex Stepney low to his left. Seven minutes to go. For Lawrie McMenemy, 'the longest seven minutes of my life' before the whistle blew and those few gamblers who had backed the rank outsiders could begin to count their winnings. For the second time in three years a team from the Second Division had won the greatest cup competition in the world. It has never happened since.

Understandably, there was little cheer in the United camp. They had been turned over by a bunch of so-called no hopers and that just made the pain even harder to bear. Docherty commented, 'I remember thinking, "This must be worse than dying. At least when you die you don't have to get up the next morning and read the newspapers."'

The people of Southampton rewarded their team with a traditional homecoming, tens of thousands cheering the players as they toured the city in an open-topped bus. Channon, who had dodged the post-match celebrations to attend a birth (of a foal!), remembered one fan was so ecstatic that he stood on top of his car to catch their attention. The fact that he was wearing not a stitch of clothing also made him stand out! That's what it meant to win the FA Cup, back in the good old 1970s. Do you think the followers of United or Liverpool get as excited these days? OK, it's a nice day out and another piece of silverware for their groaning trophy rooms ... but it's not the Champions League, is it?

Later, recalling the emotion of the day, McMenemy revealed that one of the first people to congratulate him was United manager Tommy Docherty, via a phone call in the middle of the Southampton celebration banquet. 'He congratulated me warmly,' said McMenemy. 'I said, "That's fabulous, Tom." And he said, "Don't get me wrong – I'm crying." We were both very emotional. I'll never forget that.'

For Southampton, there would never be a day like it. The nearest they have come since then was a 3-2 defeat by Nottingham Forest in the 1979 Football League Cup final, and ever since it has been a slow, agonising decline, defined by desperate money troubles, culminating in administration and relegation to League One, or the Third Division as it was more accurately, and honestly, described in the 1970s. Their revival under Argentinian coach Mauricio Pochettino provides a glimmer of hope that miracles can still happen in the 21st century, but don't rely on it.

And what about that unlikely hero Bobby Stokes? That is another sad story. His Southampton career quickly faded. Perhaps the Wembley moment had been too much of a burden. It certainly proved to be so when he made the strange, unaccountable decision to swap the Dell for Fratton Park, home of Portsmouth FC.

He was never going to be loved by his former team's worst enemies. The Pompey fans hounded him out of Hampshire. He deserved better and within a year Stokes was on the move again. But there was to be no more glory waiting for him to claim – not at Cheltenham Town, nor in the soccer wasteland of the USA. Stokes eventually came back to England, settled in Portsmouth, which was, ironically, his home town, and could always guarantee someone would want to buy him a drink, just for old times' sake. But one drink led to two and then many more. He died in 1995 from pneumonia brought on by alcoholism. Bobby Stokes was only 44.

At least United got a chance to restore their reputation a year later when Docherty took nine of the 1976 team back to Wembley to face the Division One champions and European Cup finalists Liverpool, who were intent on claiming an unprecedented treble that would eclipse the achievements of double-winning Spurs and Arsenal years before. Liverpool were clear favourites, their team simply bursting with players at the top of their game. Manager Bob Paisley chose this line-up: Ray Clemence, Phil Neal, Joey Jones, Tommy Smith, Ray Kennedy, Emlyn Hughes, Kevin Keegan, Jimmy Case, Steve Heighway, David Johnson and Terry McDermott.

United, who had finished 10 points behind Liverpool at the end of a season in which Spurs were relegated, had their own star quality but not in the same abundance. Tommy Docherty selected these players: Alex Stepney, Jimmy Nicholl, Brian Greenhoff, Martin Buchan, Arthur Albiston, Steve Coppell, Sammy McIlroy, Lou Macari, Gordon Hill, Jimmy Greenhoff and Stuart Pearson. As the two teams walked up the tunnel, Paisley, every inch the working-class hero from the Northeast, reached across to shake Docherty's hand. 'I didn't wish him luck,' said the genial Scot.

Liverpool went into the game with a lot on their minds. Could they pull off the elusive League and Cup double and then go on to lift the European Cup in Rome, only four days later? It almost certainly influenced their performance at Wembley. Kevin Keegan, in particular, was anonymous yet on the following Wednesday he ran Borussia Mönchengladbach ragged.

That FA Cup final hinged on five explosive minutes just after half-time. Stuart Pearson scored for United, outpacing Joey Jones and scoring low to Clemence's left. ITV's highly respected commentator Brian Moore, usually so restrained and conformist, chose the moment to utter perhaps the worst cliché ever inflicted on a listening audience: 'Instead of the treble ... can it possibly be trouble?' he chirped, only to have his words strangled at birth as Jimmy Case took Jones' deep pass on his instep, spun and fired a dream of a volley past Stepney. 'What an answer,' said Moore. He might have added '...to my own daft question!' but there simply wasn't time.

United attacked again, Hughes flicked on, Greenhoff tussled with Smith and Macari punted the loose ball against his own player and over Clemence, stranded and helpless.

At the final whistle, Moore this time got it spot on. 'The golden dream of the treble has been shattered,' he declared and it showed in the faces of the Liverpool players, crestfallen Hughes wiping away a tear as he led his team up to collect their losers' medals. What a contrast to the smiles of the United players, and especially their manager. It was Tommy Docherty's seventh visit to Wembley as player and manager and the first time he had experienced the heady scent of victory – 'Did it taste sweet? Not really. No sweeter than strawberries in June.'

1978 saw a new name etched on the famous old trophy: the name of a club that, to put it bluntly, could hardly be regarded among Division One's high achievers. Remarkably, under the esoteric stewardship of ex-Spurs full-back Alf Ramsey, Ipswich Town had a 1962 League Championship honour on their board at Portman Road but they had never had a sniff of an FA Cup triumph.

Enter Bobby Robson, a distinguished former England international whose managerial pedigree at that time did not really stack up, having been sacked by Fulham after two seasons in the job, but Ipswich chairman John Cobbold took the chance and the Tractor Boys embarked on the most successful period in their history, which stretched back to their amateur days in 1877.

Robson built a side packed with intelligent, thoughtful players, the likes of talented centre-forward Paul Mariner, driving midfield goal scorer John Wark, Brian Talbot, his dependable captain Mick Mills and a gifted, if somewhat troubled, young man named Kevin Beattie.

Robson, guilty on occasion of the odd bit of hyperbole, had this to say about Beattie: 'I believe Kevin Beattie was the finest player this country has produced during my time being involved in the game. See that ceiling? He could get that high to head the ball. He could be above the crossbar and head it down. He had this left foot, he could hit sixty-yard passes without looking, from left-half to outside-right and eliminate six players with that one ball. He had strength, he was quick, he was explosive and he could tackle. As a player, I would have hated to play against him.'

Sadly, there was a downside to Beattie's character; the sort of flaw someone like George Best or Paul Gascoigne would have recognised. On the day when, as a 19-year-old, he was due to join up with England, Beattie went AWOL ... and was later found playing dominoes in a Carlisle pub with his dad. Still, on FA Cup-final day 1978, he was on duty and on form.

There were plenty of stars on show that day, admittedly most of them in the colours of Arsenal FC. Manager Terry Neill picked a side bristling with talent, including Pat Rice, David O'Leary, Liam Brady, Alan Sunderland, Frank Stapleton and Alan Hudson.

Against that might, Ipswich were written off by the pundits – don't they ever learn? They under-estimated the influence of Robson, a master tactician, and he got it just about right. Unsung heroes like Clive Woods and pin-up boy David Geddis prevented Arsenal's skilful midfield from dominating play, cut down the space for the rampaging Sammy Nelson to attack from left back and, by playing only Mariner as an out-and-out striker, left Willie Young with no one to mark ... and the confusion would eventually prove fatal.

All the talk, all the headlines, were about Arsenal, their attack led by 'Supermac', at that time the best centre-forward in the country. Although Macdonald had tasted Wembley misery with Newcastle in 1974, no one seriously believed fate would do the dirty on him again. But they should know Lady Luck better than that. Macdonald suffered a knee injury during the game, which would bring a premature end to his career and at the end of 90 pulsating minutes, for him there would not even be the consolation of a cup-winners medal.

For more than an hour under a mercilessly hot sun Ipswich outplayed the Gunners, with all their vast Wembley experience, but destiny seemed determined to spoil their day. Mariner hit the bar in the first half with Pat Jennings in the Arsenal goal nowhere; twice after the break Wark smacked his shot against Jennings' right hand upright.

Cries of 'lucky Arsenal' rolled down the Wembley terraces. But as had happened with Bobby Stokes a couple of years earlier, it was all set up for a quiet man to emerge as the hero of the day. On 78 minutes blond-haired teenager Geddis, who had tormented Arsenal all afternoon, went at Nelson on the outside, did him for pace and fired low into the box. Scottish international defender Willie Young contrived to hit the lamest, girlie clearance Wembley has ever seen, straight to Ipswich midfield workhorse Roger Osborne.

Simple: quick shot, Jennings beaten, 1-0 Ipswich and the cup was theirs. It was only the second goal Osborne had scored that season – and there to watch it was a large proportion of his Suffolk family, including 11 brothers and sisters. Osborne was swamped by his delirious team mates and, starved of oxygen at the bottom of the hot blue scrum, he passed out and ended the match watching from the bench.

It is worshipped by all Ipswich supporters as the most important goal in the club's history, never mind the fact that, under Robson, European glory would shortly follow. It's that FA Cup magic again. In 1978 it was still the one trophy everyone wanted to win and Osborne, whose career hinged on that moment before taking him to America and then lowly Colchester, can dine out on it until he is in his dotage.

But there is a twist to the Roger Osborne story, later revealed by goalkeeper Paul Cooper. Osborne, an ever-present during the cup run that year, had been dropped by Bobby Robson just before the final to accommodate fit-again South African-born midfielder Colin Viljoen. Osborne's team mates did not like it one bit and the fallout was that they allowed Aston Villa to beat them 6-0.

Robson took the hint, recalled Osborne for the final and we all know what happened next. Sadly, neither Osborne nor Viljoen played for Ipswich again as Robson set about a rebuilding job with new blood arriving soon after, including Dutch masters Arnold Muhren and Frans Thijssen.

To their credit, Arsenal were back at Wembley 12 months later to give the decade the most memorable, dramatic, heart-stopping send-off in a game which would go down in history as 'the five-minute final'.

For the final against Manchester United, Arsenal boss Terry Neill was able to field most of the players who had under-performed against Ipswich, with two notable exceptions. Out was injury victim Malcolm Macdonald, in came Brian Talbot, one of Bobby Robson's bright young stars, who had moved to Highbury in January 1979 for a fee of £450,000.

United, desperate for success after a barren two-year spell under Dave Sexton, who had replaced Tommy Docherty as manager, included Sammy McIlroy, Scots Gordon McQueen and Martin Buchan at the heart of their defence, Steve Coppell and Mickey Thomas on the wings, and a potentially explosive strike partnership of Joe Jordan and Lou Macari.

Neill, clad in a startling sky-blue suit, led out the Arsenal team alongside Sexton, a more concise and undemonstrative character, wearing a much more sombre grey two-piece. The contrast was just as marked on the field; Arsenal were unrecognisable from the semi-comatose shamblers of a year before. Liam Brady was at his impish best, pulling the strings for Arsenal to cruise into a two-goal lead. Talbot celebrated his change of shirt in typically brave fashion by driving into a ruck of players on the penalty spot to ram home Rice's reverse pass, silencing the United choir, which had been filling Wembley with their anthems. Only 12 minutes had passed. And then Brady brilliantly created the second with a mazy run past flailing United tacklers. He looked up, picked out Frank Stapleton and, with a characteristic downward header at the far post, the Irish centre-forward sent the Gunners into half-time on a high, two to the good and United looking distinctly second best.

As the second-half minutes ticked inexorably by, there was nothing to promise a United comeback. When they got a free kick just outside the box, it came at a time, said ITV commentator Brian Moore, when 'hope was fading fast'. But the cross found Arsenal's defence out. It sailed over Willie Young and David O'Leary to the far side of the box, Jordan turned it back to the centre and McQueen toe-poked it past Jennings. Surely this was nothing more than a consolation? But then Coppell's long pass found McIlroy raiding on the United right. He turned inside, leaving O'Leary on his backside. Steve Walford dived in but McIlroy saw him coming and dinked the ball away, and before the onrushing Jennings could get to him, he guided the ball into the far corner. Shell-shocked Arsenal had been four minutes from an easy victory – now they faced the agonies of extra time.

The articulate Terry Neill later explained his feelings at that moment: 'A million and one thoughts go through your mind but, as a manager, you're twenty yards from the touchline and helpless. The players have given their all and suddenly we've gone from coasting to level at 2-2. You know that the TV cameras are on you so you try to look casual rather than concerned and give the impression you're not panicking, but inside your heart's pumping like mad.'

Well, it was about to go into overload. Brian Moore was busy discussing emotions on the two benches and barely watching the action as Brady seized possession and went on one last charge. He slipped the ball wide to Graham Rix; still Moore hadn't picked up the play as Rix lifted a cross beyond Gary Bailey in the United goal on to the foot of Alan Sunderland.

At last Moore got it. 'But wait a moment,' he exclaimed. 'It's there by Sunderland – what an amazing cup final!'

It was joy for Arsenal, heartbreak for United. Dave Sexton, who would be fired by United two seasons later without a trophy to his name, said, 'It was a cruel result ... we were thinking of extra time and lost concentration.'

Wembley had saved the best until last. The closing chapter, the final lines on the page, the most thrillingly explosive end to a decade of memorable Wembley occasions.

CHAPTER THREE

THE GIANT-KILLERS

Well, Peter Lorimer said it. Looking back on Leeds United's sensational 1971 FA Cup defeat at Colchester, the forceful Scottish winger with the rocket shot admitted, 'For us, it was humiliation but for the whole country at the time, because we were so hated, it was the greatest result that ever happened.'

The Leeds players knew and accepted it. No team has ever been despised like Don Revie's men. Such a pity when you consider the rich seam of talent that ran through their ranks from front to back. They had Johnny Giles and Billy Bremner, Paul Madeley and Terry Cooper, big Jack Charlton, Mick Jones and the incomparable Eddie Gray.

But Lorimer was right: no one liked them. Alongside the talent, there was a degree of cynicism that proved unacceptable. It is a sad epitaph for such gifted players – Peter Osgood said they were probably the best club side he ever faced – but there is no doubt, anyone beyond the confines of Elland Road was of the opinion that on 13 February 1971, in the FA Cup fifth round, Leeds United got their comeuppance.

Colchester of Division Four did everything they could to upset the Division One leaders, even before the match kicked off. Wily manager Dick Graham had devised a specific game plan and then added a few extra tricks – like placing chairs and benches around the ground to make it even more claustrophobic for Leeds' international stars.

The intent was not lost on Norman Hunter, who had travelled south by plane with the rest of the Leeds squad for the game. 'We'd done the Billy big time ... we flew down, which was unheard of. I walked out onto the pitch with big Jack and I looked up. The wind was blowing, the pitch was bumpy and I remember thinking, "This is not going to be easy."'

Dick Graham drummed that thought into the minds of his Colchester players. Ray Crawford, burly and tousle-haired, who had once been a Division One champion with Ipswich and an England centre-forward to boot, said, 'We were full of confidence. Deep down, we thought we might cause an upset. And I always played well against Jack Charlton.' How true was that? After 18 minutes Crawford rose unchallenged to thump a header past Gary Sprake and ignite the ram-jam crowd.

It got better. Only six minutes later Crawford collided with Sprake and, although both men were on the ground, the Colchester player reacted quickest to hook the ball over the line. Colchester, skippered by Bobby Cram, uncle of Olympic athlete Steve Cram, were in dreamland. They expected a Leeds onslaught after the break and the Yorkshiremen duly obliged but Colchester refused to take a backward step and the game went beyond Leeds' reach when Dave Simmons made it 3-0, pouncing on the sort of Paul Reaney error that was rare as hen's teeth. 3-0. Simmons raced to the crowd and was instantly smothered by delirious fans. Fast-forward to 2011 and it would be an instant booking.

Leeds rallied forth bravely, brilliantly and, as Colchester finally began to tire, Norman Hunter and Giles brought them back into the game. It was Alamo time with Graham Smith, the Colchester goalkeeper, doing his Davy Crockett bit to keep the Leeds chargers at bay. Colchester survived for a famous victory and a sixth-round trip to Everton, where the fairy tale was abruptly ended by a 5-0 defeat. Shattered by the enormity of defeat, Leeds slunk away, no doubt fully aware that they would struggle to find a sympathetic ear beyond their own particular corner of Yorkshire.

One headline writer described it as 'the most fantastic result you will ever see' and then had to think of fresh hyperbole 12 months later when Hereford United, a team of part-timers from the old Southern League, defeated Newcastle United of Division One in what has come to be regarded as the greatest giant-killing feat of them all.

If Colchester v. Leeds was a major surprise, Hereford's success over Newcastle was the mother of all cup shocks. In 2007 readers of the *Observer* voted it the best FA Cup tie ever; and given the circumstances, Ronnie Radford's goal in the third-round replay at Edgar Street stands as one of the greatest goals of any FA Cup game. The shot was struck with startling venom applied to wonderful technique and spearing accuracy – the sort of shot players probably hit time after time on the training ground but, in the tempestuous atmosphere of an FA Cup tie, it was out there with the best.

Hereford, managed by Colin Addison, were an ambitious outfit in those days, intent on making the leap into the Football

League. Addison, appointed successor to Welsh hero John Charles, had inherited a strong part-time squad and he quickly fine-tuned them for a promotion charge. But then, as now, non-leaguers would never ignore the thrill of playing in the FA Cup, nor play down its importance and, when Hereford started their run in the Fourth Qualifying Round at Cheltenham Town, all thoughts of promotion were put to one side. Their Holy Grail was to reach the third round and pull a biggie.

Well, they certainly did that and, back in the day, it did not come much bigger than a tie at St James's Park against Newcastle United. We are talking about events nearly 40 years ago and, even then, the Magpies' supporters existed on a starvation diet of silverware. But hope springs eternal on Tyneside and with the £180,000 record signing of super-confident Supermac – Malcolm Macdonald – from Luton Town to partner John Tudor up front, and the likes of Terry Hibbitt, true Tyneside legend Tony Green, Bobby Moncur, Viv Busby and Frank Clark behind them, that blind Geordie optimism was once again overflowing. Back then, there was never any question of playing kids or reserves in a cup tie. Hereford would have to face the full might of Newcastle's multi-talented squad.

Hereford United at St James's Park – what could be easier? Newcastle quickly discovered it was to be anything but easy; so quickly, in fact, that most people missed the flashing drive by Brian Owen to put the Bulls ahead after just 17 seconds, momentarily silencing the Gallowgate roar; flash in the pan. John Tudor soon had Newcastle level and when Macdonald shot the Division One side in front from the penalty spot, well, that was that, right? Howay, the lads! Er, not so.

Player-manager Addison, something of a star during his days as an attacking midfielder at Forest, with more than 60 goals to his credit, dipped into the memory bank to find a 25-yarder that fizzed past Ian McFaul in the Newcastle goal. It might not be the strike everyone remembers from that long, drawn-out cup saga but it was the goal that made history possible. United now faced a less-than-appetising replay down in cider country.

The rain had been lashing down in Hereford for days and, after a series of cancelled replays – during which time the Newcastle players were forced to spend several nights in a Worcester hotel waiting for a let-up in the weather – referee Dennis Turner finally said 'yes'. In truth, the pitch still looked more suitable for a training exercise for men of the Hereford-based SAS but, by now, it was fourth-round day and West Ham awaited their next opponents.

The official attendance was 14,313 but Edgar Street veterans reckoned a truer figure was in excess of 15,000, so tightly were they packed on the uncovered terraces, spilling over the boundary wall to sit crouched, or on upturned boxes, along the touchline. It was just like those grainy photographs you see from pre-war games; the fans were so close they could have reached out and touched the wingers. It was worth an extra man to the Hereford team who, fancifully, also seemed to have an extra player on their side – her name was Lady Luck and she played a blinder.

How else can you explain the remarkable sequence of events midway through the first half after Hereford had conceded a free kick? Mick McLaughlin's attempted clearance struck Tudor and was deflected onto the crossbar. Terry Hibbitt pounced on the loose ball but then smacked his follow-up shot against the bar. The excitement was unbearable, one heart-pounding incident following another. Saves at both ends although, to be fair, Hereford's Fred Potter was by far the busier keeper and when

Macdonald scored with a header eight minutes from time, it seemed the aforesaid Miss Luck had finally nipped off for an early bath leaving Hereford to their fate.

Cue Ronnie Radford and that goal. How many times has it been seen since? Has there ever been a televised goal with so many repeats? If Radford could have bought the image rights, he would have become a multi-millionaire. Just check the number of times it has been viewed on YouTube – it runs into the hundreds of thousands.

Radford gets the ball midway into the Newcastle half, with Macdonald looking on a few paces away. Through the middle there's not a blade of grass to be seen and into this no-man's-land Radford plays a 10-yard pass to Owen, runs onto the lay-off and whacks it. His right foot goes through the ball like a Tiger Woods' drive; McFaul's flailing dive is nothing more than a gesture. And then Radford is off, arms held high, pursued by 10 team mates and about 5,000 delirious fans. And they weren't all kids. PC Grenville Smith later recalled, 'When Ronnie scored, the crowd ran on but I was ahead of them, cheering! I threw my police hat in the air, caught it, then remembered myself and shouted, "Off the pitch!"'

What a pity the *Match of the Day* cameras did not capture that moment of FA Cup emotion.

Macdonald was the nearest player to Radford when he got his shot away. He was less than generous in his review of that wonder goal. 'The ball sat up on a divot,' said Supermac. 'He didn't know that was going to happen. Without that, it would've been a mis-hit and a throw-in to us. So all the fates colluded on Hereford's behalf.'

I have studied the YouTube footage over and over and, you know, Mac might have a point. The ball did sit up and beg to be hit – and Radford kind of agreed. 'It was an unbelievable feeling when my goal went in. It could have finished in the car park but as soon as it left my foot, I knew it was going for the top corner.'

The winning goal, by contrast, was a bit of a stumbling affair. A low, bobbling cross into the area, a sharp turn by the totally unmarked Ricky George and then a toe-poke of a shot, which was not particularly powerful but so well placed, it was way beyond McFaul's reach. Here they come again – another major pitch invasion, kids mobbing the Hereford players, smiling coppers waving an ineffectual arm to clear them off.

Had the goal been on a par with Radford's, Ricky George would be the name everyone associates with the day Hereford defeated Newcastle but the glory belongs to Radford and, whether there was an element of luck or not, it will stand the test of time as a reminder of how wonderful the FA Cup used to be.

George is deep into his 60s and retired now, like most of the men who played that day. Understandably, Colin Addison made Hereford his home and local people have never forgotten that he was the man in charge on that historic occasion. A couple of years ago he told the *Guardian*, 'Every day I walk through the town someone mentions it. I'm from Somerset but I'm adopted here. They named a street after me, Addison Court. That was nice. Five years ago I went back to St James' Park for the first time. I saw Malcolm Macdonald. The fag fell out his mouth and he said, "Fucking hell, not you again!"'

For the record, Leeds won the Cup that year, beating Arsenal 1-0.

Fast-forward a couple of years to another stunning FA Cup surprise, another one for the record books, another moment of glory for a non-league team against First Division opposition. But can you tell me the names of the two teams involved and what made this upset so special? No, I didn't remember either. In round three of the 1974–75 FA Cup competition Wimbledon wrote an indelible page in football history in becoming the first non-league team to win an FA Cup tie away from home against First Division opposition. Yet for some reason it failed to earn the romance of Hereford's victory over Newcastle; for some reason few remember a player named Mickey Mahon who scored the goal that stunned Turf Moor.

The man to blame for the resultant anonymity was Burnley butcher Bob Lord, the Lancashire club's autocratic chairman and a powerful voice in football in those days. Not a fan of television where his sport was concerned, he worried too much exposure was threatening the livelihood of the top clubs. He once exclaimed, 'If the BBC don't shift their cameras from Turf Moor, I'll be down there myself and personally burn them. They are on the ground without our consent and I don't care if even Harold Wilson [then Prime Minister] has given them permission.' What would he make of football's relationship with the small screen, were he around today?

Lord had banned television coverage of the Wimbledon cup tie. Perhaps he also had a premonition that the day's events were not going to be something he would want to remember.

Wimbledon, whose home in those days was a hotchpotch of a ground in southwest London fittingly known as Plough Lane, were another of those ambitious non-leaguers determined to break into the big time. Manager Allen Batson had compiled a decent squad of hard-working players, one or two whose names are still familiar, like Dave Bassett and goalkeeper Dickie Guy.

From the Fourth Qualifying Round on, the Dons brushed aside a succession of non-league opponents, with victory over Kettering Town earning them a third-round trip to Lancashire to play struggling First Division side Burnley, who might have been at the wrong end of the top table but, with the likes of Leighton James, Bryan Flynn and Ray Hankin in their side, were backed for an easy passage into the next round.

But even then Wimbledon, best known for their phenomenal rise in the 1980s from non-league to Division One, with an FA Cup triumph along the way, did not give a fig for reputations. Hard, uncompromising and well organised, they were difficult to break down. And Burnley were not the stiffest opposition, when compared with Liverpool or Leeds. So Wimbledon – and around 1,000 travelling supporters – went North with a fair degree of optimism. And when Mahon struck just after half-time to put the Dons in front, they proceeded to show they were made of the right stuff as Burnley threw everything at them in a bid to avoid a major embarrassment. 'It was real backs-to-the-wall stuff for pretty much the whole game,' keeper Dickie Guy recalled, years later.

But Wimbledon hung on to take their place in the fourth-round draw and this time claimed the plum tie they had been banking on, away to the champions Leeds United. And Wimbledon almost did it again. In front of 46,000 at Elland Road, they held mighty Leeds to a 0-0 draw. Leeds, desperate to avoid another FA Cup humiliation so soon after the Colchester debacle, should have won it at the first time of asking. At the end of a flowing Leeds' move from their own penalty area Eddie Gray was the victim of a tackle so clumsy that Frank Spencer could not have done a better job. Up stepped Peter Lorimer, 'about to kill the Wimbledon fairy story', according to commentator Brian Moore, but knowing his kick had to be good to get past the bearded wonder Dickie Guy, who had been in superlative form. Well, in truth, Julian Clary could have saved it. It was a weak, side-footed effort, virtually straight at Guy.

Throughout the 90 minutes Guy had pulled off one stunning stop after another. At one point commentator Moore lost a touch of his usual self-control and declared, 'This man is not human!' But the penalty save was probably the easiest of the game and it was the closest Leeds came to avoiding a replay.

Now the nation was joining hands in prayer for another major upset at Leeds' expense. Such was the clamour for tickets the replay was switched from pokey Plough Lane to Selhurst Park, where around 45,000 fans could be accommodated. And the omens were good. The referee was Dennis Turner, the same man who had officiated at Hereford's triumph over Newcastle a couple of years earlier; Leeds were without the commanding figure of Gordon McQueen in defence, and rattled manager Jimmy Armfield had punished Lorimer's penalty howler by leaving him out of the team.

It was another tense affair with Leeds, inspired by the tricky Duncan McKenzie, turning on the style but repeatedly unable to get past that guy Guy and constantly aware that a Wimbledon breakaway, a fluke, a dodgy decision, could bring more despair. Well, a fluke settled it but this time Leeds were the lucky bunch, with Johnny Giles firing in a speculative shot which took a heavy deflection and spun past Guy. It was just about the only way they were ever going to beat him.

For the record Leeds made it through to the quarter-finals, where they were beaten by Ipswich Town, the famous old trophy eventually being won by West Ham United.

The final giant-killing act of the 1970s belonged to the Northumberland coastal town of Blyth, home of the Spartans, a non-league corner of a real football hotbed. Just a few miles to the North is the town of Ashington, where the Milburns and Charltons were raised. Blyth is one of the oldest football clubs in non-league, founded in 1899 and, so the story goes, fancifully named in honour of the glorious Spartan army of Greek mythology. They have never looked likely to reach the fully professional ranks and still appear to be a lifetime away as they toil along in the Conference North. But their name is written large in FA Cup history, especially for their exploits in the 1977–78 competition when they fought their way through nine rounds and 11 ties before finally bowing out.

In Blyth they still talk about that particular Spartans team to this day; how their heroes got within a dodgy corner of meeting up with Arsenal FC. Their biggest scalp in a prolonged FA Cup campaign was Stoke City, then of the Second Division and manager-less on the day, having just got rid of one-time playing idol George Eastham after a brief and painful tenure, which included relegation from Division One.

Ex-Derby County star Alan Durban was just a week away from taking over when his new protégés got their faces rubbed in the mud by that rough, tough outfit from Blyth, a town established by coal miners and ship builders. Defensively strong, Spartans had a decent level of talent from the likes of Alan Shoulder, who later went on to a higher calling with Newcastle, and a fearsome striker by the name of Terry Johnson.

Blyth had slogged away in the qualifying rounds against local rivals like Crook, Consett and Bishop Auckland to win through to the first round proper. They drew Lancashire non-leaguers Burscough at home and duly despatched them. Next it was league opposition in the shape of Chesterfield, managed by the redoubtable Arthur Cox, but the Spireites fared no better. Then they got Enfield, who had to make the 600-mile round trip to Blyth's neat Croft Park ground just to get done 1-0. Blyth's reward in the draw for the fourth round was an away tie at the

Victoria Ground, Stoke. Not the greatest of attractions for the non-leaguers but still a decent money-spinner. And it turned out to be quite a match.

Spartans, a collection of engineers, fitters and a police officer, struck first when their robust striker Johnson was on the spot to hook the ball over the line after a bit of particularly duff goalkeeping by Stoke City's Roger Jones. City's equaliser came soon enough, from a man whose name has appeared in this chapter before: Viv Busby. Now there's a player with an album full of FA Cup memories, most of them bad. Remember, he was part of the Newcastle side who lost to Hereford.

When City went in front with a diving header by the loquacious Garth Crooks that should have been that. But, as we have seen so often, non-league spirit stirred into the FA Cup pot can achieve wondrous things. Steve Carney brought the sides level again and deep into the second half, with the Stoke defence in some disarray, Johnson ran onto a loose ball and drove it home with impressive coolness. It was hardly the finish of a part-timer.

In the fifth round Blyth were away again, this time at Wrexham, who had enjoyed an equally impressive run through the competition, having survived a 4-4 draw with Bristol City in the previous round. By rights it should have turned out to be another league scalp for Blyth. As commentator Barry Davies said, 'This is what the FA Cup is all about – the chance for the meek to have their moment.' Young fans and players today will struggle to understand just how magical the old competition was, how tantalising a prize was the trip to Wembley. Back then it was the stuff of dreams, not an unwanted intrusion in today's real competition: the accumulation of wealth.

Spartans scored first and it was that man Johnson again, then they doggedly held on to his goal until the dying minutes. But just when they needed her most, Lady Luck hitched up her skirt and farted straight in Blyth's faces. Skipper Jack Waterson tackled Wrexham winger Bobby Shinton and, as the cameras later proved with conclusive clarity, he played the ball off the attacker for a goal kick. But referee Alf Gray was in the wrong place, or didn't see it, or just guessed. His linesman was no help either. Corner. The first flag kick came to nothing ... but that referee ordered a retake and of course this time Wrexham's ace in the hole, Billy 'Dixie' McNeil, scored. That was it – a replay that shouldn't have been necessary.

Croft Park was not considered worthy of such an occasion so 42,000 Geordie lads and lasses piled into St James's Park to see if Blyth could make it through to the sixth round and a place in sporting nirvana, a quarter-final tie at home to Arsenal. But it was Alf Ippititimus again who consigned them to defeat. Two players challenge for a cross into the box, McNeil goes down. Penalty. To be fair, old Alf had a pretty good view of this one and it did look like a push in the back. Graham Whittle hammered home the spot kick.

Then it was two. A ball was floated to the far corner of the Blyth box, sparsely populated apart from the one player Blyth didn't want to see there: Dixie McNeil on the volley, top corner, 2-0, thank you very much. Just one of the more impressive strikes of a career tally that went past the 230 mark and the goal that finally brought Blyth's fairy-tale journey to an end, even though there was a fitting postscript with Johnson rounding off his exploits for the season with another fine strike.

Four great cup ties, four wonderful results; four unforgettable chapters in FA Cup history. There will no doubt be FA Cup shocks to come but, as the reputation and appeal of the grand old competition is gradually eroded, they will not match up to the triumphs of Colchester, Hereford, Wimbledon and Blyth, simply because the FA Cup ain't what it used to be.

Martin Brain, who was an 11-year-old ballboy at Hereford United FC the day they defeated Newcastle, put his finger on it as well as anyone. When asked to recall that momentous day in the lives of almost every soul in Hereford, he said, 'It was nothing like football today – a similar shock could never be repeated, neither will the run. A side like Hereford will never again play against a very top club's first-choice team.'

He's right, of course. Romance and the FA Cup used to go together like fish and chips wrapped in newspaper but now we have to eat them out of plastic boxes and it just doesn't taste the same.

CHAPTER FOUR
BERTIE'S DOUBLE WINNERS

The good folk of Nottingham like to claim Middlesbrough-born Brian Clough as one of their own and who can blame them after the unlikely glories he brought to their door? But they tend to overlook the fact that there was another genuine footballing legend who was born within the city boundaries and in 1971 he made an indelible mark on the game's history at a time when Clough was still weaving his magic down the A52 at Derby County and his only interest in Nottingham Forest was taking two points off them.

This modest hero's name was Bertram Mee, who hailed from the nondescript Nottingham suburb of Bulwell, an area of back-to-back terraced houses and modest bay-windowed semis, where men worked in the local collieries or cycled into the city for a shift at Raleigh or Players.

There was never a more unlikely character to succeed in the minefield of top football management, yet Mee engineered a feat that only one other manager in the 20th century had achieved before him: he took Arsenal to the double of Division One champions and FA Cup winners. And what made his success all the more sweet was that a decade earlier it had been Arsenal's deadliest rivals Tottenham Hotspur who had been the first team to emulate the so-called Invincibles of Preston North End, who were unbeatable way back in 1888–89.

In the 20th century, when there was so much more equality in football, most learned observers said the double could not be done. But then, in 1961, Bill Nicholson's brilliant Tottenham team, with the likes of mercurial midfield ace John White, later tragically killed by a lightning strike, thoughtful Danny Blanchflower, hard man Dave McKay and that peerless little marksman Jimmy Greaves, pulled it off.

That Spurs side was the best club team I ever saw. I remember a trip to White Hart Lane in the early 1960s to see them play Forest – I think it was Tommy Jackson who gave Forest a surprise early lead and their Channel Island striker Geoff Vowden who scored the last goal of the game. In between Spurs scored NINE! And Forest keeper Peter Grummitt was the visitors' best player. So who could blame Spurs for crowing about that double-winning side every time the north London derby came around? It stuck like a fishbone in the craw of Arsenal's supporters.

The Gunners, by contrast, had won nothing since the First Division title in 1952–53, gradually sliding into mid-table mediocrity. In 1962, in an effort to halt the demise, they took a gamble by going for celebrity, offering the manager's job to Billy Wright, at that time England's most capped player with 105 internationals to his credit but little experience as a coach. Things got worse as the easy-going Wright took them down to

14th place in Division One, their lowest finishing position since 1930, and fans deserted the grand old Highbury stadium in their droves. An end-of-season fixture against Leeds United attracted just 4,544 people through the gates. Wright's fate was well and truly sealed.

So who would Arsenal turn to? Who was big enough to fill the marble halls of Highbury, to assemble a team good enough to win a title or an FA Cup, perhaps even challenge the record of the Lilywhites from White Hart Lane?

No one was prepared for the name of Wright's successor – Bertie Mee, the club's physiotherapist since 1960 and a man with few discernible credentials for the job.

He had been a decent young player at his school back in Nottingham, a solid Gothic redbrick monolith that stood on Albert Street but has long since been replaced by an anonymous housing estate. Mee's school was around 130 miles away from Highbury, the ground where he would earn everlasting fame, but perhaps even at that tender age it was trying to tell the young man about his destiny. You see the name of the school was Highbury Boys.

Mee's playing career was hardly illustrious. He began with Basford United, a good name on the local Nottingham league scene, and then got his chance with Mansfield Town, as an amateur, and Derby County, although that was mainly for the second string. But then war broke out and Mee was called up to join the Army. It proved to be the making of the man. Mee joined the Royal Army Medical Corps, where he learned a thing or two about men and how they perform under pressure.

On the skills side, he developed an interest in the treatment of injuries and the rehabilitation of disabled soldiers. And on the human side, the qualities of soldiering were drilled into him until they became his personal Ten Commandments. Mee understood the need for discipline within the group and individually. He also believed in a set of standards to which everyone would have to adhere: he wanted people around him who were prepared to work for themselves and each other, who could obey his rules, share his vision of how best to get the job done. His philosophy was simple: 'I have been motivating people in one way or another all my life, whether they are troops, sick people or professional footballers. Basically, people are the same, whether they are footballers or factory workers.' His Arsenal side would have no prima donnas, no showboaters, no cheats and no rebels.

The Arsenal directors, with a display of common sense and intuition rarely seen at boardroom level, had noted Mee's mental toughness and his ability to handle big-name players in the treatment room: if Mee said you weren't fit, you weren't picked. They liked his strength of character, his integrity; his honesty. It suited the Arsenal image and, with that in mind, they were prepared to entrust him with the manager's chalice.

Mee, a short, dapper figure of scholarly appearance, who usually sported a dark military blazer with buttons buffed to dazzle, reluctantly agreed. But he had an amazing clause written into his contract: if he failed as Arsenal manager, he wanted a cast-iron guarantee that he could return to his old job, as physiotherapist.

Arsenal chairman Denis Hill-Wood, an old-school gentleman, thought that an entirely acceptable arrangement and in 1966 Mee replaced the over-promoted Billy Wright. Later Mee revealed his motivation for taking on such a precarious challenge: 'Mediocrity was being perpetuated. That was painfully obvious to me and that's why I went into management because I thought I could change it. The standard needed raising 30 to 40 per cent.'

It came as something of a shock to the footballing cognescenti but Arsenal had previous in this regard. One-time physio Tom Whittaker had been given the top job at Highbury in 1947 and then went on to lead Arsenal to two league titles and the FA Cup in the decade just after World War Two.

Still, that sort of history cut little ice with the players who, if the memory of double-winning captain Frank McLintock is a measure, were more than shocked by the appointment. In his autobiography *True Grit*, McLintock admitted he was 'thunderstruck' by the news, thought 'a peculiarly cruel joke' had been played on him and even accused the club of 'irresponsible thinking'.

Phrases like 'martinet' and 'pompous', and comparisons with Captain Mainwaring of *Dad's Army*, were thrown about the dressing room. McLintock says he was prepared to give Mee just six months to prove himself and then if progress was not being made, he would jump ship. In fact, it would be seven years before the tough Scot would finally say his farewells to Highbury.

Those characteristics picked out by McLintock were certainly accurate but, as he later added, Mee also had integrity and determination, a strict sense of discipline and the intelligence to know when and how it should be applied.

Life under Billy Wright had been too easy, too lax. He had hoped his natural charisma allied to respect for his achievements as a player would get his team to do what he wanted them to do. But most footballers are too shallow and self-centred to be given such freedom. They will always try to take the easy way out if the opportunity is there and Wright gave them more than enough room to manoeuvre. There would be none of that under Mee;

his was to be a very different regime – he wanted his players to be good and, to do that, they had to behave. 'Fearsomely hard but always fair,' was goalkeeper Bob Wilson's frank assessment.

Mee introduced a system of fines for anyone who fell outside the parameters of behaviour he expected. Even a minor felony like failing to wear shin-pads could incur a £10 docking of wages. Swearing, the industrial language that is part and parcel of every footballer's make-up, was something Mee abhorred and it was discouraged when he was around.

To make up for his self-confessed shortfall in coaching ability, Mee recruited boxer's son Dave Sexton, another studious character who had made his reputation at Chelsea under Tommy Docherty before taking his first tentative steps into management at Leyton Orient. Sexton sang from the same Bertie Mee songsheet when it came to hard work and conduct, on and off the field.

The duo inherited some promising young players – the likes of George Armstrong, Peter Storey, Jon Sammels, John Radford, Ray Kennedy and a precocious talent named Charlie George. Good enough to win Arsenal the 1966 FA Youth Cup, they would eventually become the nucleus of the great double-winning side.

In fact, Bertie Mee once professed that his ambition was to field an Arsenal team consisting of 11 homegrown players: 'When you live together as 15-year-olds, a close affinity develops and it is inevitably going to show on the field of play.' Perhaps that is at the root of Arsène Wenger's thinking, why he insists on sticking with youth rather than flooding his team with expensive imports. Unless you can afford the very best, there is real merit in growing your own. Taken to its logical conclusion, if the young players are good enough and are prepared to stick together, success will surely follow. Really, it is all about patience and faith.

They were qualities Mee had to display in his first months in the job. Although they did not bring the profit he had suggested would decide his future as a manager, the signs of progress were there and he gave no intimation that he was about to walk away. With Mee laying down the strict rules and regulations his players must follow and Sexton developing the cohesive pressing game that would become Arsenal's triumphant formula, there was a collective and growing belief that better days were ahead.

'Success results from a combination of hard work and a determination to figure in Arsenal's return to greatness,' he once said. 'I think our greatest qualities are confidence and character. To win the league you need a squad of footballers who will give you 45 top-class performances out of 50. Occasional brilliance is no good over a long season. That was what I set out to impress on my playing staff; that was the response I sought. We kept and recruited those who had that attitude – the others could go.'

One of Mee's first signings was to prove pivotal in the team's eventual triumphs. Having sold popular striker Joe Baker to Nottingham Forest, he brought in George Graham for £75,000 from Chelsea, a strong-willed character with a possibly-too-strong sense of self-belief but an abundance of natural ability as a counter-balance.

The foundations had been laid and that first Mee season was one of steady improvement. With the emergence of those young players and the further addition of Huddersfield Town full-back Bob McNab, another iron-willed individual unafraid to express an opinion, the squad began to add depth to its obvious quality, and Mee encouraged and engineered the collective spirit that would be needed if tangible rewards were to be achieved.

But then came what appeared to be a major setback: Dave Sexton quit to take over from Tommy Docherty as Chelsea manager. McLintock spoke for the dressing room when he described Sexton's decision as 'a huge psychological blow'. While they had every respect for Mee's man-management, they all knew he could not coach a tiddlywinks team and they could see a year's hard work and investment in the Mee vision going down the pan. But they should not have worried. Mee turned to reserve team coach Don Howe, an ex-England full-back who had played with, and then for, Billy Wright, before a broken leg ended his career. West Midlander Howe was another articulate, astute coach who believed the fittest teams were the best teams and any player who could not keep up with his demands would be left by the wayside. It proved to be a match made in soccer heaven.

In the early Mee-Howe years, Arsenal became a difficult side to beat but, equally, a team unable to establish themselves as winners. They lost the 1968 League Cup final in a suffocatingly boring match to a disputed goal from Leeds full-back Terry Cooper but a year later they were back at Wembley in the same competition. This time the opposition was Third Division Swindon Town and it was odds-on – and high time – that Arsenal would win their first trophy since 1953. But it was not to be Arsenal's day. There were extenuating circumstances for one of the greatest cup shocks on record. More than half the Arsenal team had been laid low by flu in the days leading up to the final, the Wembley pitch had been turned into First World War quagmire when a drain had been damaged during the Horse of the Year Show held shortly before the final ... and Swindon proved to be a damned good team.

Swindon scored first, Roger Smart on the spot to embarrass centre-half Ian Ure and Bob Wilson, in the Arsenal goal, after they had clumsily presented him with an open net. Just before the end another Mee recruit, Bobby Gould, grabbed the equaliser to send the match into extra time but, by then, the ailing Arsenal players had nothing left, certainly not enough pace and stamina to cope with Swindon's inspirational winger Don Rogers, who scored twice to give Swindon their moment in the sun and put their name on the honours board alongside Liverpool, Manchester United and Arsenal, for all time.

It focused attention on Rogers, who would make big money moves to Crystal Palace and Queens Park Rangers in the early 1970s, before being forced out of the game by injury. Years later, reflecting on the best day of his footballing life, Rogers remarked, 'Good old Bobby Gould for scoring. It's daft, really. If we had won 1-0, it would never have happened for me, would it?'

Despite those setbacks – or perhaps it was because of them – Arsenal kicked on. They finished fourth in Division One and qualified for the 1970 Inter Cities Fairs Cup, which later evolved into the UEFA Cup, which has now become the UEFA Europa League. All that means is that more than half a dozen teams from every league across Europe are playing in one European league or another. No wonder domestic competitions like the FA Cup have become an irritating sideshow.

Back to Arsenal in 1970 as they stood on the threshold of immortality. The team had a comfortable passage to the semi-final stage of the Inter Cities Cup but there they came up against genuine opposition in Ajax of Amsterdam, another side poised to make history. Marshalled by the brilliance of Johan Cruyff, Ajax were about to become the dominant side in Europe, going on to win the European Cup three times in a row. But over two legs against Arsenal they had to yield to the Gunners' organisation and work rate. Charlie George emerged as their match winner with two goals in the first leg at Highbury. A 1-1 draw in Amsterdam was more than enough to see Arsenal through for yet another chance to end their 17-year trophy drought. This time there would be no mistake.

The final, in those days a two-legged affair, was against RSC Anderlecht of Belgium, the first leg played at the Constant Vanden Stock Stadium in Brussels. It was a distinct clash of styles, Anderlecht parading typically European traits of patience, ball retention and measured build-up until the right opportunity to make a thrust on goal. How well it worked for them: Arsenal were defending with their usual precision and doggedness yet three times Wilson was beaten, with goals by Johan Devrindt and Jan Mulder (two). By the 70th minute it looked like Arsenal were again set to be bridesmaids, a prospect particularly galling for McLintock who, with Leicester and then Arsenal, had reached the finals of four cup competitions and lost the lot.

Fifteen minutes from time Mee (or was it Howe?) made an inspired substitution, sending on teenager Ray Kennedy in place of Charlie George. He presented Anderlecht with the sort of challenge European sides have habitually struggled to cope with – aerial power. Arsenal began to find him with crosses and he began to threaten the home goal. And with eight minutes left, he headed past Anderlecht keeper Jean-Marie Trappeniers and Arsenal had a lifeline.

What happened next is the stuff of folklore in Arsenal's particular corner of north London. Mee, Howe and especially the captain McLintock sensed that they could overturn the two-goal deficit if they pulled together and ruthlessly exposed Anderlecht's Dracula phobia – a fatal aversion to crosses. McLintock's assessment of the Belgians' centre-half, Julian

Kialunda, was classic: 'Six feet, two inches tall but he couldn't head the ball for a free haggis supper!'

When Arsenal stepped out for the second leg at Highbury on 28 April 1970, 52,000 fans were chanting and swaying and waving right into the faces of the Anderlecht players and, as Corporal Jones might have put it, they clearly did not like it up 'em. Eddie Kelly set Arsenal on the road with a blistering shot before half-time. The crowd bayed for Belgian blood. Anderlecht defended manfully but they could not hold the thin purple line against an Arsenal team that, in the end, simply out-ran them. In a breathtaking two-minute spell, John Radford and Jon Sammels took the game away from the visitors to give Arsenal victory.

The manner of the triumph was a total vindication of Bertie Mee's appointment and his style of management: Arsenal were too well organised, too fit and too determined for the Belgians to handle. And it was only the beginning.

Arsenal fans had every reason for optimism at the start of the 1970–71 season. The club's long run without a trophy had finally ended and Mee had assembled a squad with a pleasing and effective blend of youth and experience, strength and no little flair. Mee's first-choice line-up started with the urbane Bob Wilson in goal, more schoolteacher than footballer and a relative latecomer, not cementing a first-team place at Highbury until the age of 27. English-born, he won two caps for Scotland and is fondly remembered for his many years as an erudite broadcaster with the BBC.

In front of him were two highly dependable full-backs, craggy Pat Rice and the mobile Bob McNab, and centre-backs McLintock and one-club man Peter Simpson. The midfield combination was perfect. Peter Storey was the resident hard man. Every team needed one: a Norman Hunter, a Ron Harris, a Tommy Smith. Then he had to be paired with a playmaker, and Arsenal's was the elegant George Graham, aptly nicknamed 'Stroller'. The essential wideman in Arsenal's make-up was George 'Geordie' Armstrong, a tireless player with far more skill than his appearance suggested. Dead from a brain haemorrhage at 56, he is remembered as an all-time Arsenal great.

Up front was as strong a trio as any side could field at that time. John Radford was a wonderfully athletic centre-forward with steel neck muscles and a poacher's eye for goal. He scored 148 times for Arsenal, none more memorable than on a mud-heap at Anfield when he ran from inside his own half and, to hear him describe it, as Ray Clemence 'ran out like a loony', he rolled the ball beneath him and into the net. He was also the ideal foil for young Ray Kennedy. So powerful with his left foot and one of the great headers of a football, Kennedy's 21 goals would lead the way towards the double, yet he was the most undemonstrative of players, shunning the ludicrous antics expected of goal scorers today.

The front threesome was completed by the free spirit that was Charlie George: shirt over his shorts, lank hair streaming untidily across his long face, George was never the prettiest button in the box but he could do things no other Arsenal player could match and was more often than not the lynchpin for an attack which ended in a goal.

His ability to pick the ball up in the face of a packed defence and not only spot the briefest of opportunities but also exploit it led Frank McLintock to compare him to the legendary Johnny Haynes. I cannot remember the Fulham and England great, although I must have seen him as a kid, but it sounds like a glowing reference to me.

There were others in the squad who came in when required, most notably Eddie Kelly, a dependable workhorse, and Sammy Nelson, still fondly remembered for 'mooning' to the North Bank after scoring a rare goal. Less effective was Peter Marinello, a player in the mould of George Best but without the same abundance of talent. He was a fresh-faced pin-up who seemed to have the world at his feet when he came down from Scotland to join Arsenal in a £100,000 club-record transfer deal but a catalogue of misfortunes on and off the pitch meant his potential was never fulfilled. However, his much-publicised arrival at Highbury helped fuel that pre-season optimism, but not one of the North Bank faithful could have anticipated the events that were to unfold over the next nine months. Especially when things began so badly. In September 1970 Arsenal were battered at Stoke City, losing 5-0. Would anyone be throwing money at an Arsenal double?

Frank McLintock later described that miserable defeat as the defining moment of their season, the turning point when whatever disparate factions there were in the squad buried their differences and united in the common cause. Arsenal went back to doing what they did best – imposing themselves on the opposition, smothering the life out of them with their 10-man pressing game and then picking them off as they wearied of the constant stress they had been placed under. It was not always pretty but it was an effective, match-winning style, not dissimilar to that adopted by Leeds United and, in fact, it would be Don Revie's team that would mount the closest challenge to Arsenal's run on the championship.

Arsenal got there by virtue of their consistency, splicing together a string of unbeaten matches, reeling off several wins on the run, always capable of bouncing back after a bad result. They had the qualities needed for champions. It all boiled down to the final couple of games of the season and as their D-Day approached, a visibly emotional Bertie Mee gathered his players together. Compared to Henry V at Agincourt, or blue-faced Mel Gibson, it was not the longest of oratories but it made the point.

'These are our plans. I would not normally say this as a family man but I am going to ask you, for your sakes and for the sake of this football club, to put your family second for the next month. You have the chance to put your names in the record books for all time.'

Leeds had ended their fixtures with a victory over Forest, giving them a one-point lead in the title race ... and Arsenal had to go to White Hart Lane. It could not have been tougher. Of all the teams they could have faced, none would have a greater desire to spike their dreams than Spurs. Arsenal almost missed the kick-off, such was the throng of supporters cramming the streets around White Hart Lane, thousands of them without a ticket for the game. The 50,000 who were lucky enough to find a place on the terraces witnessed an epic struggle. Spurs' blood was up and they would stop at nothing to rob Arsenal of the glory of emulating Billy Nick's 1961 heroes.

The tackles flew in fast and hard, not always with the ball as primary target, Spurs being driven forward at every opportunity by their England star Alan Mullery. Arsenal knew a 0-0 draw would give them the title on goal difference but, to their credit, they scorned such a negative approach and with only four minutes to go, Armstrong pinged his cross towards the penalty spot where Kennedy, unmarked, headed over Pat Jennings and just under the bar. Arsenal were champions! Now for Wembley and the drama of the FA Cup final, with Bill Shankly's Liverpool completing the cast.

Once again Mee drew his players around him and spelled out just what awaited them and how, with one more victory, they could write an indelible chapter in the history of Arsenal FC. And so it came to pass beneath the old Twin Towers as Bertie Mee from Bulwell led his team across the Wembley turf, significantly a step ahead of Bill Shankly, who had once referred, in less than flattering tones, to Mee as 'the medicine man'.

Well, this time Shanks failed to get under the skin of his opposite number. Arsenal should have won the game in normal time. They had the pick of the chances, Graham striking the bar with perhaps the best, but it needed the energy-sapping theatre of extra time to find the moment, to provide the stage for an FA Cup image that survives 40 years on and will be repeated every time the names of Arsenal, Wembley and Charlie George are raised in conversation.

Steve Heighway gave Liverpool the lead, beating Wilson at his near post. It was an error and, had it been the winning goal, who knows how it might have affected his subsequent career prospects? But that would have been grossly unfair. Wilson had been a towering figure throughout that season and maintained his form in the final. Minutes later he made a terrific one-handed save from Brian Hall to keep Arsenal in the game and keep the ultimate prize within reach.

Substitute Eddie Kelly equalised ... or was it George Graham? Kelly's shot seemed to get a touch from the Scot, who was happy to claim the glory, although TV replays would suggest, but not categorically confirm, that he missed it altogether. No matter – Arsenal were level. Now the game needed a fitting finale and, cometh the hour, it had to be Charlie.

It was the second period of extra time and heavy legs were struggling to put in the hard yards. Radford received the ball on the left and turned inside to find George 20 yards from goal. One touch, a flash of the right foot and the ball was past the flailing dive of Clemence. George fell to the ground and lay there, arms outstretched, soaking up the immensity of his achievement, Radford imploring him, 'Get up, you lazy fucker! There are nine minutes left!'

At that moment George did not care. He could have been James Cagney in *White Heat*: 'Made it ma, top of the world.'

It was enough. As a weary McLintock hoisted the trophy for the faithful to rejoice, Bertie Mee looked on, that familiar broad smile playing across his genial face. He had taken a proven formula for success and, like some medieval alchemist, mixed in all the right ingredients to create a potent force. His players gave everything they had, laid it all on the line, travelled the extra mile. And, almost inevitably, once it was over nothing would be the same again: they could not repeat the conquest. That was where Mee came up short – he did not know how to build on what had been achieved. He had the opportunity to establish a dynasty at Highbury but lost his way. He once said, 'Having taken the title, the hardest part is winning it again.' For Mee it was a bridge too far.

First Howe left. Shamefully undervalued for his contribution, he took up the offer to manage his old club, West Brom. Then Mee brought in Alan Ball and, fine player though he was, the dynamic of the team changed. League form faltered, Ajax killed their European aspirations; Mee's control and respect began to ebb away. McLintock was allowed to leave, Graham went to QPR, then Charlie George moved on to Derby County, his potential largely unfulfilled. And most surprising of all, Mee sold Ray Kennedy to Liverpool.

Why? Some observers believe Mee was wounded by criticism.

For all that Arsenal had achieved, the reward was at best grudging praise. Despite the fact that at that time in the Football League's history the double was regarded as a near-impossible feat, no one seemed to like the style of Arsenal's triumph. Perhaps Mee thought he could do it all over again, perhaps he thought he *had* to do it again if he was to gain his place in the hall of fame. But, like a Forest or a Derby, a Villa or a Blackburn, Bertie Mee's Arsenal was one of those teams where all the stars were aligned, as much by fate as by good judgement, for just a brief moment in time.

In 1976 Bertie Mee resigned. Arsenal were back where he had found them, in the lower half of the First Division. It would be 17 years, which yielded only an FA Cup and League Cup, before they would rise to the top again.

Mee took time out from football but, incredibly, during his sabbatical there were few club chairmen beating a path to his door, demanding the services of a man who had awoken a sleeping giant and pulled off the most astounding triumph. So Mee sat down and penned a letter to Watford FC and their young, thrusting manager Graham Taylor, offering his services.

When delivering the eulogy at Mee's funeral in 2001, Taylor said,

> In 1977 I received a letter from him, after he had parted company with Arsenal, in which he offered his services should I require them. Neither Elton John nor myself could believe a man of such standing was having to write a letter to try to find a position in the game. One meeting between the three of us and Bertie Mee became assistant manager at Watford, the best signing I ever made.

Instead of Watford having just a crazy pop star as chairman and a young upstart as manager, making all sorts of noises about how they were going to go from the Fourth Division into European football, we had someone who immediately gave credibility to our ambitions. A man of great integrity, a former Double winner with bags of experience and numerous top-line contacts throughout football.

Mee was given special responsibility for scouting and youth policy, and among the players he is credited with discovering is John Barnes. With Mee's support and advice, guidance and encouragement, Taylor-led Watford embarked on a remarkable rise from Division Four into the old First Division in the space of four years, then qualification for Europe and an appearance in the FA Cup final, where they lost to Everton.

It was around this time, and long overdue, that Mee was given some recognition for his contribution to football, receiving the OBE in 1984. He stayed on at Vicarage Road as a director until his retirement in 1991.

Bertie Mee lived out the rest of his days in the Southgate area of London, where he died in 2001 at the age of 82. Among the many tributes were two that correctly locate his position in the history of football, and particularly Arsenal FC.

His old captain Frank McLintock said, 'He was probably a forerunner to most of today's top managers, a wonderful statesmanlike figure.'

And Terry Neill, who succeeded Mee at Highbury, said, 'He's up there with all of them because Bertie turned the club around at a difficult time in the mid-1960s. He laid the foundations and I think all the Arsenal managers since have followed that.'

CHAPTER FIVE
TALES FROM THE BOOT ROOM

Liverpool Football Club, until the arrival of that man Ferguson just a few miles down the M62, was the most dominant football club in the history of the English game. Five times champions of the Football League during the 1970s – plus an FA Cup, two European Cups, two UEFA Cups, a European Super Cup and four Charity Shields. Once they started collecting pots in the 1960s, they didn't know when to stop. The 1980s would be just as successful. No team in the 20th century came close to such a command of the game at club level.

But why Liverpool FC? Why not Aston Villa? They are the premier club in the nation's second city, yet their list of achievements, while notable, pales into insignificance when compared to the Merseyside Reds. Why not Arsenal, or Tottenham, or Chelsea? Each of them giants from the capital, with a proud history and glittering trophy cabinets, yet their triumphs have waxed and waned. They have had their moments, at times been the best in the land, but successive managers and owners have failed to establish a dominion that compares to Liverpool FC.

And why not Everton? Didn't the blue half of Liverpool have the same opportunities, the same fanatical support? Like all the others, they have scaled the greasy pole to the top but found it impossible to stay there. So why did it have to be Liverpool? This is not a quiz, of course. There are no prizes for answering such a no-brainer: it was Bill Shankly.

It is impossible to tell the Liverpool story within the parameters of a single decade. The story has to begin with Shankly and the day he arrived at Anfield, 1 December 1959. He did not start by beating his chest, telling the world and his dog how he was going to turn them into the greatest club side in English football history. Standing before the press, diminutive but pugnacious, much like his screen hero James Cagney, he merely told them, 'I am pleased and proud to have been chosen as manager of Liverpool. They are a club of great potential.'

History records that, pre-Shankly, Liverpool had been champions of the Football League five times ... but not since 1947; and astonishingly they had never won the FA Cup. When Liverpool chairman Tom Williams took a chance on the young manager of Huddersfield Town, his side had been languishing in Division Two for five years, too long in the shadow of their great Merseyside rivals Everton. They needed deliverance and along came their messiah in the shape of a passionate Scot, a pint-sized battler with a raw, west-coast accent and an intensity in his gaze that made people take him seriously. Charisma is a word frequently over-used, rarely in the right places. The dictionary explains it thus: 'A spiritual power or personal quality that gives an individual influence or authority over large numbers of people.'

Given that, I would not suggest Sir Alex Ferguson is a charismatic figure. A forceful personality without doubt; a man who has achieved greatness through sheer will and expertise, but the hair-dryer does not equate to charisma. Nor does it apply to the studious, charming Arsène Wenger, a manager cut from a completely different cloth yet no less qualified and adept at his job but, for my money, not a charismatic figure.

There was Shanks, Brian Clough ... it's a short list. They say that, when Clough walked into a room, you could feel his presence radiating into every corner and into the core of everyone there. It is an indefinable star quality granted to very few.

Ron Yeats, Shankly's captain during the success years of the 1960s, tells of the time when 250,000 Liverpool fans gathered in the city centre to greet their team after a successful European jaunt. They were chanting, singing, cheering – and then Shankly stepped forward, raised his hand and the whole crowd fell silent. Now that's what I call charisma and that, I would argue, was the defining characteristic he brought to Liverpool, and which made them what they are today.

A tailor's son, and one of 10 children, from the Ayrshire village of Glenbuck, young Bill Shankly was guided through his formative years by an innate sense of fair play and an insatiable desire to play football, any time, anywhere.

'We played football in the playground, of course, and sometimes we got a game with another school but we never had an organised school team. It was too small a school. If we played another school, we managed to get some kind of strip together but we played in our shoes.'

It seemed there were two career paths for young men living in Glenbuck between the wars – go down the pit or play football. For Bill Shankly, one followed the other. He experienced life on the coalface, hundreds of feet underground, shifting thousands of tons of the stuff. It must have helped develop the streak of toughness in his personality that would come into play down the line.

When he was not working, he was playing football for a local side and, when he was not playing, he was training – running up and down the local slag heaps to develop a level of stamina few could match. Shankly never stopped. 'It's a 90-minute game for sure,' he once said. 'In fact, I used tae train for a 190-minute game so that, when the whistle blew at the end of the match, I could have played for another 90 minutes.'

'For as long as I can remember,' said Shankly one day, 'my sole aim in life was to play football. When I worked down the pit, all I dreamed about was the end of the shift and legging it to the nearest field for a game.'

Fitness would be of paramount importance throughout his career. Every day of every week of every month of the year he pushed himself to the limit. And if he could do it, he argued, then no one else could have any excuses. It was reflected in his own performances as a player and thereafter in every team he went on to manage.

While still a teenager, he was rescued from the coalface by a scout from Third Division North strugglers Carlisle United FC and, in 1932, Bill became the fifth Shankly brother to join the professional ranks. But Carlisle was never going to be big enough to hold young Shankly. He was not overly ambitious in those early days but, once the mighty Preston North End came calling, he joined them like a shot ... for the princely transfer fee of £500 and a ten-bob raise to £5 a week.

The teak-hard little Scot quickly established himself at wing-half and the now-infamous Shankly characteristics soon became well known.

His wholehearted commitment to the game meant a total dedication to fitness, even through the close season. He stayed with Preston until 1948, winning FA Cup winners and losers medals before the Second World War and, when his playing days drew to a close, there was never a doubt that he would remain in the game; his passion was undimmed, even when relations with the Deepdale club were soured over a testimonial wrangle. Shankly, forever a man of principle, turned his back on the chance to become Preston's reserve team coach by taking over as the new manager of Carlisle United. He went with the best wishes of the fans and nothing good to say about the directors. A year later Preston were relegated.

At Carlisle, Shankly was able to put his theories and convictions about how to run a football club into practice. He brought into play the beliefs instilled in him as a young man growing up in a coal-hard mining community. 'The socialism I believe in is everybody working for the same goal and everybody having a share in the rewards. That's how I see football, that's how I see life.'

He expected his players to train hard, get their fitness right and then practise their ball skills, something rarely seen at English clubs in the post-war era. In return, he would look after them, encourage them, organise them. Keep the football simple, keep the ball moving; pass and go. Push and run. Basics. Master them, and the rest would follow.

Shankly lifted Carlisle to previously unheard of heights, third in Division Three and a goalless draw at Highbury in the FA Cup. They lost the replay 4-1 but he turned it to his advantage. Telling his players Arsenal were the best team in the land, he gave them pride in defeat – he could always find a positive. Years later, when he missed out on the signature of Lou Macari at Liverpool, he told his players, 'I only wanted him for the reserves.'

After Carlisle, Shankly had frustrating spells in charge at Grimsby, impoverished Workington and Huddersfield Town, where he helped to develop the talents of a crop of young players like Mike O'Grady, Ray Wilson and a slightly-built young Scottish striker named Denis Law. He was one of the few players from a rival club Shankly ever had a good word for, once commenting that he was capable of 'dancing on eggshells'!

Shankly earned a reputation as a players' manager. A hard taskmaster, he tempered that with fairness and loyalty, never criticising his players in public, never giving the opposition even the chink of a psychological opening to exploit. He reasoned that the players were the most important asset of any club and if he could keep them happy, success would automatically follow.

Other priorities were to bring supporters into the club family and keep the media onside. It is an obvious omission that the only people left off his Christmas card list were directors but Shankly had little time for the amateurs and meddlers that infested most boardrooms. 'At a football club, there's a holy trinity,' he once said. 'The players, the manager and the supporters; directors don't come into it – they are only there to sign the cheques.'

That was the problem at Huddersfield, where boardroom parsimony thwarted his ambitions for the team and so, when Liverpool came in search of his services, Shankly was ready to uproot his family and move on.

At first sight, it was not a promising engagement. Liverpool, once a mighty, title-winning First Division side, were not so much dormant as comatose. From their mediocre position in the second tier, they were forced to watch Everton rule the Merseyside roost, and it hurt. Poor attendances, no investment, Anfield was decaying, on and off the field.

But Shankly changed all that. He took over as manager in December 1959 and, as Ron Yeats put it, 'He took it by the scruff of the neck and shook it into life.' Liverpool – the city and the club – might have looked grey and unappealing to Billy's ever-loyal wife Ness but it was just what he was looking for – a sleeping giant he could awaken in his own indefatigable image. He made no promises beyond a pledge to 'put everything I have into this job I have so willingly undertaken' but that was just what the Anfield faithful wanted to hear. He was talking the talk, and he lost no time in proving he could also walk the walk.

Liverpool fans with memories going back that far will remember that, traditionally, the side wore red shirts and white shorts. It was Shankly who changed that, insisting on the now-famous all-red strip because 'I wanted to make them more imposing'.

He found kindred spirits in the club's trio of coaches, Bob Paisley, Joe Fagan and Reuben Bennett; won the respect of players like Jimmy Melia, Roger Hunt and young Gerry Byrne. All he needed was for the board to back his judgement financially and he was convinced that he would soon have Liverpool back where they belonged.

Ah, those bloody directors again! Shankly tried to sign players like Law and Jack Charlton but the cash was not forthcoming. It was a familiar story and could have led to a different version of history being written but for the intervention of major shareholder John Moores, the pools giant who had a well-heeled foot in both the Anfield and Goodison Park camps, and wanted nothing more than to see both prosper.

He was warned that Liverpool might lose a man who, potentially, was the best manager the club had ever had. And so he listened, assessed and then decided: whatever Bill Shankly wanted, he could have. The red touchpaper – it had to be red as

Shankly would never countenance anything of a more azure hue – had been lit and Liverpool were on their way.

First to arrive was Motherwell striker Ian St John. He established a blistering partnership with Roger Hunt, spearheading Liverpool towards promotion in a season that saw the team hammer in more than 100 goals. Equally important was the capture of another Scottish talent, defender Ron Yeats, only 22 years old but a colossal man, standing around 6ft 3in in his stockinged feet. 'With Yeats in defence,' Shankly once said, 'we could play Arthur Askey in goal.'

Shankly made him captain before he had set foot in the Anfield dressing room. St John, Yeats, Shankly and the club's fanatical supporters led Liverpool back to Division One in 1962, but as far as Shankly was concerned, that was only the start. From now on it would be Liverpool, as well as The Beatles, at Number One.

It took just two seasons, the catalyst being the signing of Peter Thompson, a flying winger from Preston who set up a constant supply line of opportunities for St John and Hunt. Liverpool became an irresistible force, a juggernaut that rolled over teams with ruthless efficiency, completing their championship charge with a 5-0 title-clinching victory over Arsenal. Shankly said it was the greatest moment of his football career, better than the FA Cup winners medal, his Scottish caps, and made even sweeter because the team they took the championship off was Everton.

Whether Shankly's oft-voiced disregard for Everton was genuine or mischievous we will never know but he loved nothing better than taking a rise out of the blue half of Merseyside.

'When I've got nothing better to do, I look down the league table to see how Everton are getting along'; 'If Everton were playing down the bottom of my garden, I'd draw the curtains';

'This city has two great teams – Liverpool and Liverpool reserves'. When Alan Ball signed for Everton, Shanks told him, 'Don't worry, Alan, at least you will be able to play close to a great team.' And there is a wonderful anecdote, told by Tom Darby in his 1998 biography of Shankly, of the day John Toshack came with his wife to sign for Liverpool. Seeing Mrs Toshack decked out in a blue coat, Shankly told her it had to go – 'We're red here.'

With that first title safely deposited in the Anfield trophy bank, Shankly began plotting the future. He and his faithful lieutenants would gather in a little room beneath the stand and discuss tactics, assess players and analyse opposition. The Anfield boot room became part of the Liverpool story and would be the well from which Liverpool would draw successive managers for the next 20 years or so: Paisley, Fagan, even the luckless Roy Evans.

The following season tested Liverpool's resources to the limit. The league title was relinquished, to Don Revie's Leeds United, but in a Wembley thriller that went to extra time, goals from Roger Hunt and Ian St John prevented the Elland Road team from winning the double. Liverpool celebrated their first ever triumph in the grand old competition as only Liverpool can. And then, three days later and carrying the mother of all hangovers, they were up for the cup again – this time the European Cup semi-final against the formidable Internazionale of Milan.

Shankly stoked up the fires that burn within the hearts of all Liverpool fans before the game to such a level that, when the Inter players passed under the famous 'This Is Anfield' sign and onto the pitch, they were met with a wall of sound from the heaving, swaying masses on the terraces. Inter were going to warm up in front of the Kop but visibly quailed in the face of such verbal hostility, turned round and headed up to the other end of the ground. It was no friendlier there ... and the atmosphere was about to become even more intimidating. When Liverpool ran out, it was to a roar that reached the heavens. To apply Tim Rice's brilliant lyric from the musical *Chess*, it was a night that made hard men humble.

Hunt, Ian Callaghan and St John provided the goals on a pulsating night of European football, a climactic occasion the likes of which would become so familiar in the years ahead. To their credit, Inter got a hold of their nerves to mount a creditable opposition, Sandro Mazzola scoring the goal that restricted Liverpool's advantage to two for the second leg.

That second leg became embroiled in the sort of controversy repeated many times when English clubs ventured abroad: a controversial performance from the referee, dubious goals, blatant gamesmanship. Liverpool lost 3-0 but learned some valuable lessons.

1966 brought another Division One title but again they lost out in Europe, defeated by Borussia Dortmund in the final of the Cup Winners Cup. They had gone one better than the previous season but, for Shankly, it was not good enough. For him, finishing second was like finishing nowhere. Back to the boot room and more analysis. Shankly and Co. came to an obvious, unpalatable conclusion: the side he had created and which had returned Liverpool to the A-list had gone about as far as it could go. Now he would have to build a new team; one capable of dominating for years to come and one capable of capturing the Holy Grail, the European Cup. Only one English club had done it – Manchester United – and to Liverpool that was only marginally more digestible than had it been Everton.

Shankly had won a couple of titles, a first ever FA Cup, but that wasn't enough. His vision for Liverpool was boundless.

'My idea was to build Liverpool into a bastion of invincibility,' he said. 'Napoleon had that idea – he wanted to conquer the bloody world. I wanted Liverpool to be untouchable. My idea was to build Liverpool up and up until eventually everyone would have to submit and give in.'

Between 1966 and 1973, Liverpool endured a fallow period when it came to winning trophies – they even had to sit and suffer as Everton took the 1970 Division One title under their stern and authoritarian manager Harry Catterick – but Shankly was assembling his mosaic for success. To hell with Everton!

First came Emlyn Hughes, then Ray Clemence, coltish Steve Heighway, willowy Scottish midfielder Peter Cormack and the towering, square-jawed centre-forward John Toshack. The final piece of his jigsaw was a player crafted in his own image: Kevin Keegan, short in stature but with the biggest heart in football. Not the most talented player in the world, but there was never a player who made more of his talent. Shankly paid Scunthorpe United £35,000 for Keegan's signature, gave him his debut at the age of 19 and within 12 minutes, the lad had scored!

How many times would he repay the faith Shankly had shown in him? Theirs was a relationship built on total respect for what each brought to the table. 'I think, because my dad was a miner ... he cared about me,' said Keegan. 'And he motivated me unbelievably. The second week I was training there he came over to me and said, "Son, you'll play for England." I'm not 20 yet, not even played for Liverpool, and he said that to me and I thought, "Wow!" And you knew he meant it. And I thought, "If he thinks I will, I will."'

Shankly and Keegan, sorcerer and apprentice, infused the rest of the team with a belief that anything was possible and a desire to prove the point. Emlyn Hughes, another player with a heart as big as a bucket, once said of Keegan, 'When he was with Liverpool, he was, without argument, the best player in Britain. He was magnificent, a superb, all-round professional whose consistency was incredible.'

Shankly's signings were talented in their own different ways but collectively they bought into his work and team ethic, underpinned by his insistence that they become one with the fans who could sense, as the 1970s dawned, that their team was on the verge of something special, something extraordinary, something unprecedented. Between 1966 and 1973 Liverpool won nothing, yet the faithful crammed into Anfield for every game and finally they got their reward: Anfield became the fortress Shankly had envisaged. In the championship season, 1972–73, the Reds lost only one home fixture and finished the race three points ahead of Arsenal.

In a season when Bobby Charlton announced his retirement, Gordon Banks suffered his career-ending road accident, Brian Clough broke the British transfer when he paid £225,000 for Leicester full-back David Nish, and West Ham's Bryan 'Pop' Robson topped the Division One goal-scoring charts, Liverpool's title was confirmed with victory over Leicester City in front of the delirious Kop – their 64th competitive game of the season – although it had been a virtual certainty after Liverpool's Easter defeat of double-chasing Leeds, goals from Peter Cormack and Keegan forcing Don Revie to concede to the better side.

At the final whistle, Shankly walked onto the pitch, took off his grey suit jacket to reveal a shirt of deep Liverpool red. Surrounded by a posse of photographers he raised his hands to the Kop and they yelled his name in return. The players' lap of honour ended in front of the banner-waving, swaying mass of the Kop. 'Eee-aye-addio, we won the league' rolled down the terraces in perfect harmony. Then came Shankly. A red-and-white scarf around his neck, one hand raised in recognition of the fans' vital part in their success, he acknowledged their worship, backed by a roof-raising rendition of 'You'll Never Walk Alone'. And then it was back to work.

There was still business to conclude: Shankly desperately wanted to bring European success to Liverpool. He saw it as the next step towards establishing his team as the dominant force of the decade and it is a measure of the man's awareness and tactical nous that he quickly got to grips with the different demands of European football. Back in the 1970s the UEFA Cup was much more than a consolation for clubs that failed to qualify for the European Cup, so Liverpool's march past the likes of Eintracht Frankfurt, AEK Athens, Dinamo Berlin, Dynamo Dresden and Tottenham Hotspur was cause for real excitement.

The two-legged final was against Borussia Mönchengladbach, the first tie in front of the baying Anfield hordes. Liverpool were at full strength. Even now the names trip off the tongue and each player comes instantly to mind: Ray Clemence, Chris Lawler, Alec Lindsay, Tommy Smith, Larry Lloyd, Emlyn Hughes, Kevin Keegan, Peter Cormack, John Toshack, Steve Heighway, Ian Callaghan ... What price that collection today?

Against them was ranged the likes of Gunter Netzer, Rainer Bonhof, Bertie Vogts and Jupp Heynckes, components of the German machine that had demolished England 3-1 at Wembley a year earlier. But it was to be Liverpool's night; another of those glorious floodlit European occasions at Anfield. The opening goal was classic Liverpool – Lawler crossed to Toshack, who headed back across goal and there was little Keegan diving full-length to ignite the Kop. It was the same combination for the second, Toshack heading down inside a packed Borussia box, but this time it was Keegan's bravery that made it happen, darting in among the flying boots to score.

Two Keegan goals, two Toshack assists – funny how fate plays its own game at times like these. But for a torrential rainstorm, which had forced the first leg to be abandoned after half an hour, Toshack would not have been there. He had been left out of Shankly's original line-up in favour of little Brian Hall but those 30 rain-lashed minutes had been enough for Shankly to correctly assess that the German defence could be troubled by Toshack's height – another example of Shankly's tactical shrewdness.

The third goal came in the second half, from a right-wing corner. Larry Lloyd found himself being ignored by defenders previously so disciplined but, on the night, disassembled by the passionate assault on their senses: big forehead, easy goal. That score and a late penalty save by Clemence were to prove crucial moments.

In the second leg, as thunder and lightning crackled in the Westphalian air, Borussia hammered Liverpool with 90 minutes of non-stop attacking football, scored two goals ... but they could not find the equaliser against Liverpool's resilient defence. And so Liverpool brought home the first bit of European silverware in the club's history. The city stopped to greet them. Tens of thousands of fans poured onto the streets, perhaps as many as half a million, leaning from balconies, clambering up lamp posts, swinging from shop signs, just to catch a glimpse of their heroes.

Shankly did not disappoint: he used the occasion to confirm his unique place in the community of Liverpool. In a dogmatic, finger-wagging speech of Churchillian gravitas, he told the masses, 'Since I came here ... I have drummed it into the players, time again, they are privileged to play for you and, if they didn't believe me, they do now!' There was nothing more to be said. A tumultuous chant of 'Shankly, Shankly' echoed across Merseyside.

At that moment they probably thought it would go on forever and, in some ways, it did. Liverpool are still a significant force in domestic and European soccer, still marching to Shankly's beat, but the great man was poised to shock the football world. He gave no outward signs then, nor during the following season when Liverpool again challenged for the title, this time finishing second best to Leeds before going on to take the FA Cup in an embarrassingly one-sided Wembley showdown with Newcastle. But things had changed at Anfield: John Smith had taken over as chairman. A much more hands-on administrator, that did not sit well with Shankly. He had been the heartbeat of Anfield, controlling everything the club did, from what the players wore to who was bought and sold. But under Smith, the directors wanted more say, more involvement, and Shankly wanted none of that.

And so on Friday, 12 July 1974, at the age of 58 and after 15 years of remarkable progress and success, Bill Shankly OBE announced his retirement. 'It was the most difficult thing in the world, when I went to tell the chairman. It was like walking to the electric chair, that's the way it felt,' he said. He told the world that he was tired and trotted out that politically acceptable excuse of wanting to spend more time with his family. But Liverpool FC *was* his family. To say that the city of Liverpool was stunned is the master of understatement. Kop-ites were bereaved and then, as the background of boardroom influence was revealed, their sadness turned to anger. Their perception was that Shankly was leaving reluctantly, unable to reconcile his style of management with the modern, commercial approach that came in with Smith.

To this day Liverpool command fanatical support but, it might be argued, their relationship with the club changed when Shankly retired and nothing would ever be quite the same again. Shankly had not only brought them success – League Championship (1964), FA Cup (1965), League Championship (1966), League Championship (1973), UEFA Cup (1973), FA Cup (1974) – he had established Liverpool as a monument, a symbol of the city, and given them a place on football's Olympia. Now it would be for others to take up the baton and run with it, further and faster than any team in English history, while Shankly walked away, quickly and seemingly forgotten by the club's hierarchy.

There are now the Shankly Gates and, belatedly, a statue to the great man, arms aloft in that familiar thrusting fashion. But there are also those who feel the tokens of memorial are mere notes in the margin. Kevin Keegan once said, 'I think Liverpool should be playing in the Shankly Stadium. He started it off; that stadium wouldn't be what it is now if it wasn't for Bill Shankly.'

Although Shankly had gone, the club was not foolish enough to throw the baby out with the bathwater. They could have attracted the biggest names in football but they did not want Shankly's legacy to be wasted. The next manager had to have the same tough, single-minded character; dedicated and determined. The short-list consisted of just one name: Bob Paisley.

He was the key element of Shankly's boot-room bunch. Ex-Liverpool player, physio, coach … If Shankly was the heartbeat of Anfield, Paisley was the blood flowing through its veins. Paisley was destined to become the most successful manager in the club's history. On Shankly's solid foundations he erected a palace of dreams: 13 major titles in nine seasons ... and he did not even want the job.

He told the players at their first meeting he had not wanted the job, did not know if he could do the job, and did not expect to be in the seat for long. That was not what they wanted to hear. Footballers are capricious creatures, they can be winners for one man and just as easily turn the other way if there is no connection with his successor. How could the quietly spoken, modest and reluctant new man who had been more than happy as an unnoticed backroom boy step into Shankly's shoes and walk in his large footsteps?

'I knew one thing,' Paisley said in that soft, distinctive County Durham accent. 'I had to do it my way.'

'Bob surprised us all, even himself,' Keegan recalled. 'He grew into the job, sensibly sticking with the team and the tactics he had inherited from Shanks, and slowly and gradually implanting his own ideas.'

It must have dawned on him at some early point in his tenure that there were tougher jobs than managing a football club. Raised in a typical mining village in the Northeast, Bob Paisley knew all about hard times. As a child during the 1926 strike he had scrambled over slag heaps in search of fuel. Years later he was there the day they brought his badly injured father out of the pit. During World War Two, as an anti-tank gunner, he played his part in the relief of Tobruk and victory over Rommel's Afrika Corps at El Alamein.

It is not hard to imagine Bob Paisley as a Tommie. He was working-class to his roots, small of stature, but muscular and craggy. His thick head of hair would be brushed straight back with an old-fashioned centre parting – a look so typical of the time. And he had that quiet, self-deprecating sense of humour most old soldiers who went through the horrors of war tended to adopt. He was out of step with contemporaries like Brian

Clough, Tommy Docherty, Malcolm Allison and Ron Atkinson – men who enjoyed the limelight and revelled in headlines. His affinity lay with his players and the supporters of Liverpool FC.

Had he been around today, he would have shuddered at the public bitching between top managers like Sir Alex Ferguson, Arsène Wenger and José Mourinho. Paisley kept his own counsel, never resorted to so-called 'mind games' and was always prepared to acknowledge rather than denigrate the achievements of his rivals.

Yet, paradoxically, Paisley found himself at the centre of a press storm before the ink on his new contract was dry, after his star player Kevin Keegan and Leeds United's tempestuous Billy Bremner had been sent off for fighting in the curtain-raising 1974 Charity Shield game at Wembley. Keegan got a three-match ban for the fight and a further eight for throwing off his shirt; Paisley was incensed and berated the FA – and even government interference – for succumbing to 'the hysteria and calls for examples to be made'.

It gave a hint to the steel in Paisley's nature as he laid down his own rules of engagement with the players and the board of directors. He would coach them, pick the team and decide who came in and went out. It ruffled a few high-profile feathers: Larry Lloyd was given a rapid ride out of town to Coventry City, while chairman John Smith's public utterances about transfer policy earned him a sharp, verbal rap. No one was in any doubt as to who was the new boss at Anfield and almost to a man, he was rewarded with total respect. Paisley set about rebuilding Shankly's ageing side. Phil Neal was plucked from the obscurity of Northampton's County Ground; Terry McDermott came home to Merseyside from Newcastle.

Paisley expected to win the title in his first season but was pipped by Clough's Derby County upstarts. His side was also given a lesson in the European way by Red Star Belgrade, and there was to be further disappointment in the domestic knock-out competitions. All of which left Paisley more than a little dumbfounded. 'I'll admit, right away, that I am disappointed that we did not have a major trophy to show for our efforts,' he said. 'We were in four and we had a good side, but when you count second place as failure, standards are becoming fantastically high. We never celebrate second place here.'

It proved to be something of a watershed. With Welsh defender Joey Jones added to an imposing line-up that also included Ray Clemence, Tommy Smith, ageless Ian Callaghan and young Jimmy Case, the basis of the all-conquering Liverpool machine was established. Then Paisley pulled off a stroke of genius, a touch of soccer alchemy that acted as the catalyst.

Ray Kennedy, who had made a surprising switch to Liverpool at around the time Shankly decided to call it a day, was struggling to regain his Highbury form as the youthful centre-forward of Arsenal's double-winning side. But Paisley saw something more in his make-up and, after discovering Kennedy had begun his days in midfield, he took a gamble and converted him into what was essentially an old-fashioned left-half, oddly with the number five on his back. His decision paid off in spades: Kennedy became the fulcrum of Liverpool's relentless pursuit of silverware and almost instantly was rewarded with an England call-up, even though, unknowingly, he was displaying the first signs of the Parkinson's Disease which would come to blight his life.

In his second season Paisley led Liverpool to the championship and triumph in the UEFA Cup final, defeating Bruges of Belgium over two legs. A year on they won the title again, lost an FA Cup final to Manchester United and then, four days later, walked onto the pitch of the Stadio Olimpico in Rome to contest the European Cup final against Borussia Mönchengladbach, the side they had beaten to the UEFA Cup four years earlier.

Old acquaintances were renewed: Keegan and Vogts, Hughes and Bonhof, Callaghan and Heynckes. Old memories were stirred. Paisley impishly told the press that the last time he was in the Eternal City he had been a victor, with the British Army in 1944. He repeated the story in his pre-match team talk, relaxing the players by hardly mentioning the star-studded opposition. Every man knew his job within the team framework; all they had to do was go out there and perform.

Roared on by in excess of 25,000 banner-waving Koppites, Liverpool, in a style that became their byword, slowly squeezed and then crushed the life out of the Germans after an early scare, Bonhof's bobbling shot from 25 yards, beating Clemence but not the woodwork. They went ahead when McDermott's perfectly timed run and shot gilded Steve Heighway's perfectly timed run and pass. 'Lovely stuff,' said BBC commentator Barry Davies, while Paisley later described it as 'a coaching showpiece'.

Liverpool had to shrug off the irritation of Allan Simonsen's equaliser, a screamer past Clemence just after the break, then Clemence pulled off a courageous save at the feet of Uli Stielike as the Germans, for the first and only time in the match, threatened to take control. It was that old warhorse Tommy Smith who turned the tide red with a flashing header from Heighway's corner, which German keeper Wolfgang Kneib hardly saw.

The *coup de grâce* came from Keegan. Having tormented Bertie Vogts throughout and, with time ebbing away, he made a dart into the box with Vogts snapping at his heels. Vogts slid in, might have got the ball, but French referee Robert Wurzt decided it was man first and gave the penalty. Phil Neal, for the third time in that glorious run to the title, scored from the spot. Normally so phlegmatic and taciturn, Paisley leaped from the bench, arms aloft. Liverpool were home and dry and moments later, almost lost from sight amidst the unruly mob of photographers and VIPs surrounding the presentation table, Emlyn Hughes gleefully held the huge trophy above his head, like a beacon to all victorious Liverpool fans.

Paisley had fulfilled the vision Bill Shankly had had from the day he first stepped through the doors of Anfield. Shankly said it himself: 'This is what Liverpool have been working towards for years.' Paisley, almost overcome by the emotion of it all, fell back on his natural humour, repeating his wartime anecdote for the press throng: 'This is the second time I've beaten the Germans here ... the first time was in 1944. I drove into Rome on a tank when the city was liberated. If anyone had told me I'd be back here to see us win the European Cup 33 years later, I'd have told them they were mad! But I want to savour every minute of it ... which is why I'm not having a drink tonight. I'm just drinking in the occasion.'

It was a night tinged with sadness too – the final appearance in a Liverpool shirt of their talismanic star Kevin Keegan, ironically bound for Germany and FC Hamburg. But it was the Liverpool way of doing things not to dwell on setbacks, rather to turn them to advantage – negatives had to become positives. Cue the British record transfer of Kenny Dalglish from Celtic for £440,000. King Kevin was gone, hail King Kenny!

Dalglish found everything he was looking for at Liverpool, a family club with boundless ambition, and he quickly became Paisley's lieutenant, the manager's eyes and ears on the pitch, a quick-witted, intelligent player who would be the kingpin of Liverpool's awesome domination of domestic and European football for nearly a decade to come.

Paisley's inherent ability to spot good players and then fit them into his system also brought Alan Hansen and Graeme Souness to Anfield, and within the space of six years their combined talents would capture four more Division One titles, two European Cups and three League Cups.

It is not the same any more. Paisley and Shankly have gone, foreigners run the club, trophies are much harder to come by. So fans spend a lot of time living in the past, their banners still glorifying the days of Bill and then Bob, when anything seemed possible and, with remarkable consistency, they usually proved it was.

Can Shankly and Paisley be separated? Should one sit higher than the other? One might argue that without Shankly, Paisley would not have had his chance of making such history ... who knows? Ian Callaghan played under both men and gives both equal billing: 'Liverpool wouldn't be the club it is today without Bill Shankly and Bob Paisley and the players who played there. When I first went there, it was a typical Second Division ground and look at it now!'

Alan Hansen might disagree – 'I go by records and Bob Paisley is the Number One manager ever!' His chairman David Moores echoed the view: 'Bob's knowledge of players and the game in general is unsurpassed. Football has known no equal in management or prize-winning but his modesty and dignity were overwhelming as he led this club from one triumph to another. His name will always be synonymous with Liverpool.'

But for Ron Yeats, there was only one manager, Bill Shankly, simply put: 'The greatest.'

CHAPTER SIX

CLOUGH AND TAYLOR
AT THE DOUBLE

In the bustling centre of Nottingham, just a few yards from the majestic Council House where he used to bring his Nottingham Forest team after one of their many unlikely successes to receive the tumultuous acclaim of the city, on a spot once occupied by an effigy of Queen Victoria, stands an 8ft-high bronze £70,000 statue of Brian Clough in familiar pose, hands clenched above his head in triumph.

It is rare to walk past Old Big 'Ead, appropriately located in King Street, and not see someone posing for a photograph, and it is impossible not to be reminded of the glory and excitement he brought to what is essentially a provincial footballing backwater.

And just a couple of miles away, on the banks of the River Trent – where it was rumoured he could walk across without the aid of the famous old bridge – the City Ground home of Nottingham Forest provides another powerful memorial to the great man. Step through the double doors and into the small, unfussy reception area and there he is, staring straight back at you: Cloughie captured in full cry, in a superbly sculptured bust.

And if you are lucky enough to walk past the photographs depicting moments of unforgettable triumph, past the well-stocked trophy room and down the players' tunnel, as you emerge from dark into light, dominating the scene is the towering Brian Clough Stand, his name picked out in giant red letters against a white background to leave no one in any doubt of the great man's legacy. It was originally called The Executive Stand but pressure from fans succeeded in altering its nondescript identity.

Then, if you just happen to be on a Cloughie pilgrimage, you can drive down the A52 to Derby, where he really started his campaign to shake up the football world, along a road also dedicated to him – 20 miles of major highway, which will forever be known as Brian Clough Way. And even that is not the end of the story. In 2007, in Albert Park, Middlesbrough, where the Brian Clough story began, there is another statue, this time showing him in younger guise as the brash and cocky centre-forward who graced Ayresome Park with his remarkable goal-scoring feats.

Who's to say he does not deserve such acclamation? As a player, he scored 197 goals in 213 games for 'Boro before moving to Sunderland, where he briefly blazed his trail until a crippling knee injury brought it all to an end.

And then, as the manager of two unfashionable clubs, Derby County and Nottingham Forest, he won two league titles, two European Cups and a veritable pile of League Cups, Simods, Anglo-Scottish, County Cups ... if it was made of silver, it was worth the effort for Cloughie.

But all this hero worship does not tell the whole story and, in fact, it does a disservice to the truth. Because it was not just Brian Clough, certainly not through the 1970s when he was rocking the football establishment to its very foundations, it was always Brian Clough and Peter Taylor. Football's dynamic duo, as perfectly matched as Morecambe & Wise, and never as good without the other.

In 2009, when it was announced that a statue of Clough and Taylor was to be placed on Derby County's new Pride Park campus, Brian's son Nigel commented, 'There have been a lot of individual tributes but my dad would be the first to say he would want to be sitting alongside Peter. It was a unique partnership – there are not too many partnerships stay together as long as they did, and not too many have been as successful as they were. Peter was an extremely funny, warm man. It is funny because we very rarely saw them socially but at work, it was almost a telepathic relationship.'

Old Cloughie now has more statues in his honour than Margaret Thatcher and, as a dyed-in-the-wool lifelong socialist, this would have pleased him no end. Yet in Nottingham it's a different story. Where are the Peter Taylor statues? Where is the Peter Taylor stand? Where is the public recognition of the part he played in the dazzling Brian Clough story and the riches beyond imagination bestowed on Forest?

There are some – no, make that *many* – people who believe Peter Taylor's contribution to Forest's improbable achievements during the 1970s has been shamefully overlooked, if for no other reason than he was actually born in the city, unlike Clough, a thoroughbred Yorkshireman who spent the last 30-odd years of his life in a splendid home on the outskirts of Derby.

There have been calls, supported by an online petition, to persuade the club to rename the main stand at Forest's City

Ground after Taylor, something his daughter Wendy Dickinson certainly believes is the least he deserves. She told the *Nottingham Evening Post*, 'I'm glad that we have recognised Brian as a city with the statue and Brian Clough Way, but it has been remiss that my father has been ignored. My father was Nottingham born and bred, and started his football career at Forest as a 16-year-old goalkeeper. To have two stands opposite each other named after the two men who brought so much success to Nottingham Forest would be brilliant.'

At the time of writing, at the City Ground nothing has been done to rectify this. Perhaps, should Forest eventually regain their place in the top division and finally rebuild their toytown main stand, it might happen. And despite their very public divorce, Clough would surely have wanted that recognition for Taylor. 'The Clough-Taylor managerial partnership was unique,' he said in the months before his death in 2003. 'It remains unique to this day.'

Originally I had headed this chapter *Cloughie's Triumphs* but as soon as I began to write, I realised just how misleading and disrespectful that was. I'm as prepared as any Forest supporter to eulogise Clough. I know my optimism for the team's future is exaggerated beyond the natural, my expectations unreasonable; that no one will ever take my club anywhere near the heights they attained in the 1970s. But equally, I know Clough could not have done it alone. Peter Taylor brought certain necessary qualities to the partnership that Cloughie, by his own admission, could not provide yet were essential to the mix – hence the rather more wordy but eminently more accurate chapter heading.

They were so different. Clough was tall, slim and handsome; abrasive, intimidating, insufferably arrogant, charismatic. Taylor was like a favourite uncle – silver-haired and stocky, long sideburns that were very 1960s, pulling contentedly on a torpedo-shaped cigar. He was not so articulate as Clough but in his own, reasoned manner brought a degree of calm to their partnership; the sheet anchor when Clough threatened to be swept away by a storm of emotion.

Right from the start of their relationship, back in their playing days at Middlesbrough, Taylor was the voice behind the throne, providing Clough with the reassurance of his talent, urging him to tilt at windmills, instilling in him the belief that together they could succeed. And once you put Clough up to it, there was no holding him; no one could stand up to his forceful personality. If Taylor said, 'Come on, Brian, we can do it,' that was enough for Clough because he knew how to get it done.

In his autobiography, *Walking On Water*, Clough recalled the first time Taylor spoke to him – a whispered conversation one day at Ayresome Park. Despite scoring goals for fun in Middlesbrough's second string, manager Bob Dennison was reluctant to throw the brash young centre-forward into the first team. Taylor, the reserve-team goalkeeper, took Brian to one side and told him to hang on in there because he was the best player at the club. 'He gave me the assurance I'd longed for,' wrote Clough. 'He gave me the kind of lift every footballer needs from time to time. I remembered that when I went into management.'

And so a friendship was born, one that would develop into the best managerial partnership football has ever seen. And it worked because Taylor knew his place. 'He believed in what I believed in – my talent,' said Clough, with disarming immodesty. Taylor, for his part, was happy with his lot, certainly in those early days. 'We were like brothers,' Clough said at the height of Forest's remarkable success. 'Whenever we have a crisis, he never fails me.' The players saw it too. Martin O'Neill, an astute person not prone to making outlandish, unjustified statements, said, 'There is no doubt that Clough loved Taylor, he really did.'

So, did their well-documented and irrevocable falling-out many years and many trophies later come about because Taylor stopped believing? Or was it because he simply grew tired of being Brian's crutch, making him laugh, feeding his ego and pouring oil on the troubled waters his mate left in his wake? There is only so much stress one man can take. After they had parted Clough led Forest to a few more League Cup successes but he could never reach those dizzy heights of Division One champions, European Cup winners, not even the FA Cup he coveted so much.

They had fallen out after Taylor came out of retirement to return to the Baseball Ground as manager of Derby County, and then signed Forest's great but ageing winger John Robertson without telling his old friend. Clough saw it as a great discourtesy and, in his pig-headed anger, never spoke to Taylor again. Then, in October 1990, Taylor died while on holiday in Majorca. It would haunt Clough for the rest of his days. But that is the end of their remarkable story, a story that began back in their playing days in the 1950s and would rock and roll for the next 30-odd years.

Derby County chairman Sam Longson, short, rotund and balding in the style of Elmer Fudd, had made his money in the tough world of road haulage. An old-fashioned boardroom figure, he had bought a football club as a hobby and enjoyed the swank and swagger of being the main man. Longson wanted success but not at any price and when fan pressure forced him to ditch incumbent boss Tim Ward, under whose stewardship Derby were swimming in the stagnant waters of Division Two, he looked around for a manager who could run a tight ship.

He had been keeping a watchful eye on how Clough and Taylor, with no obvious disposable income to work with, had turned a basket case like Hartlepool United from relegation regulars into a half-decent, lower-division outfit. Clough arrived for interview at Derby and had talked himself into the job within five minutes. Persuading Longson and his equally parsimonious board of directors to shell out for an assistant manager took a little longer.

Longson should have realised at that moment that he had let the foxes into the hen house. While Taylor went off talent spotting, Clough got things sorted. He moved out the players who could not play ... and also showed the door to the club secretary, the chief scout, the groundsman and even a couple of mocking tea ladies. 'My philosophy was,' said the ever-articulate Clough, 'that if there were a hundred battles to be won when you take on a new job, you might as well get them all done in the first three months, if you can.' And of course, Brian could. It was his club now, top to bottom, and old Sam might not like it but there were treasures to be had and that was something the much-maligned directors had not enjoyed for many a long year.

By the dawn of the 1970s their Derby County revolution was just about to take to the streets, ready to storm the Bastille of Old Trafford and Anfield. Clough and Taylor had learned a lot at lowly Hartlepool – how to organise a club, how to sort out the talent from the dead wood and get the best out of players, especially how to outflank a strong-willed chairman. They made important, inspired signings. The story has been told many times of how the pair of them sat through the night in Roy McFarland's house on Merseyside and refused to leave until he had agreed to come to Derby.

When asked to tell his version of the story, McFarland

remembered it like this: 'I didn't want to sign; the only team I wanted to play for was Liverpool. Then Brian said to me that he wasn't leaving until I had made my mind up. My Dad said that if he wanted me that much, I should sign. So I signed. Perhaps him and Peter were holding the pen while I did it! At one point when he was trying to get me to sign, he told me something that I thought was absolute bull. He said in 12 months' time I'd be playing for England. He was wrong ... it took 13 months!'

Clough also persuaded an overweight football legend thought long past his sell-by date named Dave Mackay to prolong a career the player himself thought was over, and join his Derby express. Mackay was 33 and the fearsome drive and power from midfield that had helped carry Spurs to the first 20th-century league and cup double in 1961 was certainly on the wane. But Clough wanted his footballing brain to help shape his team and nurture young talent like McFarland, John McGovern, Ron Webster ... players who would do the old man's running. For just £5,000 Clough got 'the best signing I ever made' and Mackay enjoyed the sort of Indian summer few sportsmen experience. Perhaps this is a good place to point out that bringing Mackay to Derby had actually been Peter Taylor's idea.

Derby charged out of Division Two with the 1969 championship in the boot. What came next was so improbable it now reads like a work of fiction. In less than 10 years Clough and Taylor took *two* decaying old clubs that had hardly won a pot to piss in for as long as anyone could remember to two league titles, a league cup and two European Cup triumphs. Only the giants of the game won back-to-back European Cups. Real Madrid, Bayern Munich, Ajax ... they added the name of Nottingham Forest. In comparative terms it was like Accrington Stanley winning the league.

CLOUGH AND TAYLOR AT THE DOUBLE

When Derby resumed membership of the old Division One for the first time in nearly 20 years, they had a near-perfect blend of youth and experience. Alongside Mackay was Welsh international Terry Hennessey who, together with winger Alan Hinton, had been plundered from Forest.

Hinton had been unkindly nicknamed 'Gladys' by the Forest fans. He was not the world's greatest tackler, kept his wavy blond locks neatly in place by dodging any requirement to head the ball, and his ungainly, flat-footed running style made him an easy target for the terrace tormentors. As the Forest fans ridiculed him, so Hinton's confidence was destroyed. But needless to say, Peter Taylor saw something few really appreciated. Hinton could cross a ball as well as anyone in the game: hard, flat and accurate. And he could thump a shot with faultless technique and awesome power. Rams fans put up with his flash white boots and his non-combative style because he was good at what he did, for a couple of seasons perhaps the best in the land, and two England caps, won during his fallow years at Forest, was scant reward.

Other key members of the side were strikers Kevin Hector, one of the few players to survive from the Tim Ward era, and John O'Hare, a canny Scot with a limpet-like ability to hold the ball with back to goal and bring others into play. Young John McGovern had been at Hartlepool when the adventure began. Clough's sort of player, he kept things simple: win the ball, pass it to a colleague – how hard is that? He never won any caps, was not always the fans' favourite ... but effective? Both Derby and later Forest were never so good without him knitting things together. Think Claude Makelele at Chelsea in recent years if you want a comparison.

Willie Carlin had been around a bit when Clough brought

him to the Baseball Ground for £60,000 – a single game for his home club, Liverpool, and then Halifax, Carlisle, Sheffield United. He was a terrier, pacey and tenacious, a bit like Archie Gemmill, the player who would eventually replace him.

Gemmill was another player, like McFarland, who signed for Clough just to get him out of the house. He fancied a move from Preston to a big-name club and Everton were hovering. Once again Clough had to call on all his persuasive skills to change his mind. Gemmill recalled, 'He [Clough] decided he was going to sleep outside in the car but my wife invited him in and he stayed the night. She cooked him breakfast in the morning ... and I ended up signing in the morning.'

Colin Todd was different. He jumped at the chance to join Clough's revolution at Derby and signed for a record transfer fee of £175,000.

In that first season Derby finished fourth in Division One. How good was that? Only a couple of years earlier they had been struggling to hang onto their Division Two status and there they were, up with the big boys, two points ahead of Liverpool, for heaven's sake! And Clough was not slow to tell people. Reporters loved his post-match press conferences. He could always be relied on for great, headline-making quotes. Suddenly, everyone was listening. Clough was in all the newspapers, and television became his friend and ally. Taylor kept his own counsel, quietly staying in the background; Sam Longson, on the other hand, was not so happy. Clough did not know – had absolutely no idea! – that Derby's success, and the way he exploited it for his own gain, would bring his world temporarily crashing down.

The following season Derby County won the First Division championship in the most dramatic fashion. It was May 1972 and the Derby players, having completed their fixtures in return for 58 points, were sunning themselves on a beach in Majorca, expecting either Leeds or Liverpool to pick up a win in their final games of the season. Taylor was with them; Clough was in the Scilly Isles. Back home in England, Leeds, who had won the FA Cup two days earlier, travelled to Wolves needing only a point, but lost 2-1 in a game that later became embroiled in controversy when rumours emerged that Leeds boss Don Revie had offered Wolves a bribe to roll over. If such a bribe was offered, it was certainly not taken and the matter was left unproven.

With Leeds losing, Liverpool could also have pipped Derby had they won at Highbury. Arsenal were still reeling from their FA Cup final defeat to Leeds at Wembley, Liverpool were on a run of a single defeat in 16 games, but Lady Luck had already decided to sprinkle her stardust down Derby way. Emlyn Hughes hit the bar, Kevin Keegan was inches wide with an overhead kick, John Toshack had a late goal disallowed for a marginal offside ... it was that close.

It was the first trophy of note that Clough had ever won and, as far as he was concerned, the most important. The cups were great for filling with champagne but the championship was the pinnacle, the result of 42 games that demanded every player deliver his last ounce of strength and skill and desire. 'It was the supreme test of management,' declared Clough. So you could hardly expect him to keep quiet about it, could you? And the more he popped up on television, the more column inches he filled in the newspapers, the more uncomfortable Sam Longson became.

The players were happy ... they were winning and, as John McGovern said, players will put up with anything if they are in a winning side. It was around this time that Clough gave his now-famous answer when asked what he did if a player challenged his point of view. With just the merest hint of an ironic smile, he replied, 'Well, I ask him which way he thinks it should be done, we get down to it, we talk about it for 20 minutes and then we decide I was right.' John O'Hare said such statements sometimes made players, and presumably directors too, 'cringe with embarrassment' before adding, 'But that was the way he was.'

The following season Derby began their assault on the European Cup, in those days a straightforward knock-out competition, and Clough was convinced they would win it. They cruised through the early rounds, got the better of mighty Benfica on a muddied Baseball Ground quagmire and fancied their chances against Italian giants Juventus in the semi-final. But for the first time, and certainly not the last, Clough and Taylor learned there can sometimes be Machiavellian influences around when European glory and riches are at stake: Derby lost 3-1 in Turin and nearly 30 years later, Clough was still ranting about the injustice of that night.

Reading between the lines of his 2002 autobiography *Walking On Water*, Clough was pointing that familiar wagging finger. The West German referee Gerhard Schulenberg booked two Derby players for nothing – but they happened to be Roy McFarland and Archie Gemmill, already sitting on a caution apiece and that meant they were out of the second leg. And the referee bought every tumble and dive perpetrated by the Italians, seemingly as well skilled in the dark arts as their reputation suggested.

Clough wrote, 'It is corrupt in my book for players to dive like dolphins at the slightest pretext.' What would Clough have written about the 21st-century divers, I wonder? Maybe even he would have been lost for words.

Clough described Derby's subsequent exit as 'unbearable heartbreak' because he was convinced his side were the best in the competition and would have won the European Cup, had they been allowed a level playing field. And he went further for he believed that the side he and Peter Taylor were building at the Baseball Ground was packed with so much young and improving talent that it would last for a decade and sweep every major trophy up in the process. But it was not to be: somewhere along the line Clough's relationship with Longson, which he once described as almost like father and son, crumbled. There is little doubt the root cause was Clough's increasingly high profile as a newspaper columnist and TV pundit, saying what he liked about whom he liked. As far as the world and his dog were concerned, *he* was Derby County. 'Hang on a minute,' roared Longson. 'I'm the one that runs Derby County, not Brian Clough!'

That vital seam of trust that has to exist between management and directors began to run out. Longson found a willing ally in his brooding battle with the club's unorthodox, controversial management duo in new director Jack Kirkland, who fertilised their growing feeling of disquiet when he began quizzing Peter Taylor to explain exactly what he did for his salary. Clough was incensed – they had lifted Derby from down among the dregs, given them a league title, European Cup semi-final place, not to mention 'sold out' signs every time they appeared at the Baseball Ground, and still certain members of the board were not satisfied. Taylor was equally disillusioned, so much so that he told his mate it was time to go. His hackles up, Clough told a board meeting they could have his and Peter's resignation. Longson did not bat an eyelid. It was over but not without the most almighty fuss.

The town was in uproar, fans demanding the board go instead, their protests so vociferous that the offending directors locked themselves in the boardroom for safety. And the players themselves reacted in the most incredible, unprecedented fashion.

It began with a letter to Longson demanding Clough and Taylor be reinstated. It ended with a threat to go on strike, which was only deflected by Clough's intervention. The furor eventually died down but never really disappeared. Over the next few years, even during the halcyon days at Forest, rumours persisted that Clough was going back, no doubt fuelled by his own assertion that resigning in the first place had been 'a crazy decision'.

The truth was that the pair of them had walked out on a club on the cusp of greatness without a penny in compensation, no job offers and with families to support. Next stop was Third Division Brighton and Hove Albion but it was no place for an ambitious young man like Brian Clough and after 32 matches, which produced only 12 wins and some distinctly embarrassing defeats, including a 4-0 FA Cup drubbing by Walton and Hersham and an 8-2 home defeat by Bristol Rovers, he began to listen to overtures from elsewhere.

In July 1974 he made the worst possible choice, accepting the job of manager at Leeds United, the club he hated and had publicly accused of cheating under Don Revie. That extraordinary episode, which lasted just 44 days, is documented elsewhere in this book.

Once again Brian Clough was out of work but this time the telephone had stopped ringing; no one wanted to take a gamble on Cloughie's capricious style of management, his volatile nature and his inherent ability to make everyone around him feel uncomfortable. The only club that showed any interest in him was ailing Nottingham Forest. He took the call from a Nottingham sub-postmaster, Forest committee man Stuart Dryden (the club was by then the only one left in the league that did not have a board of directors), who sounded him out about taking over the struggling Division Two outfit. There were distinct echoes of his entrance at Derby County but that was not the reason he took the job. Many times over the next 18 years he appeared to be on the verge of quitting Forest but he always remembered the call from Mr Dryden at a time when no one else wanted to know him, and he always pulled back.

The headlines appeared on 6 January 1975: FOREST GET CLOUGH. It was the announcement fans had been praying for, hardly daring to believe it would happen. But they were quickly warned by Clough not to expect miracles – 'We have not really got a side capable of progress at the moment and we have no money in the bank.' This statement was made to a meeting of the Derby County Supporters Protest Movement at which the ever-mischievous Clough invited them to ditch the Rams and come to the City Ground.

He began his reign with a remarkable 1-0 FA Cup victory at Tottenham, courtesy of a Neil Martin goal, but it did not even qualify as a false dawn, merely a dull glow through a very dark blanket. Forest were poor, in danger of relegation, and Clough knew he had a desperate fight on his hands – 'The problems that exist at this club have got a deep root and it will take time to sort them out.'

His first signing was a significant one: trainer Jimmy Gordon, the third constant in the management set-up and a man whose influence and input has been largely forgotten, totally overshadowed, yet proved invaluable, especially to Clough, who liked people around him he could trust. Gordon, a tough-tackling wing-half in his playing days with Newcastle and Middlesbrough, worked with Clough at Derby, Leeds and finally Forest; he also deserves his place in the spotlight, just to the left of Clough and at shoulder level.

Looking at his paper-thin squad, Clough knew it needed root

and branch repair. I remember his first two signings, two more men he knew and trusted: John McGovern and John O'Hare. Clough said, 'I'm bringing them in to show this lot how to trap a football.' Forest fans were not overly impressed with the arrival of the ex-Derby duo and McGovern in particular would have a hard time winning them over. But his was usually the first name on the team sheet and he has his own theory as to why he was one of Cloughie's favourites.

'I think what he saw in myself was, if we were losing 3-0, or winning 3-0, away from home or at home, or in a five-a-side, or in a practice game, I'll just be doing exactly the right things and I'd always, always, accept the responsibility of getting the ball to try to better whatever's happening in the team.'

Clough sold half the squad, players who had been the side's backbone under previous boss Allan Brown: John Galley, Peter Hindley, Tommy Jackson, Neil Martin, Dave Serella. He did hang on to a few of the players he inherited, although he was not altogether sure why. Martin O'Neill was an educated Irishman with a lot to say for himself; John Robertson was a scruffy, overweight, unfit Scot, who definitely needed one of Cloughie's size nines up his backside. 'You're a bloody disgrace,' he ranted at Robbo. 'You ought to be sent home!' But he wasn't, and 18 months later he was in Scotland's World Cup squad.

'I can remember his first day,' said Robertson, who was on the same transfer list as O'Neill. 'I was sat in the dressing room facing the doors and, bang, they flew open. He took off his jacket and in one movement flung it onto a peg. I didn't even know the peg was there, so how did he? You could feel the electricity. There were no pleasantries, no introductions, no shaking hands, he just told us we were going training. After that we all bucked up – we had no choice.'

CLOUGH AND TAYLOR AT THE DOUBLE

The final 17 league games under Clough produced just three wins but enough points to avoid the drop. The next season showed progress, up to a final position of ninth with the help of one or two important signings, including Colin Barrett from Manchester City, ex-Liverpool defender Larry Lloyd and, with echoes of Dave Mackay, he brought in Frank Clark, a veteran full-back from Newcastle who thought his playing days were just about done but who was about to enjoy a remarkable Indian summer.

Clough made them into winners when they were drifting into anonymity, even briefly helping Lloyd to another England cap after his international days seemed well behind him. Lloyd had this to say about his old mentor: 'I've played under Bill Shankly and Bob Paisley and Clough is a better manager than both of them. As a manager, there's no limit to my respect for him, but as a man, he's not my cup of tea. I once told him I'd never be caught at a bar having a drink with him. He said I shouldn't worry because the feeling was mutual.'

Without a doubt, the most significant signing came next. Clough persuaded Peter Taylor to join him at the City Ground and they were instantly rewarded by a piece of silverware. OK, it was only the Anglo-Scottish Cup but its significance was huge in the context of the rebuilding job they were carrying out. Then Clough signed striker Peter Withe, whose 16 goals would help fire Forest back into Division One by a single point. It had been an uneven season, unbeaten runs punctuated by surprising defeats, their equilibrium not helped by new Derby chairman George Hardy's invitation to Clough and Taylor to return to the Baseball Ground. Despite having previously described the decision to leave Derby as the biggest mistake of his career Clough, though tempted, decided to stick with Forest. They had come for him after the Leeds debacle; it was his way of saying thanks.

In the closing weeks of that 1976–77 season Peter Taylor turned detective. He donned his flat cap and mingled with the crowd at St Andrew's to run the rule over Birmingham's tearaway centre-forward Kenny Burns. The player had a reputation for trouble and Taylor wanted to find out the truth of it. What he saw was a player with courage, a player who would never take a backward step. 'Apparently Peter knew that I liked a flutter on the horses and dogs,' said Burns, 'and because of this Clough was not sure about signing me.

'I went to Perry Barr one night to have a few bets and, apparently, Taylor followed me. He was there in the shadows with a hat on and his collar up. He even wore dark glasses.'

Burns was widely regarded as a hard man in an era of hard men. He was also quick, versatile, good in the air, comfortable on the ball. Clough paid £175,000 for the Scot and then bemused everyone by sticking him alongside Larry Lloyd in the centre of Forest's defence. This proved to be a stroke of genius.

Forest fans were still reeling from that development when Clough paid a record £270,000 for Stoke goalkeeper Peter Shilton. Forest had won three of their first four Division One games, they had a decent keeper named John Middleton, so why did they need to pay such a huge sum for Shilton? 'We were mad in many people's eyes,' wrote Clough later. 'But Taylor and I knew our history in advance. History now tells us Shilton was worth twice the price. We weren't mad at all; we were magic.'

Middleton left soon after, makeweight in a deal to bring Archie Gemmill to the City Ground, but where was all this money coming from? Certainly not the Forest committee members, who were individually successful but not overtly wealthy; it came from the bank. Clough brought success to Forest on tick and no one could say no. The committee were so worried he would up sticks and leave that they simply stood to one side and let him get on with it. Years later the club would pay a heavy price for such profligacy, teetering on the brink of extinction, but you will find no one associated with Forest to say it was not worth it. The record books tell the story, the fans' memory banks richer for the experience.

Clough also introduced a couple of talented homegrown youngsters: full-back Viv Anderson and striker Tony Woodcock, who had almost been flogged to Lincoln City. Both were destined to become England internationals.

And so at the start of the 1977–78 season Forest were ready for their return to the top flight but what came next was beyond belief; a miracle of near-biblical proportions, an achievement that has never really been given the merit it deserved. From the brink of relegation to the Third Division to the best side in England in the space of three seasons, that is one giant leap. And it was almost as if no one saw them coming. Despite the fact that they lost only one of their first 13 Division One games, no one considered them championship contenders. They were sure to fade, especially when the top teams sussed them out.

Only it did not happen. Few teams could get to grips with their strategy: 11 men defending but with the capability of springing into attack with a speed and accuracy almost impossible to handle. The others finally started to take note just before Christmas 1977 when Forest went to Old Trafford and did everything right – well, *almost*: they won 4-0 but it could have been 8.

BBC commentator Barry Davies was the man who first said, informing anyone interested enough to listen, that from now on

Forest must be taken seriously as title contenders. Forest did not lose another league game all season, an unbeaten sequence that lasted well into the next season and was finally ended after 42 games – the equivalent of an entire season – by Liverpool; a record which would last for 26 years until Arsène Wenger's Arsenal went past it. It meant so much to Clough. Years later he said, 'I admire myself for the 42 undefeated games much more than the European Cup.' More Cloughie mischief? Well, of course. Forest went on to win back-to-back European Cups, a trophy Arsenal have never won.

Back then Clough did not worry much about Arsenal – Liverpool were the team to beat. Both league games were draws then they met in the final of the League Cup. It was 0-0 at Wembley and just as tight in the replay until Phil Thompson tripped John O'Hare on the edge of the penalty area. In or out? 'I had to do it,' Thompson told a TV reporter, 'but it was outside.' So the man from the BBC collared Peter Taylor. 'TV replays show it was outside the box,' he challenged the Forest man. 'They also show we've got the cup,' replied Taylor.

A month later Forest took the title with four games to spare, seven points ahead of Liverpool. Having scored 69 goals, they had conceded just 24. They had achieved a feat no club has been able to match in the 36 years that have since passed, coming straight out of Division Two and taking the league title at the first attempt. Will anyone take my bet that it will never happen again?

It could not get better than that, could it? Well, there was a chance, because Forest drew Liverpool in the first round of the European Cup. Liverpool were the holders and, once again, Forest were written off, but Clough was at his inspirational best back then. He threw into the mix an ex-carpet fitter named Garry Birtles, whom he had picked up from local semi-pro team

Long Eaton United after a spying trip at Taylor's invitation. After the game Clough cheekily declared that 'the best thing was the half-time cup of Bovril'.

Nevertheless, he gave Long Eaton a nominal few quid and, more than a season later, threw the young, inexperienced Birtles into the European mix. It was another of those intuitive Clough decisions, which was repaid not only with a memorable performance but one of the great European Cup anecdotes.

As a thin mist rolled in from the Trent, sealing the electric atmosphere within the confines of the old ground, Birtles gave Forest a shock lead in front of the Trent End faithful and, putting it mildly, Liverpool were not happy. This is what happened next, as Birtles remembers it: 'After I'd scored Phil Thompson told me a single goal wouldn't be enough to take to Anfield. So when we scored again [Colin Barrett being the man], cocky young thing that I was, I went up to him and said, "Will two be enough then?" He was speechless.'

Forest took that 2-0 lead to Anfield, defended it against relentless Liverpool pressure and the wall of sound from the Kop, to go through. Some, like Fleet Street journalist Reg Drury, thought Liverpool's defeat spelled the end of English domination in Europe. 'Forest,' he wrote, 'didn't have the know-how to win the European Cup.' But more learned folk disagreed. Liverpool boss Bob Paisley, for instance, predicted eventual success for the lads from Nottingham.

Unlike today's interminable, cash-driven competition, it was just a short sprint to the final. Forest brushed aside AEK Athens and Grasshoppers of Zurich and were into the semi-finals against top West German opponents, Cologne. The first leg, on a sodden, churned-up City Ground pitch, was a six-goal thriller that seemed to spell the end of the dream when Forest conceded a late equaliser to make the score 3-3 and weigh the odds heavily in the Germans' favour. The scorer was a Japanese player named Okudera, who had come on late in the game. It inspired the classic headline: JAP SUB SINKS FOREST.

Cologne were cock-a-hoop, Forest dejected. Peter Taylor agreed with the post-match interviewer that Forest had probably missed their chance ... and then, deliberately and obviously for the benefit of the cameras, he stuck his tongue firmly in his cheek. Cologne were so confident that they began ordering tickets for the final, booking hotel rooms in Munich, but they took their eye off the ball and were beaten in the home leg by Ian Bowyer's header.

The final was a disappointment. Swedish champs Malmo didn't have much to offer beyond blanket defence and they were undone by a piece of Robertson magic, planting a signature cross onto the head of Trevor Francis. Clough had brought the Birmingham man in for just such a moment, creating the first million-pound transfer fee in the process. Yes, it was a crazy world back then. Brian Clough's underrated collection of marvellous misfits had written a page in football history that defied logic. What glorious days to be a Forest supporter! The next season they did it again, demoralising Hamburg and giving Kevin Keegan a bad-hair day in the final in Madrid.

John McGovern, who had been a loyal servant from Hartlepool to Derby, to Leeds and finally Forest, has no doubts that what they achieved in the closing years of the 1970s topped the lot. 'In five years at Forest you win promotion, you're cheeky enough to win the League by seven points, you beat Liverpool to win the League Cup the same season and you've just got promoted. That's cheeky enough. But then you win the European Cup at the first attempt the year after. You win the League Cup again, then the following year you win the European Cup again. I mean, that's right cheeky! The speed of that success has to be his greatest ever achievement. In all due respects, it's like Crystal Palace doing it now.' Or Nottingham Forest!

All these years later it is still hard to believe. Kenny Burns, then Forest's forthright centre-back and now an equally forthright newspaper columnist, takes this view: 'Forest never got the credit we deserved. What we did was unbelievable. If it had been Manchester United, you would have heard about it every day since.' He's right, of course. For my money what happened in those few short years in a small, provincial Midlands city makes Brian Clough the greatest manager of them all.

But let's not forget that without Peter Taylor, and Jimmy Gordon, it might never have happened.

CHAPTER SEVEN

THE SCOURGE OF VIOLENCE

Cold Blow Lane. Was there ever a more apt name for a football ground? So much more than just an address too. For those who are aliens in our land, it perhaps paints a darkly romantic image of icy winds scouring the surface of a frozen landscape; for those who have been around football for these past 50 years, it drips with menace and the promise of sudden, bloody violence.

According to the website Football Hooligans, fans of Millwall FC (The Lions) have been involved in more violent incidents than any other club in Britain. I, for one, am not about to argue. It's a notoriety the combat-hardened thug element of the team's supporters positively revel in. Everyone in football knows their song: 'No One Likes Us, We Don't Care'. As a rule, their rivals prefer to hear it from behind the safety of a police cordon.

It is generally accepted that the modern scourge of football hooliganism began to infest the game in the late 1960s.

In their 2008 compendium of violence, *Hooligans 2*, Andy Nicholls and Nick Lowles credit the footballing backwater of Norwich City, and a game marred by terrace thuggery also involving fans of Crystal Palace, for bringing the scourge onto the front pages of the national press, and they date it to 1967 – which sounds about right.

But the truth is, Millwall have been at it since the dawn of the 20th century. Programme notes penned in 1919 politely appealed to Millwall fans to refrain from swearing because 'it is not nice for ladies to hear'. Sixty years later, patience with the Millwall hooligans was beginning to wear a bit thin. Reg Burr, Millwall's chairman in the late 1980s/early 1990s, and the man credited with saving the club from extinction, said after a coin-throwing incident at Highbury when Arsenal's Nigel Winterburn was struck by a 50p piece, 'What I would really like is for people who want to come and throw coins to throw them in the Serpentine instead – and then jump in after them.'

Following football in the early 1960s was the best of times. A crowd of teenage lads interested only in cheering on our team and enjoying a few pints along the way. The only disobedience, if you could call it that, came when fans threw toilet rolls onto the pitch to welcome their favourites as they emerged from the players' tunnel.

We even used to sing daft songs in the 1960s.

> In Dublin's Fair City
> Where the girls are so pretty,
> I first set my eyes on sweet Molly Malone,
> As she wheels her wheelbarrow
> Through the streets broad and narrow,
> Crying ... Joe-Joe-Joe Baker!

But at some point in time it changed. The terrace poets were replaced by Neanderthals, admittedly with a certain sense of rhyme and rhythm.

> We 'ate Nottingham Forest, we 'ate Liverpool too!
> Who the fucking 'ell are you?
> The referee's a wanker!
> You fat bastard!

Through the 1970s English teams enjoyed their most successful decade in European football, for the most part hell-bent on reversing the ultra-defensive boredom that can be traced back to Alf Ramsey's influence. Yet supporters turned their backs on football because hooliganism was blighting the game. Families stayed away and attendances slumped. Tommy Docherty built a Manchester United side designed to entertain yet besmirched by as violent a group of followers as any in the land. 'I thoroughly enjoyed football in the Seventies,' he wrote in his 2006 autobiography, *The Doc*, 'but I shudder every time I think of the hooligan problem and how, at that time, not one of us could come up with a solution.'

Yet today, remarkably, the fans have returned in ever-increasing numbers, despite the verbal violence that spews from the all-seater stands on just about every ground in the land. No one seems to care any longer if their children are exposed to a torrent of foul and abusive language. Respected author Joanna Trollope, mother, grandmother and die-hard Chelsea supporter, was quoted as saying, 'The best stand for the effing and blinding is the Matthew Harding Stand. I love it, these walls of men yelling filth at Michael Ballack. I don't join in but I do rather like it going on around me. I mean, it's terribly exciting.'

I remember Brian Clough, who abhorred soccer violence and would never shy away from taking direct action, tried to tackle the growing problem of bad language in his own singular manner. Tired of hearing foul-mouthed chants spilling from the Trent End at Forest's City Ground, he erected a banner which read: 'Gentlemen, no swearing please. Brian'. With a terrace wit that would become increasingly absent, the Forest fans, who lived with the constant worry that the mercurial Clough would one day quit the club, responded with their own plea: 'Brian, no leaving please. The Gentlemen'.

The foolish, misguided notion today is that football violence is a thing of the past. Not so. It has been controlled and largely contained, pushed out of the grounds and into the side streets, more often than not away from the public gaze. But it is still there, festering beneath the surface. Witness the Hull City–Millwall FA Cup tie in January 2009 when police in riot gear twice had to move in to break up fighting.

Sadly, fans are still dying; blood is still being spilled. In March 1998 a Fulham fan was kicked to death outside Gillingham's Priestfield Stadium when fighting broke out in a nearby alleyway; in 2002 a 17-year-old Nottingham Forest fan died after being struck with a bottle while enjoying a pre-match drink at a bar in Burnley.

And still we look for reasons why.

More than a decade ago South American author Mario Vargas Llosa wrote, 'The spectacle of hordes of drunken English hooligans attacking passers by, charging adversary fans with sticks, stones and knives, engaging in ferocious battles against the police, smashing shop windows and vehicles and, at times, the very stands of the stadium, has come to be an inevitable corollary of major matches played by England, and of many in the British League. And yet the fact is that for anyone who lives there, England is a country exceptionally peaceful and well mannered ... How do we explain this curious phenomenon?'

Football has always been a tribal affair. By its very nature, it is boisterous, noisy and confrontational.

Back in the year 1314 kickabouts in the streets of London so vexed Edward II that he banned the game.

'For as much as there is great noise in the city, caused by hustling over large balls from which many evils might arise which God forbid, we command and forbid, on behalf of the king, on pain of imprisonment, such game to be used in the city in the future,' came the sovereign's declaration.

Subsequent kings added their royal seal to a variety of laws outlawing football – Edward III was particularly worried that medieval sportsmen were spending too much time perfecting the ancient art of bending a free kick around a defensive wall at the expense of archery. When it came to defending the realm, blokes who could head a pig's bladder as hard as a Drogba piledriver were not going to be of much use.

Soccer riots have been around almost as long.

In 1539 an annual match held in Chester was abolished due to crowd violence; in 1555 the game was outlawed in Liverpool because of repeated fighting among spectators; in 1608 it was Manchester's turn, due to the behaviour of 'lewd and disordered persons'; in 1843 the Army was drafted in to help 200 police control fans at a game between Preston North End and Sunderland.

There was an infamous incident in 1885 when visiting Preston defeated Aston Villa 5-1. The North End players were trapped on the pitch by a mob of 2,000 'howling roughs' who attacked them with all manner of weapons from sticks and stones to umbrellas and spit ... and so it went on: fights, pitch invasions, missiles, drunkenness, train-wrecking. From the first days of organised soccer hardly a season went by without some headline-grabbing incident.

But it was not until the 1960s, when the number of recorded outbreaks of hooliganism doubled, that the menace began to manifest itself on a more regular and terrifying basis.

The 1960s was a time of great social upheaval, the emergence from the grim austerity of the post-war decade, a time when young people found their voice and began to question and even challenge authority ... the arrival of the ubiquitous angry young man.

Arthur Seaton put flesh on the bones. 'Don't let the bastards grind you down,' declared the anti-social hero of Alan Sillitoe's novel *Saturday Night And Sunday Morning*, thereby setting the tone for his generation. 'I'm only out for a good time and the rest is propaganda,' he told anyone who cared to listen.

With jobs easy to come by and money in their pockets, testosterone-fuelled adolescents needed a focus for their anger and a sense of belonging to something outside the parameters of what stood for normal, acceptable, civilised society. So they ganged up to follow their teams into enemy territory. It was one thing to win a game at an away ground but real glory came from taking the home supporters' end of the stadium – 'Come over 'ere if you think you're 'ard enough.'

Charge and counter-charge, the Zulu Warriors of Birmingham, Chelsea's Headhunters, West Ham's notorious Inter City Firm and the Millwall Bushwackers all became crews to be feared.

Nottingham Forest secretary Ken Smales collected some of the weaponry used by these armies and built up a 'black museum' in his office. Alongside the usual bricks and coins, it included a replica hand grenade, a lump of lead with the word 'Villa' gouged into it, and a heavy black cosh.

But why did they do it? For the buzz, the adrenalin rush.

Reformed soccer hooligan Dougie Brimstone, now a successful and respected author, once said, 'I've fought in two wars, flown in fighter jets, raced cars and motorbikes, but being involved in soccer violence is without a doubt the most exciting and enjoyable thing I have ever known. A statement like that to anyone who has not been a part of it will sound astonishing but is, nevertheless, the truth.'

When teams with some of the more notorious fans came to town, commercial activity came to an apprehensive halt. Shops were boarded up, pubs were closed, all police leave cancelled. The authorities didn't know how to handle it. Until they learned more sophisticated policing methods and were able to acquire greater intelligence about the underworld of organised soccer violence, the only solution was manpower and containment.

Manchester United was one of those teams with a following to be feared during the 1970s. When 7,000 of those fans descended on Nottingham for a match against Notts County at Meadow Lane, they could not find anywhere to buy a pint or even a bag of chips. 'Ridiculous panic measures,' raged United supporters' club chairman Dave Smith. 'This is the kind of provocation that stokes the fires of hooliganism.'

As early as 1968, and just a few days after two Wolverhampton Wanderers fans had been stabbed in clashes with Tottenham Hotspur followers, sports minister and ex-referee Denis Howell convened a working party to study crowd control, improved seating, better liaison with fans' groups.

When the working party reported back – fully 19 months later – it made some interesting and prescient recommendations:

> Police and clubs should work together to beat the troublemakers
> Seating should replace the terraces
> The referee is always right and his decision must be obeyed by everyone.

A match at Elland Road, Leeds, in April 1971 perfectly illustrated the wisdom of that last recommendation. Leeds United were at home to West Bromwich Albion. It was a vital match in Leeds' quest for the Division One title. With 65 minutes on the clock and leading 1-0, Albion, aided by referee Ray Tinkler, enraged United's players and fans by scoring a second goal, which was dubious to say the least. As Leeds threw men forward, Albion's Tony Brown raced onto a pass in the Leeds half, past his team mate Colin Suggett, who was clearly in an offside position, but, it was later argued, was not interfering with play. Brown laid the ball across the penalty area for Jeff Astle to score. He, too, seemed in advance of the ball with only the keeper to beat but Mr Tinkler decided it was a good goal and so it stood. Suddenly Leeds' title hopes had blown up in their faces.

'Leeds will go mad,' blurted the normally urbane BBC commentator Barry Davies, 'and they have every justification.'

What ensued was at first ugly and later reprehensible. Virtually to a man, the Leeds players surrounded Tinkler, jostling, protesting, abusing. Then came a pitch invasion, 30 to 40 home fans racing full pelt towards the referee. The players did their best to protect the official but could do nothing to stop a linesman being struck on the head with a stone. Five minutes and 32 arrests later, police finally cleared the pitch.

When asked for his reaction, the Leeds manager Don Revie was quoted thus: 'I don't blame them [the fans] at all. The referee's decision in allowing West Bromwich's second goal was diabolical.' Leeds chairman Alderman Percy Woodward was similarly quoted thus: 'I am not blaming the spectators, there was every justification for it.' At no time did anyone from Leeds United stand up and condemn the brutish reaction of the crowd, nor did they acknowledge the behaviour of some of their players had contributed to the mayhem.

It was a watershed in the insidious rise of soccer hooliganism, a tacit approval for fans to riot if they did not like what they saw. *The Times'* David Miller later described it as 'the definitive moment of moral corruption in English soccer' and lumped the blame squarely, and eloquently, on the backs of the Leeds players – 'They should have been prosecuted by the police for provoking public disorder.'

Welcome to the 1970s.

That Howell working-party report had echoed the sentiment. Describing players as 'prima donnas', it concluded, 'There can be little doubt that bad behaviour on the part of players, frequently the idols of many in the crowd, can lead to misbehaviour and increased misbehaviour among the crowd.' I think 30-odd years and numerous ref-baiting incidents later it is safe to assert that the players did not take a blind bit of notice.

In 1974 rioting fans at an FA Cup tie effectively changed the course of history. Second Division Nottingham Forest were playing a sixth-round tie at First Division Newcastle United. Tormented by the mesmeric skills of Forest's Duncan McKenzie, Newcastle, as desperate then to end their trophyless run as they are now, looked on course for a shock exit from the competition.

Early in the second half, with Forest leading 2-1 and looking good value for it, Yorkshire referee Gordon Kew awarded them a penalty when McKenzie was brought down by David Craig's thunderous challenge. The home fans packed on the terraces at the Leaze End began to push and sway in their anger and that fire was fuelled further when Kew sent off Pat Howard for overstepping the mark with his protests.

Forest schemer George Lyall then thumped home the penalty to make it 3-1, much to the delight of the visiting fans, who danced behind the touchline ... and right in the faces of the Geordie faithful.

They could not restrain themselves. Led by a middle-aged pot-bellied man, bizarrely wearing a collar and tie, around 500 Newcastle fans charged across the pitch. The players were momentarily stunned before being engulfed by the raging mob. Forest's Dave Serella and Martin O'Neill later claimed they had been physically assaulted before they and the rest of the players could escape to the sanctuary of the dressing rooms.

As they waited out of sight more than 100 police officers, many with dogs, moved in to restore order. Ten minutes later Kew asked both teams if they were ready to resume. Forest, 3-1 up against 10 men and with only 25 minutes to hold out, were up for it ... Newcastle, given an unexpected chance to regroup, knew their best hope was to win it there and then rather than face a difficult replay.

Newcastle attacked from the whistle, driving back a Forest side that had lost all their earlier poise and cohesion. The Second Division outfit were clearly unnerved by the violence, which had left 23 fans needing hospital treatment, two people with fractured skulls, and more than 100 receiving first-aid treatment at the ground. Youngsters had been crushed against the barriers and fainted; others were knocked to the ground and trampled on.

A number of police officers received minor injuries and, in all, 39 people were later charged with violent conduct and another 40 ejected from the ground. Leonard Conroy, one of the pitch-invaders, was sentenced to six months imprisonment for breach of the peace and assaulting a police officer.

Forest, almost certainly with one eye on the crowd, which was being whipped into a frenzy by Newcastle's kamikaze attacks, wilted and crumbled. Tinkler gave Newcastle a penalty, which Terry McDermott converted to make it 3-2, and John Tudor equalised with a brilliant diving header. Mayhem in the Forest defence; pandemonium on the terraces. In the 89th minute Malcolm Macdonald headed down for Bobby Moncur to volley home the Newcastle winner.

But it was never going to end there, not after the battle of St James's Park. Forest boss Allan Brown told reporters, 'The crowd and the referee undoubtedly won the game for Newcastle. When we were taken off, we were playing brilliant stuff. Newcastle were finished. But after the hold-up, with the crowd baying all the time, the referee gave everything to Newcastle.'

Urged on by a hysterical media reaction, which delivered a majority verdict that the tie should be awarded to Forest, the Second Division side lodged a formal protest and an FA investigation was quickly called for. Although referee Gordon Kew urged the authorities to let the result stand, there was a feeling that some action must be taken, if only to send out a message to fans that such direct intervention would not – could not – be allowed to succeed.

FA secretary Ted Croker announced, 'Newcastle could be

disqualified. We do not have the power to order a replay as the game was completed.' And the FA decision? To order a replay.

They decided it should be played at a neutral ground – Everton's Goodison Park – and also added a ban on Newcastle staging home FA Cup ties for five years. The reaction from both camps was interesting. 'Supermac', England centre-forward and Tyneside hero Malcolm Macdonald, said, 'My reaction is one of total disgust but not surprise. I have expected a ridiculous solution and they certainly have come up with one.' He was later charged with bringing the game into disrepute.

Forest's George Lyall said, 'For the good of the game, Newcastle had to be punished so hooligans all over the country wouldn't be given the go-ahead to do it ... but deep down I feel we didn't deserve to go through. We just weren't professional about it ... when we came back, we were a shambles.'

The first replay ended 1-1. Forest believed, with some justification it might be argued, that they had earned the right to stage the second replay at their own City Ground. And the FA decision? Replay it at Goodison again. Forest lost 1-0 to a Malcolm Macdonald goal. Newcastle went on to Wembley; Forest went home with a sob story to tell.

That same year, on a UEFA Cup trip to play Feyenoord in Rotterdam, supporters of Tottenham Hotspur went on the rampage, both inside the ground and in the old city centre. As the game was being played, hundreds of Spurs fans rioted. They tore up chairs, set fire to anything that would burn and, in a concerted attack on home supporters, hospitalised around 150 Feyenoord followers. Seventy Spurs fans were arrested.

At half-time Tottenham chairman Sydney Wale appealed for calm. His words echoed around the ground via the public-address system. 'You hooligans are a disgrace to Tottenham and

England. This is a football game, not a war.' Once again, no one was listening. Legendary Spurs manager Bill Nicholson was deeply shocked by the violence and it had a hastening effect on his decision to retire from football. A sad end for a master technician who believed the beautiful game should be presented as a simple and exciting form of entertainment.

The incident was dismissed as another example of 'the English disease' – neatly convenient for the perennially mealy-mouthed European football authorities who, a decade later in the wake of Heysel, would decide to ban English teams from Europe ... while ignoring the Ultras of Italy, the Feyenoord Legion, the persistent violence that was occurring in Turkey, Germany and, of all places, Sweden. In 1970 fans of IFK Göteborg invaded the pitch, destroyed the goalposts and fought the police at the end of a match that saw them relegated.

The 1975 European Cup final was held at the Parc de Prince stadium in Paris, and Leeds United and their fans were again under the critical spotlight for their behaviour on and off the field. Leeds, who had had Duncan McKenzie and Gordon McQueen sent off in a bruising semi-final against Ujpest Dozsa, were in a typically uncompromising mood against the German champions Bayern Munich, led by Franz Beckenbauer.

Bayern's Swedish defender Bjorn Andersson was carried off after only four minutes, victim of a ferocious challenge by Terry Yorath and, before half-time, Bayern's key midfielder Uli Hoeness limped off with a knee injury that would effectively end his career at the age of 27.

Although Leeds were the dominant side, they could not get the better of French referee Michel Kitabdjian, who turned down two confident appeals for penalties and disallowed a Peter Lorimer goal for an offside that was marginal at best. The Elland

Road army took that as the signal to intervene and began ripping up seats and throwing them at the French riot police. One enraged fan even got over the moat, scaled the wire fence and ran on to the pitch. He was swiftly and harshly dealt with by stewards, further infuriating the Leeds fans, who continued their violent protests long after Franz Roth and Gerd Müller had scored the crucial goals to take the trophy.

Leeds United were punished with a four-year ban from European competition.

That was at the end of a season that had started with the shameful fight involving Leeds captain Billy Bremner and Liverpool hero Kevin Keegan at the Charity Shield game at Wembley. This was supposed to be a showpiece encounter, being shown live for the first time. Football was in a new shop window with a chance to sell itself to a wider audience. But the match was full of niggles and nastiness, which culminated in a punch-up between the two international stars. Keegan obstructs Bremner, Bremner kicks Keegan, Keegan thumps Bremner ... Cue a mass brawl involving most of the players. Wembley had never seen anything like it. Even then referee Bob Matthewson was not going to send either of them off but Keegan and Bremner would not let it lie. They bawled and bleated until Matthewson decided he had had enough and pointed to the dressing rooms. These two high-profile stars of the game then reacted with a level of petulance previously unseen, tearing off their shirts to leave the pitch bare-chested.

And from the terraces, although which set of supporters was in such fine voice no one was quite sure, came the time-honoured chant, 'You're gonna get your fuckin' 'eads kicked in'.

Could it get any worse?

Well, yes, actually.

THE SCOURGE OF VIOLENCE

The litany of violence continued in that same depressing vein throughout the 1970s, only the venues altered.

Back to Carrow Road, Norwich. The date: April 1977. The visitors: Manchester United. A series of violent skirmishes broke out around the town. One United fan was stabbed, his life saved only by the transfusion of seven pints of blood. Shocking scenes, later televised, included a United fan climbing onto the roof of the Barclay Stand and then falling onto the concrete terrace below. As he lay injured there, he was attacked by City supporters. The casualty toll that day was 30 injured, including eight police officers, and 19 Manchester United fans charged and convicted.

It was a disease, a scourge, a plague – and it affected every level of football in England. On the same day that Derby County fans fought a running battle through the streets of Sheffield, rampaging gangs left a swathe of damage in their wake ... in the small Lincolnshire market town of Boston, home of non-league Boston United, who had just lost an FA Cup tie against Lancaster. The visitors had to be escorted out of town by police outriders.

In 1977 the normally well-behaved followers of Scotland besmirched their reputation after a 2-1 victory at Wembley. Hundreds of well-oiled Scots invaded the pitch after the final whistle, broke down the goal posts and ripped up chunks of Wembley turf to take home as souvenirs that probably gave birth to a thousand lawns across Strathclyde.

Nowhere was safe. It was on an April day in 1979 after a 2-0 win for Forest at Birmingham City that my car got stoned as we drove away from St Andrews. That was also the day I witnessed one of the bravest examples of police work I have ever seen, when a pint-sized PC fronted up a large group of chanting, menacing Blues fans, reached into their midst and pulled out one of their number by the collar. The crowd did nothing, perhaps in deference to the uniform, perhaps because they were scared stiff of his snarling Alsatian, desperate to get among them but held by the officer's very short leash.

At Liverpool a Scouser urinated down the back of my legs; at Maine Road I had to hand over a quid to two young scallies who promised to look after my car; on the Tube to West Ham someone pulled a knife; in the street near Hillsborough I was asked by a burly thug what I thought of the result – I was acutely aware that the wrong answer could lead to a kicking but, fortunately, a sudden chase down a side street was enough to distract him.

Nottingham was no better. After a game against Everton, as two lanes of traffic crawled along the ring road, Forest fans weaved among the cars looking for anyone sporting blue colours. Then they tried to force open vehicle doors and, if they failed, a few panels got kicked in.

Finally, two incidents which graphically illustrate that, despite all the committees, recommendations, fines, prison sentences, ground closures and life bans, the violence that had come in at the beginning of the decade showed no signs of diminishing as the 1970s drew to a close.

In December 1979 a 17-year-old youth was hauled before magistrates in Nottingham to face the music for throwing a dart at Arsenal goalkeeper Pat Jennings during a match at the City Ground. The Irish international had been picking up the ball near the penalty spot when the dart hit him. It embedded itself well over an inch deep into his arm. The culprit was caught after an appeal by the Nottingham club for fans to give him up. He was subsequently banned for life by the club.

Just a few months later, serving as a reminder that the 1980s would be no better – in fact, far worse – a 17-year-old Middlesbrough supporter was kicked to death in a fans' brawl outside Ayresome Park stadium.

What could be done about it?

Suggestions for solving the problem were many.

Politicians took centre stage at every opportunity. Labour Home Secretary James Callaghan announced his determination to stamp out soccer hooliganism ... without actually saying how. When the Conservatives took office, their man Reginald Maudling soon trotted out similar words of defiance, saying he had drawn up plans for tackling the thugs ... in secret.

Labour were back in charge in 1974 and guess what? Denis Howell set up a working party. Manchester United fans had just laid waste to a shopping area in Ostend en route to a European tie. 'The authorities are determined to get the matter under control,' he wailed politically.

While such worthies were following that depressingly familiar and fruitless path, others called for more drastic action. Football League President Len Shipman wanted to see a return of the birch. He was supported by Don Revie, who said, 'We have tried everything else, we might as well try this drastic deterrent.' Notts County secretary Dennis Marshall suggested a ban on away supporters – 'The trouble at grounds seems to be caused when rival supporters bait each other.'

There was a call to introduce identity cards but Eddie Plumley, secretary of Coventry City, and Alan Hardaker of the Football League, both dismissed this as a crackpot idea.

In 1977 Chelsea finally went the extra yard and installed fences at Stamford Bridge. They soon became a hideous feature of grounds across the land although, thankfully, Ken Bates' suggestion that they should also be electrified never came to pass.

It was around this time that criminology expert Ian Taylor stood up in front of a conference and talked about soccer violence being 'a symptom of ill health' and how 'expressive violence is a feature of all Western societies'. A bit academic perhaps but Taylor also made a comment that really should have been heeded: 'The fencing-in of crowds in situations of high excitement could have fatal consequences.'

Measures that have been introduced have served only to contain the problem: segregation, close-circuit television, all-ticket matches, stiffer penalties, restrictions on alcohol and banning orders.

Dougie Brimstone argued that the answer had to come from within. Why, for instance, was the scourge of soccer violence, particularly that which attached itself to the national side, not nearly so apparent north of the border for an international side that boasts a following as passionate as any in the world ... and a reputation for hard-drinking? Brimstone says the simple answer is positive peer pressure.

'The Scots took the decision they did not want to be linked with hooliganism,' said ex-RAF serviceman Brimson. 'They said, "We are better than that," and they reinvented themselves through peer pressure.'

Thankfully, we do not see the widespread violence that characterised the 1970s and 1980s. That is down to better policing and all-seater stadia. But do not be fooled: the will is still there, a hardcore at the heart of almost every club's fan base still exists and, if the police and governing authorities ever let their guard drop, the hooligans will fill the void faster than you can sing, 'Who are ye, who are ye?'

CHAPTER EIGHT
THE ENTERTAINERS

Tough guy actor Sean Bean is a Sheffield United man through and through – it says so on his shoulder; a £5 tattoo proclaiming him to be a Blades man. I like his no-nonsense, unpretentious acting style – a real working-class hero. Of the 80-odd movies he has made, none can have given him greater pleasure or meant more to him than the football drama *When Saturday Comes*, the story of a hard-drinking bloke with a talent for football who has to battle his demons to succeed. The movie was built around Sheffield United and Bean got to appear in front of 30,000 extras at Bramall Lane. 'It is a dream part,' he said at the time. 'If you could think of a part that you'd like to play, could write yourself and include all the things you want to do in a film, this is it!'

The film's best moment comes with a cup tie against Manchester United, final minute, penalty to the Blades. The ground falls silent; fans watching TV in nearby pubs hold their breath. Bean's character, Jimmy Muir, steps up to place the ball on the spot. If he scores, Sheffield win. The director draws out the action in theatrical slow motion, cutting from keeper to Bean, to the terraces, the pub, and to the dug-out, where a familiar face can be spotted among the anonymous extras. Blond-haired, broad shouldered, he watches nervously, intently, as Muir takes three steps and spears the ball to the keeper's left. Cue exultation. The crowd's arms go up, beer spills in the boozer and on the bench the back-room boys hug each other with delight. It might have required a few takes for Bean to get the ball into the net but who knows or cares? It looks real enough on screen and the little cameo by that chap on the bench seems genuine as well. It was Tony Currie, by the way.

That was, perhaps, the greatest moment for Bean, in his favourite movie, sharing the billing with his teenage hero, Tony Currie. 'Like many Blades, I loved Tony Currie ... his flair, his vision and his amazing talent. When able to grow my hair long and get my sideburns going, I wasn't a bad Currie look-alike.' He's right. You can see the resemblance up there on the screen, although no one is pretending Currie could act like Bean, and Bean would be the first to tell you that neither he, nor most footballers in the 1970s, could play like Tony Currie.

Currie was a London boy who dreamed of playing for one of the capital's top teams. Only the talent spotters they employed back in the late 1960s seem to have been suffering from a collective myopia as far as Currie was concerned: Chelsea did not want him, QPR saw nothing special. Currie was reduced to playing Sunday-morning football until someone with a bit more wisdom persuaded Watford he was worth a go.

Currie, a striker in those early days, did not disappoint, took his chance, made his mark and was soon on his way to better things with Second Division Sheffield United, where astute manager John Harris saw more talent in the lad than just scoring goals. Harris pulled him back into midfield where his sublime, easy-on-the-eye skills married to considerable power and had the team dancing to his beat. Blades fans worshipped at his altar and, judging by the fanzines and official polls, he is still Bramall Lane's all-time Number One. Promotion soon followed, then the start of an England career that would stretch from 1972 to 1979, yet yield a paltry 17 caps. As has been said elsewhere, successive England managers simply could not cope with or accommodate individuals like Currie within the national-team framework.

With Currie as conductor, Sheffield United came within a few points of winning the First Division championship for the first time since 1898 but just a season later they were relegated. How did it happen? Did manager Ken Furphy lose the dressing room before losing his job? Certainly, players had to be sold as United built a new stand on the open side of the ground they had once shared with Yorkshire County Cricket Club. And perhaps Currie lost a bit of focus. Relegation affected him badly. He was struggling with his weight, struggling with his form and needed a new challenge.

At the age of 26 and still with one eye on the M1 heading south, Currie finally made the big-money move that most people had realised was inevitable, but the surprise was that he travelled 34 miles north to Leeds United. Jimmy Armfield was prepared to take a chance on Currie's ability against his perceived indolence and paid £250,000 for him. Currie's task was straightforward: he was expected to be the new Johnny Giles. You could see the Leeds faithful dismissing that particular ambition yet it was just the impetus Currie needed. He loved proving people wrong and over the next three seasons under Armfield, and then Jock Stein, he carved himself a place in the hearts of the Elland Road faithful.

You see there was actually not much Currie could not do with the ball at his feet. There is one goal, there for all to see on YouTube, which says everything you ever need to know about him. The opposition was Southampton but that's irrelevant. Even Inter Milan's *catenaccio* could not have prevented it. He was outside the penalty area, had a defender in his face and the keeper was well positioned but, with his right boot, Currie put a yard of bend on his shot to steer it just inside the post. Then he stood there, arms aloft, applauding himself. 'Oh my goodness,' exclaimed Barry Davies in commentary. 'Currie milks the applause that is so deserved.'

Currie spent three highly successful seasons at Leeds – if you can call three losing semi-finals successful – playing the best football of his career. At the same time, he saw intermittent action with England, first for Don Revie and then Ron Greenwood. But ever the perfectionist, he never felt comfortable with his international appearances and his England career petered out when he was substituted in a lifeless 0-0 draw against Sweden in June 1979.

Two months later, much to the disappointment of the Leeds fans, his manager Jimmy Adamson, and even Currie himself, he finally moved south to Queens Park Rangers, primarily to try and save his marriage. However, it ended in divorce a year later. The 1970s had seen the best of Tony Currie, a player of great skill, heart and natural showmanship. Just ask Alan Birchenall.

Well, I could not rest the Tony Currie case without mentioning that kiss. It was one of those wonderfully spontaneous moments that simply would not be countenanced today. Can you imagine the headlines and the charges of ungentlemanly behaviour that would follow? Actually, it is probably a red-card offence. A sense of humour is no longer tolerated on the football pitch.

If it had been any other player than Birchenall that Currie found himself sitting next to on the Bramall Lane turf that April day in 1975, nothing would have happened. But Birch was always up for an on-field laugh and jokingly said, 'Give us a kiss.' Currie, never backwards at coming forwards, puckered up and a moment of magical mirth became legend, particularly among the gay community, who have raised the image to iconic proportions.

Over the years Currie, these days Football in the Community co-ordinator at his beloved Blades, has kept his thoughts on that kiss pretty much to himself. Birchenall, on the other hand, has been a bit more forthcoming, admitting that at the time his wife was less than impressed. And when asked the question about his worst moment in football, he once said, 'Kissing Tony Currie ... every year we have to re-enact the kiss and he gets uglier by the year.'

Duncan McKenzie was an enigmatic footballer; impish and easy-going. He often flattered to deceive, frustratingly drifting out of games until no one really knew he was there but, without a doubt, he was outrageously gifted and, in a perverse way, that sometimes worked against him and certainly held back his hopes of international recognition. Because it was difficult to fit McKenzie into a team plan: he was a free-flowing individual who played without shackles, capable of manoeuvres that others never saw, and that could lead to frustration, for him and his colleagues.

But when it worked, it was sublime. I can hear the song now, echoing round some nondescript Second Division ground he had just lit up with an outrageous piece of skill: 'We all agree, Duncan McKenzie is magic'. His finest hour came on 27 January 1974, a Sunday afternoon fourth-round FA Cup tie at the City Ground between Second Division Nottingham Forest and high-flying Manchester City of Division One. There was a miners' strike on. Nottinghamshire's coalfield protestors wanted a bit of light relief and funnelled through the turnstiles until the attendance topped the 41,000 mark. Manchester City, a thrifty outfit under the no-nonsense management of gnarled old Ron Saunders, came with more glitter than Marc Bolan. From back to front they bristled with big name players like Willie Donachie, Mike Doyle, Tommy Booth, Mike Summerbee, Colin Bell, Francis Lee and Rodney Marsh – a coterie of class for which the Eastlands sheikhs would flog an oil well today.

But on that day they were flummoxed by McKenzie's wizardry – Harry Potter against the hordes of Voldemort. McKenzie danced past three bemused defenders to create the first goal for Ian Bowyer, at that time a striker who had been sold off by City boss Malcolm Allision but later to become of one of Brian Clough's most influential midfield lieutenants. McKenzie hooked in the second himself and then, just before the break, came the *pièce de résistance*: a quickstep through the visitors' defence, a cross, a goal. This was how local reporter John Lawson described it: 'Donachie gave him the ball on the right, he slipped past the City full-back with nonchalant and contemptuous ease, nut-megged Booth, beat Mike Doyle and pushed the ball between another defender and MacRae [the City goalkeeper] for Bowyer to accept the simplest of tasks.'

Ectasy on Trentside. As the dazed Sky Blues trooped off for a half-time shellacking, they were serenaded by a charming little ditty from the local wags suggesting that, as Forest had McKenzie, City could position their superstar Rodney Marsh in a bodily orifice where the sun suffered perpetual eclipse. The moment was not lost on the flamboyant City star. 'If McKenzie could play like that every week, he would be an England regular,' Marsh remarked after Forest's stunning 4-1 victory. But, of course, there was the rub: like so many players blessed with extravagant ability, McKenzie could not turn it on like a tap. There were days and games where nothing much happened and then, as now, managers were not the most patient of individuals.

Brian Clough, who took him to Leeds from Forest for a huge fee for the time of £250,000, during his infamous 44-day Elland Road sojourn, once described McKenzie – a chain-smoking footballer whose party pieces included jumping over a mini and throwing a golf ball the length of a football field – as 'flamboyant' and then quickly corrected himself. 'Eccentric would be more accurate,' said the manager famous for his own particular foibles.

McKenzie was everything above and more ... but, in a word, he was an entertainer. One of that rare breed of footballer you would single out and say, 'Yes, I'd pay money to watch him'. Back in the 1970s there were quite a few such characters, all, of course, emerging from the home nations. As mentioned elsewhere, it is remarkable that England could not win an eggcup when they had some extravagantly blessed footballers to call on. Perhaps there is a flaw to be detected here. All those characters – I think of Tony Currie, Rodney Marsh, Stan Bowles, Charlie George and Frank Worthington among the best – were coloured by a streak of individualism and rebellion; you were never quite sure what they would do next. That was what made them so compelling.

BEST, PELE AND A HALF-TIME BOVRIL

It is interesting that England have never been able to make the best of players who would be at the core of teams like Brazil and Italy, Spain and even Holland. Countries not afraid to give flair its place, to embrace players who might flit in and out of the action but could win you a game in a heartbeat. England always look for the pragmatic approach, or at least they did back in the 1970s when the table was groaning under the weight of so much ability. It's not like that anymore. There were probably eight English players in every Division One side for the likes of Alf Ramsey, Don Revie and Ron Greenwood to pick from.

Now, if he is lucky, when Roy Hodgson takes in a top Premiership match, there might be two or three from both sides who fill the qualification criteria for the home country. What would Roy Hodgson give to have the artistry of a Glenn Hoddle, the guile of an Alan Hudson or the arrogance of a Charlie George that he could select? It is staggering to consider that, between them, Duncan McKenzie, Frank Worthington, Alan Hudson, Charlie George, Rodney Marsh, Tony Currie and Peter Osgood won a total of 41 caps – and Currie's 17 (spread over seven seasons, it should be pointed out) account for nearly half that figure.

Yet it is also not surprising, when you consider the defensive attitude of successive England managers, summed up by this comment from Ron Greenwood when explaining a controversial team selection to the media. Greenwood had left out one of the most exciting talents in the First Divison because he thought he was too young. This is what he said: 'We tend to rush players forward in this country. We don't realise maturity is relative to their physical development.' He was talking about Glenn Hoddle, who was 22 years old.

Although he was called into a couple of Alf Ramsey squads,

McKenzie never made an appearance for his country. This was partly due to his formative years being spent at Nottingham Forest, struggling along in the early 1970s under the yoke of an inept manager named Allan Brown and Forest's anachronistic committee hierarchy. Forest were a selling club back in the day, allowing their best players to be taken from them: Terry Hennessey, Henry Newton and Ian Storey-Moore being the prime examples. McKenzie was left behind, at times his skills carrying the side. In 111 games he scored 41 times, a ratio any striker would envy, and that gave him an appreciation of his worth that he felt was not entirely shared by his employers. In the end, he tired of all the backstage machinations and actually went on strike, threatening at one point to give up the game altogether. He was rescued by Brian Clough and Leeds in a record £275,000 transfer deal that should have been the making of him.

The switch to the mighty Leeds should have given him his place among the elite, surrounded by quality players who could ensure his peculiar skills were harnessed for the common good. Had that happened, his claims for international recognition would have been hard to resist. But, of course, it all turned sour at Elland Road. Such was the fallout from Clough's disastrous reign the players he brought in – McKenzie, John McGovern and John O'Hare – were hardly welcomed into the fold.

'He [McKenzie] wasn't what you would call a team player,' wrote Norman Hunter in his 2004 autobiography, *Biting Talk*. 'He was very skilful ... he scored goals and was a big favourite with the fans and you couldn't knock that.' But ... there was always a 'but'. As Hunter pointed out, where other equally gifted players in the Leeds team, like Eddie Gray, for instance, would be content with beating two or three defenders before making the right pass, McKenzie would usually go back for one more trick. New Leeds boss Jimmy Armfield, not a man likely to swim against the tide, was brought in to repair the Clough damage and quickly sussed out upon which side his bread was buttered. He had little choice but to keep faith with the old guard and week after week, match after match, he gave McKenzie a nice warm seat on the subs bench, a position that included Leeds' losing the European Cup Final against Bayern Munich in 1975.

Yet when he played, he delivered: 27 goals in 66 appearances, not far off a goal every two games. And the fans loved him. 'One of the few good things to come out of Brian Clough's short and unlamented reign,' enthuses a Leeds United blog. McKenzie finished the 1975–76 season as the team's top scorer but that summer Armfield sold him to Belgian club Anderlecht, then holders of the European Cup Winners Cup and intent on establishing themselves among the continent's elite club sides. 'I don't think I could have bettered myself,' McKenzie concluded. But six months later he was back in England, preferring to sign for Everton rather than join Brian Clough's revolution at his old club Forest.

Although he looks back on his two seasons at Everton – 'my spiritual home' – with fondness, once again McKenzie's timing was all wrong. The manager who signed him was Billy Bingham but within weeks the genial Irishman had been sacked and new boss Gordon Lee was not so enamoured with McKenzie's idiosyncrasies. Still, McKenzie continued to score goals in his limited appearances (14 from 48 games), just as he did for every club he represented. There would later be spells at Blackburn and Chelsea, even Tulsa Roughnecks and Chicago Sting, but it is fair to say that no one really got the best out of him.

I was surprised to discover that much the same could be said of Rodney Marsh, certainly from the Manchester City and England point of view. My hazy memories were of another excessively gifted player, languid in possession but possessed of quick feet, who played with an attractive *joie de vivre*. But then I saw an old Allison interview in which he admitted that the signing of Marsh for Manchester City at a time when they were four points clear at the top of Division One had not worked. 'He was not the right player,' said Allison, suggesting that Marsh had a particular problem with training and fitness. 'He had never trained before ... he said he didn't realise you had to work so hard.'

Allison paid out a record £200,000 to Queens Park Rangers for Marsh in 1972. 'I had always liked Marsh, from the time he was with Fulham,' said Allison, who thought he could bring the same cutting edge to Maine Road that had been his forte with QPR, where he scored 106 goals in 211 games. But it did not work. The huge fee proved a heavy burden for the player, especially in his first few games for City, and the general consensus is that the transfer cost them the title that season.

Colin Bell, City's powerhouse midfield star, certainly believes this to be the case. 'His arrival ruined our game for a while because everything we worked on was based on a one-touch or two-touch. Unfortunately, once Rodney was involved, he'd take three or four unnecessary touches, beating one player and then another.' Marsh's great friend Mike Summerbee later emphasised the point: 'Rodney at that time wasn't the right player for us.' And Marsh himself put it in a typically robust nutshell – 'They fucked up by signing me. I didn't play badly, I just upset the rhythm of the team.'

It is, almost word for word, the Duncan McKenzie story. And, of course, while Marsh was frustrating the hell out of his teammates, the fans were lapping it up. They loved all that showmanship and, to be fair, the many goals he scored, all delivered with that trademark Marsh bravura and panache. This is what Graham Green once wrote about him in *The Times*: 'As for Marsh himself he remains the individualist and the entertainer he will always be. Hooked up a number of times in full artistic flow he always managed to turn the ire of others to laughter in the fluent manner of his falling. He should be a tumbler or a clown in a circus. Yet as a footballer he is no clown. He may not suit the planners or those who worship method. But he makes the crowd purr.' In 118 games for City, he scored 36 goals but the bottom line is that he failed to bring them success. A solitary League Cup final appearance in 1974 and they lost that 2-1 to Wolves, the winner from John Richards being deflected into his path by Rodney Marsh. He was so dejected by the defeat that he refused to collect his runners-up tankard.

The sand timer was running out on Rodney Marsh's days at Maine Road. By the end of 1975, although installed as club captain, he was becoming disillusioned, having seen the shape of the team change inexorably as the flamboyance of Malcolm Allison gave way to the pragmatism of Ron Saunders, followed by the laboured, safety-first approach of former player Tony Book. Marsh, never one to keep an opinion to himself, confronted the manager with his frustrations in a fairly hands-on sort of way. It signalled not just the end of his City career but, to all intents and purposes, his career at the top level. He was only 28 yet over the next 12 seasons he would play less than 130 games in a variety of shirts belonging to Cork Hibernians, Fulham and Tampa Bay Rowdies. It should have been much better; there should have been much more.

Marsh himself knows that and has said so on many occasions.

'I was born a free spirit and I played the game the same way. You either loved it or you hated it. I make no excuses for that and I wouldn't change a thing. Did that contribute to me only getting nine caps? Probably. I would hold my hand up and say that I was a luxury player and I make no bones about that.'

And that surely is the way to remember Marsh. Remember the way he enchanted us with his skills and gave us something to smile about with his style? This was the man who once answered a fatuous question about whether he was the white Pele with the riposte, 'Actually, Pele is the black Rodney Marsh!' And this was the man who effectively ended his England career by shooting from the lip once again. You must have heard the story. Marsh is about to win his ninth international cap. In his pre-match team talk England manager Alf Ramsey, by then suffering the habitual media abuse visited on all who take the job, was laying down the law, urging his men to work harder. 'Rodney, you in particular,' he said, adding, 'If you don't work hard, I'm going to pull you off at half-time.' And without a thought to the consequences, Marsh said, 'Christ, at Man City all we get is a cup of tea and an orange!' Strait-laced Ramsey was not amused and Marsh would never be invited to take his international tally into double figures.

The Rodney Marsh story is interlaced with the career of another genuinely individualistic character who definitely did things his way – Stan Bowles. By an entertainingly circular route, he went the opposite way to Marsh, starting his career with his home club, Manchester City. See, not a lot of people know that. Most assume Stanley is a London boy, no doubt because of his most successful association with QPR. But no, the truth is that he began at City under Joe Mercer as a 17-year-old outside left. Mercer once said, 'Straightaway we realised that Stan was something special as a player but what we didn't know was that by the time he was 21, he would be impossible to handle.' Stan had that same streak of cussedness that often went hand in hand with singular ability – George Best, Frank Worthington, Charlie George, etc., etc.

Through the dozens of books I have trawled to put some flesh on the bones of fading recollections from three decades ago, Stan Bowles receives few mentions – far too few when measured alongside his talent. I've never met the guy but I am fairly confident I can predict his response to those continual omissions and oversights. 'I don't give a fuck,' he would have said, and he never did. Football did not get in the way of Stan Bowles having a good time, simply because he did not let it. If ever a bloke did it his way, it was Bowles. But he should be forever grateful to the game because, had it not been for the magic in his feet, Stan Bowles' life would have turned out to be very different.

Born in a tough part of Manchester and raised on the wrong side of the tracks, he was always comfortable in the company of villains. Perhaps that is what kept his feet firmly on the ground. If he had ever become the big time Charlie, he might have found those feet being kicked from under him. Perhaps that is what also gave him his 'take no shit' attitude to football and to life: we are here only once, this is no rehearsal, so grab it while you can and to hell with the consequences.

At Maine Road Bowles was a wild child – late nights spent gambling, drinking. It was all too much. The day he failed to turn up at the airport for a trip to Amsterdam, preferring the inside of a betting shop to a plane ride and a friendly against Ajax, was the final straw. 'He had brilliant ability,' said Malcolm Allison, 'but I couldn't control him.'

Bowles doesn't argue with this. 'I got the sack from City

because Joe Mercer and Malcolm Allison thought I was barmy. It was in my wild days and they couldn't stand it.' It was his 21st birthday. Bowles was shipped out to Bury on loan but that did not last long. After seven weeks his relationship with the manager had deteriorated so rapidly that he was returned marked 'damaged goods'. City tore up his contract and Bowles, by then a married man with a family to support, drifted back to his own neighbourhood, 'doing little errands, putting bets on' to earn a crust.

His salvation would come in the shape of a part-time landlord named Ernie Tagg who was also manager of Division Four club, Crewe Alexandra. On the recommendation of a friend who loaned him the train fare to Crewe, Bowles met Tagg, whose other string to a unique bow was part-time milkman, and a highly unusual partnership was formed. Tagg also proved to be a gambling man, taking a chance on a player every other club was scared of signing. But he gave Bowles an ultimatum: Crewe was the end of the line, the last chance saloon. If he screwed things up at Gresty Road, there would be no more takers. But the penny seemed to drop and Bowles buckled down under Tagg's close, fatherly attention. He scored 18 goals in 51 games and, in such modest company, shone like a Vesta in the dark. The big clubs could not fail to be impressed but Tagg wisely steered him towards the more rural delights of Carlisle United, where his growing maturity would be given a little more time to put down some roots.

He did not play a full season at Carlisle – just 33 games, in fact – but his departure from Brunton Park had nothing to do with his waywardness. In 1972 a £110,000 cheque – worth about a million today – was more than enough for a Division Two chairman to throw up his arms and run round the boardroom yelling, 'I've won, I've won!' The man who coughed up the cash was Gordon Jago, manager of Second Division QPR. He wanted Bowles for a specific task: to take over the number 10 shirt worn by Loftus Road idol Rodney Marsh, who had just joined Manchester City.

To some it would have been like carrying a record transfer fee onto the field but not Stan; remember, he did not give a toss ... and he believed he was a better player than Marsh. In fact, he once cheekily claimed that, coming from the North, he had never even heard of Rodney Marsh and years later, in typically straightforward fashion, he said, 'For me, Rodney Marsh only did it in the lower leagues – I did it in the higher ones. When he went to Manchester City, they were 12 points clear and they lost the league, so that tells you everything! I don't think he was a bad player but at the end of the day that is up to the QPR supporters to decide.' Well, suffice to say that in an unofficial poll those same QPR fans voted Stan Bowles the best player in their history. Enough said!

Bowles earned their everlasting respect and admiration over a seven-year period when he was a crucial component in the best years the club has ever experienced. They almost did a Derby County/Nottingham Forest, getting within a couple of points of winning the old First Division title. In return, QPR gave Bowles the best years of his career and he was not slow to recognise the fact. Promotion came quickly, prompting him to indulge in a rare moment of introspection. 'Nobody knows how lucky I am to be here,' he told an interviewer. 'Playing for Queens Park Rangers in the First Division is the easy part. The tough part was being reborn, and keeping in football when it seemed I was destined for the scrapheap.

'You could say that as a teenager I had the ability to be a useful footballer but I got the idea I was training to be a playboy instead. Now it is like a dream here as we are proving that we have got what it takes in the First Division.' The remarks came just after QPR had stuffed Arsenal 2-0. Bowles, whippet-slim with dazzling ball skills and a predator's eye for goal, was both architect and assassin. His best position was hard to pin down. His ability to spot and make a pass pointed him towards midfield, but had he been allowed to develop purely as a striker, more honours might have come his way. One star of a previous era, ex-Spurs favourite Eddie Bailey, went so far as to compare him to Jimmy Greaves: 'I think the business of shuttling Bowles between the front and midfield was wrong. He was too good a finisher to play in midfield. Of course, Jimmy was great – but, in my opinion, Bowles is up there in the same bracket.'

Soon the clamour for international recognition would become irresistible, only for it to add another frustrating, controversial chapter to the Bowles' story. His five-game England career began under Alf Ramsey but then Ramsey was sacked and none other than Stan's old Maine Road boss, Joe Mercer, stepped in. It was never going to work, was it? In his second game in charge Mercer subbed Bowles. Bowles didn't much care for the decision, packed his bags and left the team hotel. Destination: White City dog track. 'I'm not surprised,' said Mercer. 'Nothing Stan Bowles does surprises me.'

The white-knuckle ride that was Bowles' life continued. With Gordon Jago (now a big cheese in American soccer) ousted from QPR, Bowles told new boss Dave Sexton he wanted a transfer ... but within weeks he said he wanted to stay. Then Don Revie called him back into the England squad but that did not amount to much and in 1977 he played his last international game against Holland. Five caps in three years while players who could not hold a candle to Bowles were racking up appearances. But it did not bother Stan – 'I do think I deserved more caps but if I'd never played for England, it wouldn't have bothered me.'

All good things come to pass and so it was at Loftus Road. As the team started to grow old together, results suffered, disillusionment set in. Chairman Jim Gregory called Bowles into his office one day and asked if he would be interested in a move. Stan, 31, wasn't at all interested until Gregory told him who was asking – 'It's Big 'Ead and his mate.' Ten minutes later Stan Bowles had agreed a £250,000 transfer to European Cup holders Nottingham Forest. In hindsight, it is easy to see this was another non-starter. There was only ever room for one ego at the City Ground and Bowles was not the first, nor the last, to learn that Clough ruled and anyone who did not like it would quickly be shown the door. 'We got off on the wrong foot straightaway when he said, "You cockneys are all the same," and I told him, "Excuse me, I'm from Manchester." I also told him once that I had a load of "O" Levels and "A" Levels and, when he found out that was all bollocks, he went mad!'

Bowles found himself sitting out as many games as he played, Clough deciding that his talents were more suited to home games than away. Of course he did not like it one bit but the chance to appear in a European Cup final, as Forest approached their 1980 Madrid showdown with Hamburg, was a tantalising one, especially considering he had never won a meaningful medal in his career. But it was not to be. A few weeks before the final Forest played a full-strength team in a testimonial match and Bowles was not selected. Once again, our man Stan packed his bags and left in a huff, passing up possible selection for the game and a few thousand in squad bonus money.

'It's the principle of the thing that was at stake,' said Bowles.

'I've won nothing that matters in football and I would have loved a European Cup medal.' Clough did not shed a tear. After just 19 games he sold him to Leyton Orient for £150,000 without a backward glance, although, interestingly, there was regret from Peter Taylor: 'I watched him go with a tinge of sadness. He is not a bad sort and there has never been the slightest doubt about his ability.' Within a couple of years it was all over for Bowles. After Orient he turned out for Brentford but, typically, he called time. 'I just got fed up,' he declared.

If Stan Bowles was the *enfant terrible* of the 1970s, the big daddy was certainly Frank Worthington, a rough diamond from the back streets of Halifax with more than a hint of the Elvis about him. He was football's answer to Bill Wyman, a lover with so many notches on his bedpost it looked like woodworm, a gigolo who gave new meaning to the phrase 'playing between two strikers'. Worthington looked just as comfortable in a crushed velvet suit as he did in the stripes of Huddersfield Town, where he began a peripatetic career that took him to 21 different clubs across numerous time zones and to places where that strong Yorkshire accent was an alien sound. It also brought him a grand total of eight England caps and stands him up as another example of a breed of flair players around in the 1970s who were criminally ignored or under-used by successive England managers who, to be perfectly frank, were scared of their own shadows. 'I've no time for England managers like Don Revie and Graham Taylor,' Worthington once said. 'They just seemed determined to squeeze out individual flair.'

He remembered a squad session with Revie when he called Worthington, Alan Hudson, Stan Bowles and Tony Currie together for a chat. 'You have all the skill in the world,' Revie told them, before adding that he thought there was something missing, without making any attempt to say what that something was. Worthington later wrote, 'His intentions were crystal clear. In effect it was two fingers to skill and up the workhorses, which is the complete opposite of how it should be at international level.'

Worthington never abandoned his footballing principles; skill came first and never forget that you are out there to entertain the paying public. He did that into his 40s and despite suffering the sort of setbacks that might have broken lesser men. The biggest came when his dad Eric died at the age of 52. Eric Worthington lived long enough to see his three sons, Frank and brothers Bob and Dave, all play league football but not long enough to witness Frank's recognition at international level.

Then there was Worthington's much-publicised on-off transfer to Liverpool in 1972. The deal was done and dusted, signatures on the contract, Frank himself on Cloud Nine, just the medical to sort out and Anfield, here we come. Only it never happened. High blood pressure meant that Shanks was not about to risk a record £150,000. Worthington regards it as the biggest regret of his life, justifiably arguing that, had he become part of the Shankly regime, it would have been the making of him and that a whole lot more honours would have come his way. He recognises that his lifestyle at the time was probably behind the diagnosis – a case of burning the candle at both ends.

Somehow Worthington managed to shrug off that huge disappointment and give good service to every club he represented up to an age few players reach and are still able to kick a ball competitively: more than 700 Football League appearances, more than 200 goals, including, of course, that one against Ipswich. It is, for me, one of the best goals I have ever seen. Twenty-five yard pile-drivers are spectacular and require a degree of technique such as Dutch ace Marco van Basten once produced but goals conjured up by intuitive skill and unashamed talent, which leave players and fans alike open mouthed in admiration, come along all too rarely. Matthew Le Tissier has one or two in his locker, Paul Gascoigne against Scotland comes to mind, but Frank Worthington's was the best of the lot. Back to goal, a flick over his head took out the entire Ipswich defensive line and then, with just a tad of arrogance and a huge measure of cool, he stroked it into the corner of the net. Lovely jubbly!

I want to finish this chapter with one more Worthington story, one anecdote that captures the multi-faceted essence of the character. There are a few to pick from. I mean, this is the man who bedded, among many others, Miss Barbados Lindy Field and notorious Profumo scandal witness Mandy Rice-Davies. Somewhere in his highly entertaining autobiography, *One Hump Or Two* – clever title, that – he describes the seduction of an attractive Swedish lady ... and her daughter. But within the pages of that self-same tome I found the perfect passage. Young Frank, who had helped Huddersfield back into the First Division for the first time in eons, has just been tapped up by Jimmy Bloomfield, manager at Leicester City, and called up for the England U-23 side for the first time. He is on Cloud Nine.

The international is away in Poland – Warsaw, to be exact – a capital city that instantly strikes Frank as drab and grey. He is about to brighten up the landscape. As he walks towards baggage control he spots Alf Ramsey speaking to the press and decides to walk across. This is how Frank himself recalled the incident: 'Not normally one to ever utter a profanity, Ramsey turned to his audience and said, "Whooooo the fuck is that?"' Why? Because there was Frankie boy dressed in a green velvet jacket, a flowered shirt, leather trousers and cowboy boots. He hardly looked like your average footballer but then Frank Worthington was above average. In the game against Poland U-23s Frank was at the corner of the penalty area when a left-wing cross floated towards him. He controlled it on his thigh, turned and, as the ball dropped, he volleyed from 20 yards into the top corner. Frank Worthington in a nutshell: pretty as a peacock· but, oh boy, could he play!

CHAPTER NINE
THE MANAGERS

We had Shanks and Bob Paisley at Liverpool, Tommy Doc's star-crossed reign at United, Joe Mercer and the flamboyant Big Mal at City, the unlikely success of Bertie Mee at Arsenal, Keith Birkinshaw who brought the samba to Spurs, Jimmy Armfield and then Jock Stein at Leeds, Lawrie McMenemy at Southampton.

They all wrote their names in the encyclopedia of football history, for one reason or another but no one really talks about them now. Only two names from the 1970s continue to dominate the managerial album of memories. They are still writing books and making films about Messrs Clough and Revie, two individualistic managers who went about their jobs in different ways, yet had so much in common.

They could not stand each other yet the capricious nature of fate decreed that their paths would meet and cross. Clough, the outspoken younger man who never hid behind a platitude, never betrayed his inner feelings; and Revie, a superstitious character, more reserved, suspiciously so in many eyes, lacking his rival's public confidence and bravura.

If there is one moment when their differences were publicly laid bare, it was shortly after Clough's 44-day reign at Leeds when both men were invited to share a television studio with chirpy TV presenter-turned-MP Austin Mitchell. It was Revie's chance to challenge Clough; to ask him what he had been trying to do in vilifying the team he had built and denigrating his every achievement.

But it was Clough, hectoring and badgering in his branded style, who took the high ground as Revie slumped lower and lower into his chair. Revie, an old fashioned figure with his long sideburns and powder-blue jacket, tried to list Leeds' attributes but Clough, irritatingly smug and overtly prosperous after his life-changing pay-off from Leeds, rudely interjected with a jibe about their disciplinary record. Revie was floundering and Clough beamed at his little bit of mischief.

'I wanted to do it better than you,' Clough then declared.

'How could you?' exclaimed an incredulous Revie. 'We won the championship and only lost four matches.'

'Well, I could only lose three!' countered Clough, while Revie just shook his head: 'No, no, no, no!'

Perversely, despite their overstated differences, Clough and Revie came from the same lowly Yorkshire environment, born in Middlesbrough – a beer-and-football town according to J. B. Priestley – and both made their playing reputations as centre-forward. Both later took rudderless Second Division clubs and moulded them in their own image into all-conquering teams. They did it by imposing their will and vision on everyone from the chairman to the charlady until it reached the point where, without them, the clubs could never function in the same successful way. Looking back, it could be said that Clough and Revie left Nottingham Forest and Leeds United pretty much where they found them: in the backwaters. Provincial teams with great history, wonderful tradition but limited hope to match unrealistic expectation.

The Clough story has become part of soccer folklore and is told elsewhere among these pages. The Revie story is not quite so well worn, primarily because he has become a figure of hate in all football centres beyond the LE1 postcode. It is a fairly basic and understandable reaction to a man whose team was seen to take professionalism to, and occasionally beyond, its acceptable limits and whose career ended in ignominious controversy. 'One has to admire them,' wrote Brian Glanville, 'but it's still hard to like them.'

But as with most things in life, there are several shades to the Revie story and it is easy to forget they were more, much more, than just 'dirty Leeds'. George Best probably got the players' verdict about right. 'I hated playing against them, I really did,' he once said. 'But they also had a hell of a lot of skill.'

Revie played his junior football for Middlesbrough Swifts, coached by a train driver named Bill Saunderson, a working-class man who took his football very seriously, even to the point of compiling dossiers on opposition youth teams. The lessons were not lost on young Revie. He was picked up by Leicester, played for Hull City, but it was at Maine Road where he enjoyed his best days and where he first revealed a tactical awareness that would become the cornerstone of his managerial success in the years ahead.

Revie was used as a deep-lying centre-forward, a position inspired by the legendary Hungarian Nandor Hidegkuti, who had famously scored a hat-trick against England in the national side's first ever defeat at Wembley in 1953. England had been unable to handle it back then and First Division defences were just as confused a decade later as Revie fed the forwards around him before darting into a goal-scoring position. It was so successful that it became known as the 'Revie Plan'. Revie's rewards were the accolade of Footballer of the Year in 1955, an FA Cup winners medal in 1956 and six England caps ... four more than a certain Brian Howard Clough.

After a brief spell with Sunderland, Revie was transferred to Leeds United, then in Division Two, in 1958. Although he could not help Leeds play their way into the top tier, he showed anyone interested or astute enough to notice what he was about. Billy Bremner's assessment, for instance: 'What impressed me more than anything else was his vision on a football park ... it was tremendous. And after he had struck the ball, he would pose, as if for a photograph.' Jack Charlton had his say as well: 'Good striker of the ball, good passer was Don – though he couldn't tackle to save his life.'

There was enough in Don Revie's locker to persuade Leeds chairman Harry Reynolds to make him player-manager in 1961 and although the first couple of years were a constant battle against relegation to Division Three, he also made the first of so many crucial signings when former Leeds hero John Charles was persuaded to return to the club from Juventus. Taking that as his lift-off point, Revie built not just the team but the club from top to bottom. He plotted and schemed, nurtured and orchestrated down to the finest detail, almost as if he had laid the very bricks and mortar that held Elland Road together. And it was all done with a single purpose in mind: to win at all costs.

Along the way he collected a group of players who bought into his philosophy and saw a handsome return on their investment. No one can deny they were a talented bunch. Once he had replaced the hapless Gary Sprake with David Harvey in goal, Revie had a line-up that rarely changed through the glory years and which rolled over opposition with a swaggering ruthlessness.

They were all internationals. England full-backs Paul Reaney and Terry Cooper; versatile Paul Madeley; World Cup winner Jack Charlton; Norman Hunter, one of the era's real hard men; Irish talisman Johnny Giles, the artist of the team, although he, too, could replace the brush with a switchblade; Peter Lorimer, a player with dynamite in his shooting boots; unselfish centre-forward Mick Jones; and his goal-poaching partner Allan 'Sniffer' Clarke. On the wing was Eddie Gray, about whom Revie once said, 'When he plays on snow, he doesn't leave any footprints.'

And, of course, Revie's lieutenant Billy Bremner, the player who epitomised all facets of his manager's character. Abrasive? Of course he was. Aggressive, arrogant, belligerent, uncompromising too. 10ST OF BARBED WIRE, according to a 1970 headline. But it must be said, he was also supremely talented. Esteemed observer John Arlott once declared that he was the best footballer in Britain and the one any manager would want. 'Some, no doubt, would toy with the idea of Best; but the realists, to a man, would have Bremner.'

Recently I watched a clip of the day Leeds demolished Southampton 7-0 and it told me everything you ever thought about Leeds. They bullied Southampton, skilfully dismembered them and finally, with little back heels and cross-footed passes, dismissed them with a cruel display of contemptuous artistry designed to ridicule and humiliate.

Revie's Leeds compiled an enviable list of triumphs: Division

Two champions in 1964, two First Division titles, an FA Cup and a European Fairs cup – yet it could, perhaps should, have been an even more glittering decade as they developed a habit of finishing second more times than the losing Boat Race crew, and it never sat well with Revie.

Revie's achievements stand up against the likes of Shankly, Clough and Busby, but despite an OBE and three Manager of the Year awards, there is no golden glow to his reputation. He is identified by his team's dark side and the sly way he abandoned England. But would Revie have forfeited any of his club's successes for a more favourable position in the football firmament? 'You get nowt for finishing second,' he once said and by God, he knew that to be the truth.

The bedrock of Revie's success with Leeds had been the club as a family. His loyalty to his players was beyond question, he ignored criticism and dissected advice.

It was a different story with England. The national team could not give him what he had at Leeds. He could not get close to the players, he tinkered with the team as he searched for that singular blend he had achieved at Elland Road, realising that the England pool of talent could never give him a Bremner or Giles. Like so many who have followed, he allowed himself to be influenced by the media and he clashed with the FA hierarchy. He failed to get England to the European championships of 1976 and the World Cup of 1978. And so he quit.

But the manner of his mutiny only added to Revie's notoriety for underhandedness. He got a £60,000-a-year job coaching the United Arab Emirates ... tax-free. Considering the inflation rate, that equates to a cool quarter of a million today. It was an offer he could not refuse and who could really blame him? Revie's error was to announce his defection through the columns of the

Daily Mail, rather than by informing his employers. Signal the inevitable witch-hunt. The FA, led by their vindictive, doddery chairman Sir Harold Thompson, banned Revie from any participation in domestic football for 10 years and, although he fought and won a High Court action to overturn that decision, there would be no significant return for him when he ended his desert sojourn, seven years later.

The media also, gleefully, took off their gloves. Rumours of bribery and bungs had stained the Revie years at Leeds and now the tabloids had just the excuse they needed to throw them into the public domain. Nothing was ever proven. In fact, Billy Bremner successfully sued one newspaper; but think smoke and fire and sticking mud. Revie and his team became damned united forever.

Except in Leeds, of course, where the glories he provided still motivate the Elland Road crowd, just as Clough's legacy continues to colour hope and expectation down the M1 in Nottingham. There is a poignant photograph of Revie, crippled by motor neurone disease, at a reunion with his family of Leeds players, shortly before his death in 1989 at the age of 61. Speaking for his team mates, Terry Cooper said, 'He was a great man and a great manager, who looked after us by wrapping us in cotton wool. On the field of play he made you feel ten feet tall, so that you wanted to die for Leeds United.'

The 1970s were dominated by Clough and Revie, reducing other managers to bit-part status, which, in retrospect, seems a little unfair. Where, for instance, do we place Tommy Docherty? Well, something of a clown, wasn't he? All those clubs, got the sack more times than Santa Claus, *and* he had a bit on the side. We cannot take him seriously, can we? Well, the truth about Tommy Docherty, although highly colourful, is a little more prosaic. In fact, he was a pretty good manager if records are anything to go by. He won cups and leagues, his sides played entertaining football and his personal story of infidelity was far from a typical football dalliance. His love for another man's wife was one of those relationships that happen and there is nothing anyone can do about it. It was an irresistible, unstoppable force of nature, which brought with it inevitable heartache and pain ... and it cost Tommy Docherty the best job of his career.

If the Doc had a fault, it stemmed from his poverty-stricken upbringing in Glasgow's notorious Gorbals, where you had to be quick with your wits to survive. It taught him to stand up for himself, to speak his mind and any fools who got in his way had better watch out. Unfortunately, certainly back in the 1970s, there were a vast number of football-club chairmen who could accurately be described as fools and that usually meant a relationship with the Doc was bound to end in tears. 'When I want your opinion,' he once told a director of a club where he was gainfully employed, 'I will give it to you.' Not the recommended way to make friends and influence people.

That was the attitude that came back to bite him at Manchester United where, in most people's eyes, he was doing a better than decent job and where, for those with long enough memories, he is still regarded as something of an Old Trafford hero. But there was a clique within the club – 'junior directors' he called them – who did not naturally warm to the diminutive Scot's abrasive persona and were continually sharpening their knives, waiting for Docherty to step out of line.

United was Docherty's 11th club in a coaching career that began at Chelsea in 1961, where he established his reputation as a brilliant motivator with an in-built ability to spot a good player. The Chelsea side he nurtured saw the emergence of a

Above: It's there … oh no it's not! Gordon Banks pulls off his remarkable save from Pele's header in the World Cup group game against Brazil at the Estadio Jalisco in Guadalajara. Pele later said, 'I could not believe what I saw. At that moment, I hated Banks more than any man in football. When I cooled down, I could only applaud him in my heart. It was the greatest save I have ever seen.'

© Getty Images

Left: Everyone was looking to get on England's 1970 World Cup bandwagon – including the RAC, which gave the squad honorary membership and set up this publicity shot.   © Getty Images

Right: German striker Gerd Muller drives in the winning goal of the 1970 World Cup quarter final to complete West Germany's comeback from two goals down in a dramatic match England should have won.

© Popperfoto/Getty Images

Above Left: Sunderland manager Bob Stokoe hugs his goalkeeper Jim Montgomery after his remarkable double save helped the Second Division side pull off a shock win over mighty Leeds United in the 1973 FA Cup final. © *Mirrorpix*

Above Right: Charlie George lies in triumph on the Wembley turf after his winner against Liverpool in the 1971 FA Cup final clinched an historic league and cup double for Arsenal. © *Getty Images*

Below Left: Mayhem at Edgar Street as Ronnie Radford leads the charge after scoring Hereford United's equaliser in the FA Cup 3rd Round Replay against First Division Newcastle United. Hereford won the tie 2-1 to become the first non-league side to beat a First Division club in the cup. © *Popperfoto/Getty Images*

Below Right: Bertie Mee shows his delight after he defied the odds to pull off a remarkable double triumph as manager of Arsenal, winning the First Division championship and FA Cup in 1971. © *Mirrorpix*

Above: Brian Clough and Peter Taylor celebrate in the dressing room after they brought the Division One championship to Nottingham Forest in 1978. © *Mirrorpix*

Centre: The Liverpool mutual admiration society. Legendary manager Bill Shankly celebrates with the Anfield faithful. © *Press Association Images*

Below: Kevin Keegan's moment of disagreement with Leeds United captain Billy Bremner during the 1974 Charity Shield final. Both players were sent off.

© *Mirrorpix*

Above Left: Ex-Forest star Viv Anderson comes up against Forest fullback Brian Laws following his £250,000 switch to Arsenal. © *Nottingham Post*

Above Right: Frank Worthington, part footballer, part playboy, struts his stuff with The Grumbleweeds pop group in 1975. © *Mirrorpix*

Below Left: Stan Bowles answers the jeers of Manchester United fans in typical fashion. © *Mirrorpix*

Below Right: Tony Currie, of Sheffield United, puckers up to Leicester City's Alan Birchenall for the kind of laugh you never see these days! © *Mirrorpix*

Above Left: Colourful referee George Flint. © *Nottingham Post*

Above Right: Hooliganism was a serious problem in the 1970s. Scottish fans invade the Wembley pitch after their heroes inflicted a 2-1 defeat on England. © *Mirrorpix*

Below: On 11 March 1978, an FA Cup quarter-final at The Den between Millwall and Ipswich descended into chaos as fighting began on the terraces, then spilled out on to the pitch and into the narrow streets around the ground, resulting in a number of injuries. Bobby Robson, the manager of Ipswich, who were winning 6-1 when the violence erupted, later commented, 'They (the police) should have turned the flamethrowers on them'. © *Mirrorpix*

Above Left: West Bromwich Albion's black trio Lawrie Cunningham, Brendan Batson and Cyrille Regis, nicknamed The Three Degrees by manager Ron Atkinson, posing with the real Three Degrees.

© *Mirrorpix*

Above Right: Clive Thomas was one of the most respected, but often controversial, referees of the 1970s.

© *Bob Thomas/Getty Images*

Below Left: Malcolm Allison, arguably the most flamboyant and charismatic manager of the 1970s.

© *Getty Images*

Below Right: Tommy Docherty and George Best pictured together in 1974, not long after playing his final game for Manchester United, a 3-0 defeat at QPR on New Year's Day.

© *Mirrorpix*

Left: Ipswich Town's Dutch imports Arnold Muhren and Frans Thijssen pictured after winning the UEFA Cup.

© *Mirrorpix*

Right: Ossie Ardiles in action for Spurs in a 1979 FA Cup tie at White Hart Lane.

© *Mirrorpix*

Left: George Best comes up against old adversary Norman Hunter in an FA Cup tie between Manchester United and Leeds United. © *Mirrorpix*

Above Left: George Best with one of his favourites teams … a group of Playboy Bunny girls!   © *Mirrorpix*

Above Right: Pele and Best share a moment together … but which one was the greatest player of the 1970s?   © *GEORGE BIRCH/AP/Press Association Images*

Below: It will never happen again – two years and three months after they sat in eighth place in the Second Division, Nottingham Forest were winners of the European Cup, defeating Malmo 1-0 in Munich. The Forest heroes pictured are, standing left to right, Viv Anderson, Peter Shilton, sub Chris Woods, John McGovern, Ian Bowyer, sub David Needham, trainer Jimmy Gordon, Trevor Francis, Frank Clark (nearly hidden) and sub John O'Hare. Crouching are Larry Lloyd, John Robertson, Tony Woodcock and Garry Birtles with Kenny Burns in a headlock.   © *Mirrorpix*

clutch of hugely talented players including Bobby Tambling, Peter Bonetti, Barry Bridges and Terry Venables – incidentally, the first player to be capped at school, amateur, youth, U-23 and full international level. Don't you just love trivia?

By the time he resigned in 1967, Docherty had also introduced Peter Osgood, Charlie Cooke, Ron Harris and John Hollins. If any man can lay claim to being the founder of the modern Chelsea, it is Tommy Docherty.

It was at that point the Doc got on the managerial carousel with stops at Rotherham and QPR, where he lasted for 28 days of total frustration due entirely to the intransigence of dictatorial chairman Jim Gregory. It culminated in a telephone call at the end of which, politely, Tom told Gregory to stuff his job. At Aston Villa he was the first manager to work with another strong chairman, Doug Ellis, and the first to be sacked by the man who became affectionately known as 'Deadly Doug'.

In 1970 Docherty was handed a very different challenge, as coach of struggling Portuguese club Porto. As he would do at just about every club he took over, Docherty's methods brought quick results. Porto charged up the league table and Mr Docherty became a hero in a foreign land. But there was no place like home and at the end of his two-year contract he came back, first as assistant at Hull City and then, the opportunity of a lifetime, manager of his country. Scotland came calling. For a proud and patriotric ex-player who had collected 25 international caps, it was an easy decision. And Docherty's timing was pretty good because he had some half-decent players to draw on: George Graham, Archie Gemmill, John O'Hare, Martin Buchan, Eddie Gray, Peter Lorimer, Willie Donachie, Denis Law and a talented youngster who was setting Celtic Park alight by the name of Kenny Dalglish.

Under Docherty's influence the Scottish team gave their passionate and perennially optimistic supporters performances that would gladden hearts on a cold night in Aucterader. As 1972 drew to a close they were on course for World Cup qualification, fresh off a group victory over the talented Danes, and Docherty was the toast of the highlands and lowlands. But Fate can be a capricious bitch when in the mood and, as Docherty stood on the threshold of a long-held dream, he was made an offer he couldn't refuse. Matt Busby invited him to become manager of Manchester United, then as now, the biggest football club on the planet, and as much as Docherty was revelling in his success as an international manager, he missed the day-to-day involvement of club football.

But there was one minor irritation, a single source of worry, a reason for a moment's hesitation. In a word, Manchester United were rubbish. Bottom of the table, their star players all getting old together, the club was in freefall. They sacked old-school manager Frank O'Farrell and, at the same time, told George Best enough was enough. They had won nothing since that glorious Wembley night in 1968 when they lifted the European Cup and, heaven forbid, there was even a chance of the unimaginable – relegation. 'It will be like turning an oil tanker round, only bigger,' Sir Matt Busby warned his fellow Scot. However Docherty was not fazed and on Friday, 22 December 1972, he was unveiled to the world as the new manager of Manchester United. The next day they drew 1-1 at home with Leeds United.

After making 'nice guy' appointments of Wilf McGuinness and Frank O'Farrell in the wake of Sir Matt Busby's retirement, the United board had realised there was no room for nice guys at the top of football; someone had to come in and shake the club to its foundations. Tommy Docherty was not afraid to take that on. He made some hard decisions, shipping out European heroes like Tony Dunne, Pat Crerand, John Sadler and even the idol of the Stretford End, Denis Law. In came Stewart Houston, Jim McCalliog and, briefly, the prodigal son George Best returned. The Doc reasoned that Best was still in his prime and, if he could be influenced to give his heart and soul to the cause, United would rise again.

But the genie had long been let out of the bottle and after a handful of games provided only glimpses of the glory that had once been George in full flow, he went AWOL yet again. Docherty suspended him and put him on the transfer list. Best responded by announcing his retirement from football. It was over. There would be comebacks at various clubs but after United it was all a bit demeaning and you sensed Best's heart was not beating for the game he once graced.

Without him, United survived. But it was only a temporary reprieve. The following season, for the first time in 40 years, Manchester United were relegated from the First Division ... and the man who hammered the final nail in their coffin? None other than Denis Law.

The Manchester derby that bright, late spring day in 1974 had never held so much significance. If they were to have any chance of survival, United had to win and the cause dragged 57,000 into Old Trafford. They would need other results to help but, if they could beat the old enemy, there was a chance. It was a daunting task. City in those days could draw on the talents of players like Colin Bell, Dennis Tueart and Francis Lee as well as the old Scottish warhorse Law up front. Just eight minutes from time, after 82 minutes of non-stop excitement, City broke up a United attack and Bell surged towards the box and found Lee running to the right. Lee fired the ball back into the area where Law, facing away from goal and unmarked, back-heeled it over the line and sent United into Division Two.

Law did not want to be there but his innate striker's sense had led him to the right spot and his instinctive ability to conjure a goal from any situation did the rest. There was not a flicker of emotion from Law. Team mates came to congratulate him, arms aloft, but Law walked sombrely away. It was the last time Denis Law kicked a ball in the Football League.

A pitch invasion brought a premature end to the game and so the curtain fell on a colourful career in the worst possible circumstances. Only six years after conquering Europe, United had been relegated. 'What's more,' wrote Docherty, 'I had the stigma of being manager when it happened.' Had that happened today Docherty would almost certainly have been sacked. Managers are fired if they lose two or three games in a row. Just ask Bryan Gunn, idolised in his days as Norwich City goalkeeper, who took charge at Carrow Road and was then summarily dismissed by Delia Smith and her board just one week into the 2009–10 season, having lost the first game of the season 7-1 – before winning their second 4-0.

United were wise enough to give Docherty time to continue his rebuilding job and over the coming months the revolving doors of Old Trafford were spinning like a roulette wheel as players came and went: Brian Kidd and Jim McCalliog out; Stuart Pearson and Steve Coppell in ... at a net profit. United stormed out of Division Two as champions and, true to say, both players and fans enjoyed the experience. United played to packed houses everywhere they went. Well, how often have Leyton Orient been able to match up to the mighty in the search for points? And they were winning just about every game they played.

They went back to where they belonged in some style and Docherty was in his element, fashioning a side that played expansive, entertaining football with a decisiveness that brought results. The capture of Coppell from Tranmere had been a masterstroke, Pearson liaised perfectly with Macari, Martin Buchan was the accomplished defensive leader and around them were players like Sammy Mclroy, David McCreery and another flying winger named Gordon Hill. For most of that returning season, they were in with a sniff of a championship and FA Cup double but the lure of Wembley proved a distraction in the league and they were beaten to the title by Liverpool.

Still, the cup would have been a suitable consolation only United did not turn up for the final against Southampton. Understandably, they had failed to give the Second Division side quite the respect they deserved. United's free-flowing football was stifled, they could not find the impetus to break out and they were punished by Bobby Stokes' winning goal. For Docherty, it was a desperate blow. Six times a Wembley loser.

But at least United were back in Europe, back near the peak of English football, back competing for the big prizes. Docherty had done everything the board had asked of him. The following season he took them back to Wembley and this time his team got to climb the steps after their opponents. Goals from Pearson and Macari had shattered Liverpool's dreams of a League-FA Cup-European Cup treble. Docherty was now officially entitled to claim legendary status at Old Trafford.

And then the roof fell in.

Tommy Docherty, a married man with four children, had fallen in love with Mary Brown, wife of Manchester United's physiotherapist Laurie Brown. The papers called it an 'affair', a label the Doc detests. Thirty-odd years later, they are still together, grandparents now. Some affair. Perhaps that led to an oft-repeated Docherty quote: 'I've always said there's a place for the press but they haven't dug it yet.'

The United board reacted to the revelations with almost puritanical outrage, claiming Docherty had 'broken the moral code of the club'. They demanded his resignation but Docherty refused, so they sacked him. The best job in club football had been taken away from him 'because I fell in love'. When you consider the yobbish behaviour of the modern footballer, which goes virtually unpunished, you can only shake your head at the game's moral descent in the decades that have passed since Tommy Docherty committed his 'crime of passion'.

Docherty returned to the managerial merry-go-round – Derby and QPR again and then into the 1980s with stipends at clubs as disparate as Sydney Olympic, Preston North End, South Melbourne, Wolverhampton Wanderers and Altrincham, the appointments often ending in dismissal. Looking through the cuttings, there is a palpable sense of treading water, playing out time in his career. Management was never the same for the Doc after Old Trafford – how could it be? Just like Best and Law, it was hardly a finale befitting his achievements.

Through the 1970s, like Shankly, Clough and Revie, the mug shot of Tommy Docherty beneath a screaming headline quoting something he had said or done was a regular occurrence. Whether they craved the spotlight of publicity or not, they certainly did nothing to avoid its glare.

Not so a thoughtful, talented young coach who was quietly making something of a reputation for himself in the sleepy soccer outpost of Suffolk. At Ipswich Town, Bobby Robson was proving that nice guys could succeed in the self-centred world of football management.

There is a constant linking all these prominent managerial figures and it was mostly notably manifested in the person of Bobby Robson: an unquenchable passion for the game of football. Even in retirement, these giants of the game lived for football, talked about it, thought of little else. Bobby Robson was the epitome of that obsession. In his final days, when Robson accepted that he could no longer hold back the inevitable, when he knew the pernicious tentacles of cancer were squirming inexorably, painfully into the recesses of his failing body, football sustained him. When he no longer had the strength to walk, he was happy to be wheeled onto the pitch at his beloved St James's Park, his once-handsome face pale and crumpled by the ravages of his illness, framed by a Newcastle United scarf. His shock of white hair had gone, his baldness hidden beneath a snappy trilby, yet still he maintained that thin, slightly lop-sided smile, a smile that so endeared him to the public. His well-publicised battle against cancer had taken him beyond the football community into the hearts and minds of non-sporting folk who simply admired a warrior.

It was the joy he took from every aspect of football that had made him a more than decent player, capable of winning 20 England caps, and when those days were long forgotten, into an international coach respected the world over.

It was football that brought him into the light as a 15-year-old, while working underground in his northeast homeland. He would forever thank his lucky stars that a scout from Fulham spotted him and the Cottagers' manager Bill Dodgin did the rest. 'Seven pounds a week, lad,' Robson was told as the contract was placed before him. He signed, knowing off-pitch work as an electrician would bring it up to a decent wage, but no extras. 'I certainly didn't go to pubs,' he says. 'The game has changed so much. Then we didn't have the money to buy flash cars and champagne.' The year was 1950.

He played alongside the legendary Johnny Haynes for six years at Craven Cottage, spent seven years at West Brom after a £25,000 transfer and then went back to Fulham to end his Division One career. In all those years he never won a cup or championship but he was storing up knowledge, urged on by football scholars like Walter Winterbottom and Don Howe. He would use that knowledge to achieve the glories he never managed as a player and to write his name, indelibly, into the sport's hall of fame.

He dipped his toe into management waters in the soccer millpond of North America, with Vancouver Royals, before taking charge of Fulham, the club he had graced as a player, in January 1968. There he quickly learned a harsh lesson in the realities of his chosen profession. Before the year was out the struggling Londoners had sacked him. So much for past loyalties. But he was soon back in work, hired by the wealthy and distinctly upper-crust Cobbold family, who had run Ipswich Town since its foundation in 1878. It was one of the quietest corners of the Football League with a reputation for hiring thinking managers. In 1962, managed by Alf Ramsey, Ipswich Town won the First Division title, thanks in a large part to the goals of a wonderful centre-forward named Ray Crawford. It was a golden era for football when such feats by such unprepossessing clubs were still possible.

When Ramsey left to manage England, Ipswich's fortunes dwindled ... until they entrusted their revival to Bobby Robson. It was something of a struggle to begin with; two seasons followed in which they diced with relegation but Robson kept Ipswich in the top tier as he reshaped the team. He rarely moved into the transfer market, preferring to bring young players through the ranks. Few clubs did it better than Ipswich with a roll call of talent such as Mick Mills, Brain Talbot, George Burley, Trevor Whymark, Roger Osborne, John Wark and the incomparable Kevin Beattie. When he did spend a bit of money, he was equally astute. Paul Mariner was a big signing, and an influential one, as were the Dutch duo Arnold Muhren and Frans Thijssen. His sides played attractive football, winning football. In a 10-year run from 1972, Ipswich were twice runners-up in Division One, finished third three times and fourth twice. Today those positions belong almost exclusively to the 'Big Four' cabal. 'I think,' Robson once said with typical understatement, 'we were playing the sort of football they had not seen here for many, many years.'

He also led Ipswich to their famous FA Cup victory of 1978 and the UEFA Cup in 1980. What a record and all achieved with a quiet dignity and a sincere generosity of spirit. Beyond the 1970s, of course, his prestige was immeasurably enhanced, first with England and then abroad with Sporting Lisbon, Porto, Barcelona and PSV Eindhoven ... but that is a chapter for another volume.

Robson is also remembered for his humour, mostly unwitting but endearingly harmless and innocent. My favourites include such gems as: 'Manchester United dropped points, Liverpool dropped points, Chelsea dropped points, Everton dropped points, so in a way we haven't lost anything at all really, although we dropped all three...'; 'They've probably played better than they've ever done for a few weeks' and 'We didn't underestimate them, they were just a lot better than we thought.' But there are other words that more accurately capture the soul and fortitude of a man who truly deserved the accolade of legend. As he faced up to his fifth tussle with cancer and, ultimately, the battle he would finally lose, Robson said, 'I am going to die sooner rather than later but then everyone has to go sometime and I have enjoyed every minute.'

So who else is worthy of mention from the managerial merry-go-round of the 1970s? Ron Saunders for one. A hard man, taciturn, rarely seen with a smile, desperately uncomfortable in front of the cameras, but a manager who could make ordinary players do great things. He made his reputation at Norwich City, taking them into the top flight for the first time in their history, and to Wembley, for a losing League Cup final appearance. It prompted Manchester City's chairman Peter Swales, a hi-fi tycoon with an even better comb-over than Bobby Charlton's, to take him on. City had been a formidable power in the late 1960s and early 1970s but had slipped somewhat when Saunders arrived at Maine Road. After two largely forgettable seasons, including another losing League Cup final appearance, he switched to Aston Villa for the most fruitful years of his managerial career.

He led Villa out of Division Two, picked up two League Cups and, before the inevitable fall-out with chairman Doug Ellis, guided them to the 1981 Football League Championship. A few months after he quit, the side he built would also collect the European Cup – the sixth successive English champions.

Saunders had gone to Maine Road in 1973 to draw a line under the wretched end to one of the best managerial partnerships in English football. Popular opinion would probably nominate Brian Clough and Peter Taylor as the first successful duo but Joe Mercer and Malcolm Allison actually beat them to the punch. If Clough and Taylor could be compared to Morecambe & Wise, the Mercer-Allison show was up there with Hale & Pace, or maybe Cannon & Ball.

Mercer was the straight man, the experienced man, the old man. Past 50, he was recovering from a stroke when he arrived at Maine Road in 1965, taking over a club looking nervously towards the Third Division. He needed a youthful, passionate foil and chose ex-West Ham coach Malcolm Allison. Allison had been responsible for nurturing a bunch of young starlets at Upton Park, including a lad called Bobby Moore, whom he had first spotted at the tender age of 12.

Ambitious to prove his managerial worth, Allison introduced his innovative thoughts on training and tactics to the journeymen of Bath City and Plymouth Argyle. Joe Mercer liked what he was hearing and persuaded the brash young coach to move north to Maine Road, despite the fact that he carried a fair bit of personal baggage, including a liking for a punt on the horses and a twinkle in his eye that women found irresistible. Unfortunately, one of his conquests was an Argyle director's wife, which resulted in him being obliged to pick up his P45.

Between them, Mercer and Allison fashioned arguably the best team City fans had ever seen, bringing in the likes of Mike Summerbee, Francis Lee and Bury's Colin Bell. Bell was the fulcrum of that City side, 'a world-class player ... the key piece in the jigsaw', according to Allison, who had stolen his signature from under the noses of several Division One managers who used to fill the directors' box at Gigg Lane to watch the talented young midfield star.

Allison asked Bury to name their price. £45,000 was the reply – a lot of money in the mid-1960s. 'I told them they were asking too much for such a young player,' recalled Allison but he did not give up on his quest. 'I carried on going to watch him and would sit in the stands at Bury telling everyone within earshot that he was hopeless in the air and too one-footed, to try to put any other interested clubs off from trying to sign him.' In the end, Allison just had to have him in the team and City coughed up the 45 grand. They got their money's worth, the complete player who became known over the next 13 years, 394 games and 117 goals as the King of the Kippax; a player good enough to make 68 appearances for England. If any young people happen to be reading this and want a modern-day comparison, think Steven Gerrard and you won't be far away.

Between 1966 and 1970 City won promotion, the First Division title, FA Cup, European Cup Winners Cup and the League Cup. But, inevitably, it all ended in tears. Part of the bait old Joe had dangled in front of Allison to bring him to Maine Road had been the promise that the top job would be his within a couple of seasons.

But, a bit like the relationship between Tony Blair and Gordon Brown, Joe found life at the top rather agreeable and was not so keen to let go, especially at his time of life. It sparked a bitter takeover tug-of-war with Mercer in one camp, Allison in the other. Allison won, broken-hearted Mercer was forced out and his apprentice took over his wood-panelled office, only to find the seat was too hot for him to fly solo as he frittered away the treasures he and Mercer had amassed. City would pay the price for the next 30 years.

Mercer had a couple of years left in him, managing Coventry City as well as a seven-match stint in charge of England before he retired to a life sadly eroded by the pernicious onset of Alzheimer's. He died in 1990 at the age of 76.

Allison re-emerged from his brief, disastrous solo gig at Maine Road, as manager of Third Division Crystal Palace, with an even more flamboyant persona, and that image has survived as an icon of the 1970s: the fat cigar, white fedora and long overcoat with a collar big enough to put round Irish racehorse Shergar's neck. The hat, he later explained, had been a gift from a girlfriend of the time, which he brought out as a good-luck charm when Palace embarked on a remarkable FA Cup run to the semi-final. 'We'll win the FA Cup with this hat,' he predicted and Palace duly rolled over Leeds, Chelsea and Sunderland – thanks in no small part to the brilliance of his young winger Peter Taylor. Sadly for Allison and Palace, he was forced to doff his cap to Southampton in the semi-finals. Nor could he lift Palace out of the Third Division and in 1976 he resigned from arguably the most enjoyable job of his managerial career to globe-trot from Turkey to Kuwait to Portugal and a few English stops in between, including a romantic but foolhardy return to Maine Road in 1979, before he retired in 1993. 'I had a lot of fun,' he once told Garth Crooks in interview, 'but I worked hard at it.'

Considering the negatives of his life – too much booze, too many women, losing a lung to TB – it is a near-miracle that Malcolm Allison made it to the age of 83 before he checked out in 2010. He will not be forgotten, that is for sure. A torrent of tributes poured in from the men, and one or two women, who knew him best. This from Steve Daley, one of his expensive Manchester City misfits, says it all: 'Malcolm was a guy who just oozed charisma. He was so buoyant and up for everything ... a fantastic guy.'

And the best of the rest in the 1970s? Lawrie McMenemy by a mile. The ex-Guardsman with the instantly recognisable Tyneside accent had to step into an oversized pair of shoes when he became Southampton manager in 1973, succeeding Ted Bates who had been the boss for 18 years. Before the decade was out McMenemy had taken the Second Division club to unprecedented success, winning the FA Cup, promotion and to the League Cup final. And remember, he would be the man who persuaded big stars like Alan Ball and especially European Footballer of the Year Kevin Keegan to come and play at The Dell. Lawrie Mac stayed with the Saints for 12 seasons ... that's two managers in 30 years. Look at Southampton since: the list of failures is epic.

I ought to mention Harry Catterick because he ushered us into the 1970s as manager of Everton, the decade's first title winners. He was from that same principled line of team bosses that gave us Bertie Mee, Alf Ramsey, Billy Nicholson and Matt Busby. Quietly spoken, but his very appearance, always suited and booted, gave him an authoritarian demeanour that demanded respect. He had been in charge at Goodison since 1961, quickly winning the Division One title followed by the 1966 FA Cup. But the side he assembled and guided to the 1969–70 crown was the best of the lot. They were strong in defence, a line built around the uncompromising Brian Labone at centre-half; in midfield there were three players who complemented each other totally. They were Alan Ball, Howard Kendall and Colin Harvey. And up front they had Joe Royle – quite a team. When they won that title, with that roster of stars, Everton had their chance to establish a dynasty on Merseyside that could have rivalled Liverpool's to come. But it did not happen and there are still those from the blue side of Stanley Park who wonder why. Everton's championship captain Brian Labone, who died in 2006 at the age of 66, was once asked to explain it but simply replied, 'I could not tell you why that team didn't go on to achieve more.'

There are probably others deserving of a line or two, but to be honest, none come readily to mind. These were the managers who achieved great things with style and panache, generally with a smile on their faces, and you cannot ask for much more than that.

CHAPTER TEN

BLACK IS BLACK

The first black footballer I ever saw rejoiced in the splendid name of Lloyd Lindbergh Delapenha. That was the reason I remember him. I was barely into double figures and still wearing short trousers, with braces (thanks, Mum!), when I saw Lindy, as he was universally known, playing for Mansfield Town with a fair degree of success in the late 1950s.

It was the twilight of an illustrious career for the small, round-faced Jamaican with an engaging smile and a lilting Caribbean accent that would serve him well as a broadcaster in retirement. I don't remember it registering at the time that he was black, nor do I recall him scoring any of the 27 goals he got for Mansfield in more than 100 appearances. Then, as now, I was a rare visitor to Field Mill, but I just remember the name.

At a time when Mansfield fielded players with solid Anglo-Saxon names like Bradley (Don), Humble (Wilf) and Watson (Sid), including a Delapenha on the team sheet added an exotic touch, conjuring up images of places that, back in the 1950s, young schoolboys only saw in geography books.

Delapenha was a rarity then, a rarity and a pioneer. He was certainly the first Jamaican to play First Division football in England – in fact, the first from that island to become a professional over here. At Portsmouth he won a championship medal, at Middlesbrough he became a free-scoring winger who might even have played for England had it not been for a certain outside-right at Blackpool named Stanley Matthews.

He struck up a close friendship at Ayresome Park with an up-and-coming centre-forward named Brian Clough, who spoke fondly of Lindy in his autobiography *Walking On Water*, recalling the time they appeared together on the stage of a local theatre ... playing head tennis. Clough also remembered that, as the team's star turn, Lindy was the only player with a car – a rusting model with a door that had a tendency to fall off. How things have changed.

Lindy was still playing into his 40s, back home in Kingston, before retiring to become a commentator, and then he took his place in the Jamaican hall of fame alongside people like Colin Powell, Lennox Lewis and Cleo Laine.

Until the 1970s Delapenha was one of a mere handful of black players who graced the English game. The trickle had begun with Arthur Wharton, born in what was then the Gold Coast of Africa in 1865 to wealthy parents, whose future seemed to be as a missionary until he began to reveal an enviable talent for sport that would see him become the first black professional in English football as well as a record-breaking cyclist and pro-sprinter.

But whatever living sport gave him – he was a goalkeeper with Preston North End, Darlington, Rotherham and Sheffield United among others – his days ended in poverty and an unmarked grave in Doncaster, a shameful snub that was not corrected until 1997. It was thanks to the research of the author Phil Vasili, recognised as *the* authority on black footballers in England, that Wharton's name was brought back into the public domain and he finally received the recognition his place in football history deserves.

Apart from Delapenha, there were only two other notable black players I saw in action in the days before the flood: a tricky, flying winger from South Africa named Albert Johanneson, who spent nine years in the all-white of Leeds United through the 1960s and Mike Trebilcock, who scored two goals in Everton's 1966 3-2 FA Cup final win over Sheffield Wednesday, becoming the first black player to score in an FA Cup final – but he was rarely heard of again and ended his playing days in Australian football.

Johanneson was a sad tale of a player touched with greatness yet never able to fulfill his promise and unable to come to terms with that disappointment. Perhaps, if Don Revie had not discovered a better winger in the shape of Eddie Gray, Johanneson's career, and life, might have turned out for the better. As it was, he was something of a bit player at Elland Road, capable of dragging fans out of their seats with his eccentric skills but never consistent enough to please his manager. Just 167 appearances in nine years tells its own story and, when Johanneson drifted away to York City for his final season, his only solace on a downward spiral into despair came from the bottle. He died, another lonely and pitiful figure, in 1995.

There were others plying their trade around that time despite, it must be emphasised, varying degrees of prejudice, but names like Steve Mokone (Coventry City), Elkaneh Onyeali (Tranmere Rovers), John Mensah and Francis Fayemi (Cambridge City) certainly passed me by and are little more than marginal notes in the story of black footballers in England.

But with the dawn of the 1970s the narrative began to change. The integration of black people into British culture and life, kick-started by the Windrush generation who arrived from the West Indies just after World War Two, was about to manifest itself in the national game. And the suspicion among the less enlightened football folk, that black players were best equipped to be nippy wingers but lacked the substance for more centrally responsible roles, was about to be demolished.

So where do we start? Probably with a powerhouse centre-forward from Bermuda named Clyde Best, who looked more suited to a heavyweight contest with Sonny Liston than a first-team place at the football academy that was West Ham United, yet who would prove to be an inspiration for many a black player who had previously questioned their ability – perhaps even their right – to become a professional footballer.

Discovered by Ron Greenwood at the age of 17, Best had already played football at international level for his native Bermuda. Greenwood said of his new protégé, 'At 17 he was the best player of that age I had ever seen. He has the ability to make as big an impact as Pele or Eusebio.'

Well, due to an inconsistency that mirrored the Johanneson story, Best did not quite scale such lofty heights but he handled it much better and in the eyes of young black footballers, he was the man. He had a presence on a football field, which had something to do with his colour but as much for the way he married a magnificent physique with exciting skills. And with admirable dignity he showed them how to conquer all the mountains they would have to climb to succeed in the English game.

Best arrived at a deserted Upton Park on a Sunday afternoon

in 1968, a stranger in a strange land. 'It was not easy to settle down, in a strange country, 3,500 miles from home. The climate, the pitches and even the houses were all different,' he told journalist John Morris in a 1972 interview. 'So was the way in which the game is played here. It is quicker, harder and, of course, the marking is a great deal closer.'

The first game in England for the man from the island of sunshine was for West Ham Reserves in the bleak mid-winter on a snow-covered pitch in front of 5,000 fans, gathered to see Moore and Hurst on their return from injuries. Those faithful supporters had their heads turned by an altogether more imposing figure.

'Clyde had never seen snow before,' recalled Greenwood, 'and there were plenty of icy patches too. Yet, despite the conditions, you could see that the lad had something. I know I was excited.'

Best was fast-tracked into the first team and over the next seven seasons would plunder more than 50 goals and be on the way to legendary status, especially for aspiring young black players. Ex-England full-back Chris Powell is one who cites the Best influence for his place in the game.

It almost goes without saying that along the way Best had to endure the kind of racist abuse that was a fact of life at the time. Greenwood said that Best's disarming attitude was a perfect template for any non-white footballer, or any sportsman of colour, to adopt. 'He smacks any barrackers in the face with an act of courtesy that comes naturally to him – going to get the ball, helping an opponent or something like that.'

In response to the monkey chants and hurled bananas Best said, 'You just had to get on with it. I just ignored it and concentrated on playing the game for West Ham. Sure, the supporters pay their money and are entitled to their opinions but sometimes people cross the line. You will always come up against nutters in your life but you can't let these people see they are getting under your skin. All you can do is just get on with your job – in my case, scoring goals – and do all your talking on the pitch.' When he sees players like Didier Drogba react in an altogether more truculent and thoughtless manner, it angers and disappointments him. After Drogba's suspension in 2009 for retaliation – he threw a coin, originally aimed in his direction, back into a crowd of Burnley fans – Best commented, 'I thought Drogba was wrong to do that.

'I can understand the player's frustration and it is wrong a coin was thrown at him from the stands. But you have to try and stay calm and thoughtful, no matter how difficult it gets.'

Nearly 40 years down the line it is hard to find footage of Best doing his job but deep in the archives of ITV's *The Big Match*, highlights exist that provide a fascinating glimpse of his laidback style. I will mention one match because it throws up a number of ancillary but nonetheless fascinating vignettes: Spurs v. West Ham 1971. On the Spurs side, former West Ham legend Martin Peters; in the West Ham line-up former Spurs legend Jimmy Greaves.

There were other familiar names like Martin Chivers. I had forgotten he could effortlessly hurl a throw-in onto the penalty spot from a standing start; and Bobby Moore, imperious as ever, despite his recent disappointment of World Cup defeat in Mexico, the turmoil of that infamous jewellery incident and then a bizarre kidnapping threat against his wife. For me, however, that game is worthy of note in my review of the 1970s for two related incidents. Frank Lampard Senior, forever a swashbuckling full-back with a tendency for recklessness in the tackle, went through the back of Spurs' Scottish striker Alan

Gilzean. Gilzean limped away briefly, a pained expression the only giveaway of any annoyance, while referee Bob Matthewson had the briefest of words with Lampard. Minutes later Gilzean sideswipes Lampard in mid-clearance. No histrionics, no rolling around in feigned mortal injury, no chin-to-chin confrontation. Honours even. Isn't that how it should be?

But that was then. Football has changed beyond all recognition, in some small part for the better, with pioneers like Best responsible. 'When I look at the game now, it has changed so much it is mind-boggling,' he says. 'You couldn't imagine football now without black players, or any of the other nationalities who now ply their trade in England.'

His playing days done, Best went back home to Bermuda, where he has since been inducted into the Bermudan Hall of Fame and deservedly awarded an MBE. The official accolade notes his services to football and the community of Bermuda; unofficially, it rewards his tolerance in the face of provocation and the example he laid down for others to follow.

The profile of black players in England, defined by the emergence of Clyde Best as a role model and fans' favourite, was then enhanced even further at The Hawthorns, home of West Bromwich Albion and the first team to go multi-racial. When Ron Atkinson left Cambridge United in 1978 to take over as Albion manager he inherited the services of Cyrille Regis, born in French Guiana, and Laurie Cunningham, London-born son of a Jamaican jockey. Atkinson added his Cambridge defender Brendan Batson, born in Grenada, and subsequently included the trio on the same team sheet, at the same time giving them the amusing soubriquet The Three Degrees ... 'to our lasting embarrassment,' says Batson, incidentally the first black player to appear in Arsenal's senior team as a youngster in 1971.

'Players like Justin Fashanu, Luther Blissett and Garth Crooks were coming through at that time but what happened at West Brom was radical. Three black guys in one side was incredible,' Regis said, years later.

If individual black players had been targeted by the pondlife that swam in every club's fan pool, to have a trio among the opposition simply cranked up the abuse. 'The racism was quite abhorrent,' said Regis, an explosive centre-forward who arguably had the most successful playing career of the three with five full England caps, 200 career goals and an FA Cup winners medal.

How bad? This other quote from Regis tells it like it was: 'Back then you had thousands of people screaming "nigger, nigger, lick my boots" at you and the authorities just said "disgraceful" and did nothing.'

It would be through the efforts of people like Regis and particularly Batson, long-serving chairman of the Professional Footballers Association and a prime mover of the anti-racism campaign in the 1990s, that the pernicious evil on the terraces would eventually be confronted and socially outlawed.

Sadly, Cunningham, the most gifted of the three, could not be part of the drive to bring equality to football. Like a Roman candle, his career flared spectacularly before burning out. Cunningham is down in the record books as the first black player to be capped by England at any level – a goal-scoring debut for the Under-21s. Its significance probably registered more with headline writers and statisticians than the player himself. Batson once said that black players were never interested in being the first to do this, the first to do that – they just wanted to be footballers per se.

Cunningham was both a provider and a goal scorer; a player of great pace and wonderful control who could cross on the run and could be relied upon to keep his head in front of goal. He was also a brave player, denying the erroneous view held by many who should have known better that black players in some way lacked the courage needed at the top level. Atkinson said of him, 'We didn't put any restrictions on Laurie – I just told him to get the ball at his feet and go and do damage with it.'

Collectively and individually, the threesome were never better than in a game against Manchester United at Old Trafford in 1979, which West Brom won 5-3. It should not be forgotten that Atkinson had built an exciting side by then with his three black players an integral part of the whole, which also included Bryan Robson, Tony Brown, John Wile and Len Cantello.

But on this day it was Regis and Cunningham, booed by the moronic among United's following every time he touched the ball, who destroyed United; a day that would, in retrospect, change Cunningham's short life. Most of the goals were magnificent. Albion's first equaliser came when Cunningham rode two flying tackles before threading the ball through the proverbial eye of a needle to Regis, who instantly back-heeled it into the path of Cantello, who then lashed it into the net. It was the sort of passing move we have come to expect of today's Arsenal team.

Cunningham got one of the five, his pace too much for Stewart Houston's scything attempt to bring him down, his composure too certain for Gary Bailey in the United goal. Regis got the best of five, his on-the-run finish sending commentator Gerald Sinstadt into a tenor exultation.

That performance probably clinched it for the watching scouts from Real Madrid. Not long after, they slapped a near £1 million cheque into Albion's bank account and Cunningham was on his way to the Bernabéu. In his first season Cunningham was a star turn for the Spanish giants, who won La Liga and the Copa Del Rey. But that was as good as it got for the shy young Londoner as one setback followed another.

It was a great disappointment to him that he could not force his way into Ron Greenwood's England team, a victim of the view that wingers were a luxury at international level. It was another disappointment that, after scoring for Real Madrid in the first leg of the European Cup semi-final against Hamburg, Real lost the second leg 5-1 and Cunningham's hopes of a European medal were dashed.

Two seasons later he was on the losing side in the final against Liverpool and by then injuries were starting to take their toll and eventually he was moved on, hawking his talents around some of Europe's lesser lights for a couple of seasons before returning to Spain, where he signed for Second Division side Real Vallecano. Cunningham's story ended in tragedy, in the early hours of 15 July 1989, when he was killed in a car crash in Madrid. Married to a Spanish woman and with a young child, Cunningham was only 33 when he died. He is remembered at the clubs where he starred, particularly Leyton Orient and West Brom, as the most gifted footballer to wear their colours. Surely the epitaph any player would crave.

The aforementioned Justin Fashanu would go on to write his own little piece of history when Brian Clough made him the first black player to be transferred for £1 million, in 1981, from Norwich to Forest, largely on the back of a single, quite stupendous goal he scored for the Canaries against Liverpool; Luther Blissett's rise to the top began in the mid-1970s and by the early 1980s he had scored goals in all four divisions as Graham Taylor's Watford stormed their way to the top tier; and

Garth Crooks established his CV at hometown club Stoke City, scoring nearly 50 goals for the Potters before Spurs paid big money to team him with Steve Archibald in 1980.

Because they were very much a minority group, these were the players who had to brave the torrent of abuse with quiet sufferance and dignity so that others would not be dissuaded from following their lead. They set an example that should have shamed their detractors had they possessed the mental capacity to understand who the winners were and who the losers were in their pathetic ritual.

There is one more black player from the 1970s to talk about and I have left him until last simply because he was one of my Forest heroes – a local boy who became the first black footballer to be capped at full international level by England. He was Viv Anderson and he said, 'It was a really big thing at the time, to be the first black player to pull on an England shirt in a full international – I can see why people made a bit of a fuss.'

That was in a friendly at Wembley in November 1978 – a 1-0 win over Czechoslovakia. Anderson's selection had given the red tops something to write about and gave rise to Ron Greenwood's now-famous quote, 'Yellow, purple or black – if they're good enough, I'll pick them.'

Anderson had made his first team debut for Forest only four years previously while his team were floundering in the lower reaches of the old Second Division. Talented though he was, it is probably fair to say Anderson would not have claimed his particular place in the history books had it not been for Brian Clough. And equally, Nottingham Forest would not have been able to bathe in the reflected glory of Anderson's selection. Without Clough transforming that wretched side of the early 1970s into something rather special, Anderson would either have settled for one-club mediocrity or, more likely given his natural talents, moved on much earlier in his career.

But he was one of the sitting tenants of the City Ground when Clough arrived and he survived the inevitable clearout once Clough 'turfed out the crap'. Anderson, tall and slim with elongated legs that earned him the nickname 'Spider', quickly developed into a modern full-back, good at defending but always prepared to rampage forward.

Anderson came out of the Clifton estate in Nottingham, a sprawling council development, which once had the dubious claim to fame of being the largest in Europe. But despite its size, Clifton was always regarded as a close-knit community without any overt signs of racial tension. It certainly did not dawn on Anderson in his formative years that bigotry was something he would have to contend with further down the line.

'There may not have been many black people around then,' he told his local newspaper, 'but those I played football with I saw as being my mates and that's how it was. I didn't see colour as an issue.'

But once he got out into the big wide world, his perception of people's attitudes quickly changed. In fact, not long after his debut at the age of 17 – 'I can remember a Milk Cup tie away at Newcastle. The crowd were very hostile when I went out to have a look at the pitch. I was getting a lot of abuse, all sorts. You have to remember that in those days Newcastle was a place where you didn't see a lot of black people. Because of the abuse I didn't go out for the warm-up.'

Clough soon put him right. Anderson had to learn how to take it, how to cope with it, if he wanted to progress. It was the only way he could win, not just for himself but for every other black player.

Anderson heeded the lesson but, years later and with

characteristic modesty, he commented, 'It was a lot easier for me than, say, Laurie Cunningham or Cyrille Regis. They were flamboyant forwards so they were identified much more. Cyrille got a bullet through the post with the message, "This one's for you if you play for England". I never got anything like that because I was just a defender who used to boot people.'

Of course, he was better than that but he had to come through an uncertain start at Forest, which was as much to do with his own doubts in his ability as anything else. Brian Clough's number two Peter Taylor later claimed some of the credit for Anderson's development, revealing the psychology that had helped Anderson fulfil his potential.

'His big problem when I first came to the club was that he was not walking tall. Having natural ability is only one part of the game, I had to get him to believe in himself. I smashed him verbally but Viv's not the sort of lad who will have a go back at you – he's one of the quietest lads you could meet. But he got the message pretty quickly. I told Viv that I had got another right-back lined up.'

With Clough in one ear and Taylor in the other, Anderson's career blossomed and he became first choice right-back in the Forest team that won the First Division title at the first attempt after promotion, carried off a couple of European Cups, League Cups and all sorts of minor silverware. And he was a key member of a defence that helped Forest establish a record-breaking run of 42 league games without defeat. He also showed a liking for a punt at goal, one of his most memorable coming just a couple of weeks before his England call-up when he let fly from 20 yards or more and then shared in the amazement and delight of his fans as the ball flew past Everton goalkeeper George Wood in an arc from out to in off the post.

It said everything England boss Ron Greenwood needed to know and the historic decision to hand the number-two shirt to Anderson for a friendly against Czechoslovakia at an icy-cold Wembley on 29 November 1978 dominated headlines in the build-up to the game.

Anderson, who was only 22 years of age remember, took it in his stride, refusing to invest in all the hype surrounding his selection, which included good-luck messages from HM The Queen and Elton John. It was an attitude indicative of his upbringing. His mum Myrtle, a nurse at a Nottingham hospital who had to work her shift on the day of the match, said, 'Viv has rung me up from London and he's enjoying being with the England side but he's not the sort who will get carried away with what is happening to him.'

Quite the opposite, in fact. On the eve of his senior international debut Anderson found time to acknowledge the debt he owed to Clough and Taylor. 'The boss and Peter Taylor just tell me to go out and enjoy myself. They say to me that I would not be in the side if I didn't have the ability so there is no point in not showing it.'

As Anderson walked out of the Wembley tunnel and into his own special immortality, there was no ugly chanting or abuse from the 92,000 crowd, only warm applause when his name was announced. 'It was a very positive reaction from the terraces,' said Anderson. 'To them, it was all about the football.'

For the record, it was not much of a match – typical England friendly, to be honest. Anderson, watched by his dad Audley and brother Donald, did OK and had a part to play in the only goal of the game, scored by Steve Coppell. Greenwood, trying to keep a lid on things, commented, 'Viv can be pleased with his first performance for England.'

In the greater scheme of things, the match and the result were less than important when compared with the significance it held for a generation of young black people. Ex-Arsenal and England centre-forward Ian Wright was in no doubt about what it meant, writing in 1997, 'Winning that first cap may have been a small step for him in his career but it was a huge leap forward for black footballers in this country.'

And the contribution he had made did eventually register with Anderson. 'At the time all I thought about was doing my job and trying to impress the manager enough to get selected again,' he recalls. 'It is only looking back that I realise the importance of it all and the responsibility I was carrying.'

Because he was in direct competition with the ever-reliable Phil Neal for the England spot, Anderson would collect only 29 more caps over a 10-year period. It seems scant reward for a player of such outstanding ability and consistency, rarely missing a match for any of his clubs: Forest, Arsenal, Manchester United, Sheffield Wednesday. But Anderson has no regrets, no bitterness, no sense that he deserved more.

'I played in an age where it wasn't the norm for a black man to represent his country, so to do it not just once but 30 times is more than I could've ever asked for,' he said.

His place in history is assured. He can be found on the website dedicated to the 100 Great Black Britons, along with other players including Brendan Batson, Paul Ince and Ian Wright. Anderson has taken his rightful place in the National Football Museum's Hall of Fame. In 2000 he collected an MBE and 96 per cent of Nottingham Forest fans believe he is the best full-back the club has ever had.

He has also stood up for his colour whenever, and wherever, he has been asked and worked passionately to break down old prejudices, which still exist in sport. Anderson was one of the first voices to support renewed sporting ties with South Africa. As far back as 1980 he realised there would be no end to apartheid by isolating it from the rest of the world. 'I have no doubts at all that we should play sport against South Africa at every opportunity. We must break down the remaining barriers and this is the way to do it.'

He became a patron of the Kick Racism Out Of Football campaign, which began in 1993 and has been a forceful voice when moved by events. After the controversy surrounding Ron Atkinson's 'off-air' derogatory comments about black French player Marcel Desailly, Anderson revealed, 'I played for Ron for three years and I can never remember him saying anything racist. But I spoke to him the day after the incident and said, "You can't get away with that sort of thing. If you say things like that, you should lose your job."'

In 2010, Mario Ballotelli followed in Anderson's pioneering boots by becoming the first black player to be capped by Italy … and in a friendly international against Romania he was subjected to a barrage of racial abuse by the Italian fans, who even raised a banner which read: 'No to a multi racial Italian team'.

Anderson reacted angrily, telling reporters: 'The late, great Brian Clough once advised me to ignore the racists and not let them get to me. If they did, he said, I'd end up working in Sainsbury's. Balotelli is only a young man and he is out to make a name for himself. Maybe he would make a name for himself by walking off the pitch when his own fans abuse him. But I personally wouldn't do that. I'd try to let my football do the talking. But that means that FIFA should now step in and punish the Italian FA. Not with the kind of pathetic fines Uefa have given to European clubs after racist incidents. Fines should be more stringent. If they fine them a million pounds they would take notice. Then they would try to winkle out the culprits and ban them from their grounds.'

Despite the influence and example of black pioneers like Batson and Best, Regis and Anderson, the cancer of racism still infests the world of football. But at last, the world governing body seems to be waking up to the menace. In May 2013, FIFA president Sepp Blatter announced: 'There have been despicable events this year that have cast a long shadow over football and the rest of society. I am speaking of the politics of hate – racism, ignorance, discrimination, intolerance, small-minded prejudice, that uncivilised, immoral and self-destructive force that we all detest.'

The hope is that FIFA is as good as the word of its boss.

CHAPTER ELEVEN
THE MAN IN THE MIDDLE

G eorge Flint was a miner – the son of a miner – and, for all I know, his grandfather was a miner too. That was the way it was back in the days when coal was king; generation followed generation down the pit.

It bred a particular kind of person: hard, blunt, brave, caring; armed with a great sense of humour. That was how they survived. Flint was born, lived and died in a typical mining town, like a thousand mining towns across the coalfields of England, where back-to-back terraced houses, with outside lavs and a tin bath on the wall, were once the norm. The air was thick with the soot of the railway sidings, the sound of the pithead whistle and a hundred pairs of hobnail boots clattering across the cobblestones leading to and from the colliery gates.

When he wasn't working at the pit, likely as not George was enjoying a pint at the Welfare. And like all pitmen he had a hobby that would take him away from the grime and danger of the colliery and into the open air. For George, it was not pigeons or whippets, darts and dominoes: it was always football. And he had skill – real skill that carried him to the very top of his chosen game. George Flint was not a player, however. During the 1970s he was one of the best referees on the Football League list. He got the top fixtures, home and abroad, and, because of his working-class roots, he was as popular with the players as any referee you could find.

George spoke their language, more often than not littered with the sort of words grafters shared in their place of work. He was the sort of man who called a spade a bloody great shovel. If a player swore at him, he swore back. He saw football as a man's game and treated the players accordingly. A person of strong principle so typical of a mining background, he believed in fair play and common sense and, before his time, it cost him his career.

For George was never cut out to be a schmoozer; he did not do the social things expected of referees. He was nobody's yes man. If he had tried any of that, his mates would have kicked his legs from under him, back home in the Welfare on a Friday night. So the day authority pushed too hard, George did not push back, he was too proud for that – he just walked away. Turned his back on the big games, the huge crowds, the foreign trips. George Flint walked his own line, marched to his own tune and in so doing, the sport lost one of its finest officials.

The 1970s was undeniably a better era for referees. There was not so much money swilling about in the game and there were still people who went about their work with a smile on their faces. George Flint was certainly one of them. There was not quite the same pressure on referees: not so much was at stake, so not every decision was analysed and dissected like crows picking at road kill.

THE MAN IN THE MIDDLE

I knew George quite well. I would be covering Mansfield Town and there he would be at Field Mill on a night off, watching, enjoying; relaxing. And in a corner of the directors' bar he would spin a few yarns over a pint or two. In his broad East Midlands accent he could make the banal sound funny.

George Flint's name is legendary in Nottinghamshire local football circles. Like the tales of Cloughie, everyone has a favourite George Flint story. I'm going to share one or two with you and let you make your own minds up. I'll let you decide if the game would not be better if there were a few referees around today like George Flint; if a few of them adopted his attitude to the game and did not buy into bullshit. You see them strutting about, martinets in a black uniform, desperate to be stars, to claim centre stage, wanting to be seen when they should be anonymous.

I sometimes wonder how George would have reacted to the mouthy players like Craig Bellamy or Wayne Rooney; what would he have done, had he been on the end of a four-letter fusillade? From what I remember of George, he would have told them to 'fucking grow up and get a couple of shifts at the coalface under your belt, then you would have something to swear about!'.

But referees cannot do that these days; cannot answer back to the multi-millionaires who grace our game. 'Don't you know who I am, ref?' 'No,' George would have said, 'but if you ask the nurse, she'll be able to tell you.'

George Flint refereed at the highest level, all over the world. He followed the unwritten 18th rule of football: use your common sense. He loved a bit of banter with the players, like the time he gave Nobby Stiles a veiled warning after a series of crunching tackles. 'Do you think you can win the game with 10 men, Nobby?' To which the great England player replied, 'With you reffing we couldn't win with the reserves and colts playing for us!' They both laughed. No need to reach for the card or sharpen the pencil.

Then there was the day when George scored the winning goal in a Yorkshire derby. It could only happen to George: the final minute, Hull City v. Huddersfield Town, the score 0-0. Hull get a corner and George takes up the approved referee's position, just inside the penalty area, near post. The corner comes in hard and low but Town's keeper has it covered ... until the ball smacks referee Flint's not inconsiderable backside, wrongfoots the keeper and goes into the net. According to the laws of football, the referee is part of the play and so George points to the centre for a goal, Huddersfield's players go crazy and a few moments later, he blows the whistle for time. 'You can't allow that, surely,' the keeper protests. 'We can't have lost this game.' To which one of George's helpful linesmen suggests, 'Watch the bloody results in a bit, mate, and you will see you have!'

Or the story about the England striker who was winding George up throughout an important Division One game until, finally, he won a penalty. But this was where George got his own back by delaying the kick for as long as he could. Eventually, the grumbling star took the penalty, blazed it over the bar and fell to the ground, shouting, 'I could kick myself.' George leaned over him and said, 'Better let me do it, pal, tha'll probably miss.'

But it was that easy-going attitude that made enemies among the more strait-laced officials who ran the sport. George called time on his illustrious career as a Football League referee in 1982, on the day he was carpeted for finishing a match between Rochdale and Crewe five minutes early. He knew he had made a mistake and accepted his temporary suspension but promptly resigned when the FA called him in and tried to impose a 'second punishment'.

Often he had been at odds with the hierarchy. George remembered the day he refereed a game at Kettering when a dog ran onto the field. Players chased the mischievous mutt and a policeman lost his helmet in a vain attempt to catch the animal. Suddenly, the dog came to a halt in front of George, who was holding the ball, and sat up and begged. George, capturing the spirit of the moment, wagged his finger in admonishment, then showed the dog the red card and ordered him off. The spectators thought it was hilarious ... especially when the dog cocked his back leg against George's stockings before trotting off. But then came the assessor's report: 'Was it necessary to lower the dignity of yourself and football in general by showing the dog the red card?'

Although he enjoyed the lighter side of football, George was always prepared to offer a measured opinion on the game. He was convinced that the way to improve relations between players and officials was to let them mix – he remembered receiving FA memos denying match officials the privilege of drinking in the players' lounge after a game. But George usually ignored such edicts, taking the view that 'football is a man's game and, as such, we should do away once and for all with the "them and us" situation'.

But George was not a one-man band. When compiling a list of referees from the 1970s I was amazed at how many names came instantly to mind: Jack Taylor, George Courtney, Pat Partridge, Gordon Kew, Neil Midgeley, Joe Worrall, Roger Kirkpatrick, Don Shaw, Keith Hackett, Ken Burns, Ray Lewin, Clive Thomas. All good referees – can you come up with a list from today's batch to match them?

Of them all, Clive Thomas, a stickler for the laws of the game and as decisive a referee as ever blew a whistle, had perhaps the highest profile and more than 30 years later he is still remembered for two of the most controversial decisions since a Russian linesman named Tofik Bakhramov decided Geoff Hurst's shot had crossed the line for England's third goal against West Germany in the 1966 World Cup final.

The first came in the 1977 FA Cup semi-final between Liverpool and Everton, and the outcome still grieves the blue half of Merseyside. Passions always run high on Merseyside; what is good for the Reds is a dagger in the heart for the Blues, and vice versa. But in 1977 the great divide carried added pain for Evertonians, simply because Liverpool were kings of the castle, winning championships and cups at will. Since winning the title in 1970, Everton had achieved sod all. They had tired of hearing Bill Shankly take the piss and, when he retired in 1964, they had to suffer Bob Paisley's even greater success. The 1977 FA Cup offered some salvation. If only they could beat that lot from Anfield, they could assuage seven years of suffering and take the bragging rights from one side of Stanley Park to the other.

The venue was Maine Road, Manchester; the date 23 April 1977, and it proved to be a classic encounter. Twice Liverpool led, through Terry McDermott and Jimmy Case, and twice Everton came back, with goals from Duncan McKenzie and Bruce Rioch. As the minutes ticked away, Maine Road became a cauldron of noise. Everton pushed for a winner. Ronnie Goodlass was the architect of what, to this day, every Everton supporter believes was a legitimate goal – his cross was flicked on by McKenzie for Bryan Hamilton to bundle in at the far post. GOAL! NO! As Everton whirled away in delight and Liverpool dejectedly accepted their fate, attention turned to the referee, Clive Thomas, who was in no doubt that an infringement had occurred.

This was how Thomas saw the incident: 'Duncan McKenzie crossed the ball but Bryan had moved on and by the time he got the ball, he was a yard offside. My linesman, Colin Seel, was satisfied it was a goal and so, too, were the Everton fans. I saw Gordon Lee [Everton manager] jump up on the touchline and I swear Bryan had tears in his eyes as he pleaded with me that it had to be a goal. But in my opinion, he was definitively offside and, even if he wasn't, I would have ruled it because there is no way he could have controlled the ball without using his hand.'

Although Jimmy Hill, at that time regarded as the voice of football, came out in support of Thomas after studying the video evidence, you will not find many people who agree with the decision made by the man from Treorchy in the Rhondda Valley. Certainly not ex-Everton player Ronnie Goodlass, who was central to the moment: 'There was no way it was offside – I put the cross in and could see that clearly. As for handball, well, Bryan's arms were up as the ball came in and it hit him on the hip. These days, when you have replays from every angle, those arguments would have been cleared up straightaway. But it says a lot about that decision that there's not really a lot of debate about it. We were hard done by and everyone knows it.' It's a measure of where the FA Cup stood in the hearts and minds of players, adminstrators and supporters back in the 1970s. Everton's manager Gordon Lee said, 'I still feel so hurt about it and for the Everton supporters really. I was at Wembley and I think Bob Paisley, God rest his soul, also thought we were at Wembley – we had won the game. But these things happen.'

Before we continue with the adventures of Mr Thomas, this is a good place to mention another controversial incident involving Everton and the laws of the game. We have to go back to 1970 and a game at Highfield Road, Coventry. City are awarded a free kick about 20 yards out and, in what was clearly a move straight off the training ground, ginger-haired midfielder Willie Carr stood with the ball between his feet. On the whistle he flicked it up and behind him for Ernie Hunt to volley it into the far corner of Everton's net.

It was a stunner, a moment of sheer football genius. BBC commentator Barry Davies loved it. 'Well, they don't come much better than that!' he exclaimed. 'Right out of the book and on the first line too!' No one had ever seen anything like it before and it is a certain fact that no one has seen anything like it since ... because FIFA immediately outlawed it. To hell with the fact that it was a sublime piece of skill and wonderful entertainment for the paying customers ... it was declared illegal because the two-footed flick was deemed to be a double touch – and the kicker may only touch the ball once. Glad they got that one sorted out.

And so to the World Cup of 1978 in Argentina and Clive Thomas's other well-documented moment of controversy. It came at the end of a Group Three qualifier between Sweden and a distinctly below-par Brazil, whose progress in the tournament was in doubt after a draw with Spain. Victory over Sweden would virtually guarantee a place in the next phase, anything less and they would be relying on results elsewhere.

Thomas Sjoberg gave Sweden a shock lead before Reinaldo equalised, interestingly 50 seconds into first-half injury time. Brazil then missed a hatful of chances but, with only seconds of the second half remaining, they launched one final attack, forcing a corner on the right. Clive Thomas could clearly be seen looking closely at his watch, yet Nelinho seemed in no hurry to take the kick, replacing the ball in the quadrant before delivery. His tardiness would instantly prove crucial. As the ball was floated into the six-yard box Zico got in a scoring header ... just as Clive Thomas blew the whistle for time and pointed to the centre circle.

Sweden celebrated while Brazilian players chased the striding Thomas in protest. Bearing a fleeting resemblance to Mr Bean, Thomas waved his arms dismissively, pointed again to the watch on his outstretched wrist and clearly had no intention of changing his mind. In the end, it proved academic. Brazil beat Austria in the final group match to go through, Sweden finished bottom with just that one point to their credit.

Brian Saunders, a Football League linesman through the 1970s, ran the touchline for most of the top referees of the day, giving him a unique view of their different styles. Thomas, he remembers, was a stickler for the rules and certainly not a referee to be challenged or disrespected.

> I admired Clive Thomas' style for that. Before the game he would tell the managers, 'If any of your players want to start arguing, I will book him and, if he continues, I will send him off.'
>
> In my view, the difference between then and now: the referees had a rapport with the players, Neil Midgely would crack jokes, Gordon Hill could swear better than any player. If Wayne Rooney had gone on one of his four-letter rants like he did against Andy D'Urso, the old-style refs would have just stood the ground, not backed down an inch and, likely as not, shown him a card.

George Courtney would stand there, keep blowing his whistle and just say, 'Six or eight ... here.' He was a headmaster, you know.

I will give you a couple of for-instances ... and you try to imagine this happening today.

I was running the line for Pat Partridge, Barnsley v. Huddersfield, and Dave Cowling, one of the Huddersfield players, said something to me, a bit nasty. He went to take a right-wing corner – I was running the left wing. Pat Partridge made him come right across the pitch to apologise to me. Same thing happened when I was linesman for George Courtney. Someone said something and Courtney told him he would not blow for play to restart until he had apologised.

And Cloughie. He was a ref's man, was Cloughie. I was reffing a behind-closed-doors game when Dave Serella [the Forest defender] made some throwaway remark. Clough told him to shake hands with me and apologise.

Like everyone who ever met the great man, I have my favourite Clough story. Forest were playing Tampa Bay Rowdies, seventh minute, and Larry Lloyd refused to go back ten yards for a free kick ... so Clough substituted him, telling the ref, 'If he won't go back for you, he'll get back for me.'

Diminutive Joe Worrall – 'so fast he could catch pigeons' according to Saunders – was another big fan of Clough and his teams. 'I always liked refereeing Forest. If we had 92 managers like Brian Clough, there would be no problems on the field. He had some hard men in his team – Kenny Burns, Larry Lloyd – but they always showed you respect.' Worrall, who lives in Warrington and is part of the referees' set-up as an assessor these days, agrees with Saunders that man management is the key difference between the referees of his era and today. 'It was easier to work with the players back then ... today Howard Webb is one of the the best, always buzzing round the players and there is no doubt, it helps.'

No one will argue that without referees there would be no football, yet they are, without doubt, the most vilified branch of the sport, particularly in the modern era where every split-second heat-of-the-moment decision they take can be analysed in super slo-mo, just to prove they have dropped a clanger and thoroughly deserve all the opprobrium heaped on them from the terraces ... and by the so-called experts who pontificate from their studio armchairs.

Perhaps that is why there are so few referees you would describe as characters, referees who take a little humour and personality on to the pitch with them. That breed of official, victims of a more rigid authoritarian approach, died out in the 1970s. It goes back to what old George Flint used to preach about common sense. Today, referees are not given such leeway. If a certain foul is regarded as a yellow-card offence, a yellow card it is without consideration of the circumstances; if a goal scorer celebrates in a manner perceived to be ungentlemanly or provocative, it is a yellow card; if a player requires on-field treatment, he is then ordered by the referee to go beyond the touchline ... and then waved back on. Give me a break!

Referees are not automatons. They go through the same emotions before a big game as the players do; a heady mixture of excitement and apprehension that can sometimes blur the judgement. I can remember watching Gordon Hill at the start of a match at Anfield. As the noise built to a crescendo he checked his watch, blew his whistle and then gave a little clenched-fist gesture like a golfer sinking a 10ft putt. It was a simple expression of his feeling of being part of something special and there is nothing wrong with that.

The late Wilf Mannion, great Middlesbrough and England forward of the 1940s and early 1950s, once wrote an appreciation of referees that is as relevant today as it was 60 years ago.

> [The] most abused and maligned official in a football match is the referee and frequently the abuse is entirely unwarranted, being hurled at him by spectators who, to say the least of it, often have but only a rudimentary knowledge of the rules for all their enthusiasm.
>
> But that official can surely mar a game by playing too closely to the rules without allowing for 'advantage' to the player he thinks has been wrongly dealt with. But the position is of exceptional difficulty, let that be clearly understood.
>
> Too much whistle can ruin the best game; too little can just as surely spoil it too. Where is the happy medium? It is hard for me to say, since, as a player, I am almost bound to be biased in my judgment. Referees can be too strict ... and they often are far too lenient. Some come to the dressing rooms before the game and make it clear that they will severely punish offenders or anyone who imagines that they can dispute each and every decision. Others merely come along and upset the

players by dictatorial methods before the game commences at all.

Referees ought to be chosen as much for their ability to control men as anything else; and they must be able to treat players as men and not as disobedient children at school. Showmanship in refereeing is all well and good as long as it does not mean making a player feel small in front of a large crowd of spectators.

A good referee need not halt play for any offence while he administers a classroom lecture to an offending player with much wagging of the fingers and repeated pointing to the dressing room. He should have such faith in himself that all that is required is a word in the player's ear which cannot be misunderstood. 'Next time, my lad, you will be sent off'; that is sufficient so long as he actually does order a player off next time that offence is committed.

That sort of referee soon becomes known and players treat him with respect. The type who continually threatens and never does anything is equally soon known to all and, regretfully, treated accordingly. I do not advocate the sending off of players for offences committed in the heat of the moment. We are all but human and can do things which we instantly regret. The average player is not often guilty of this sort of thing. The regular offenders are the players who want dealing with and referees know them as well as their fellow players do.

What a pity there were no video recorders around to allow us a glimpse of the development of football in its early years when there were no referees. Can you imagine the mayhem? It was not until the formation of the Football Association in 1863 that the game had a coherent set of rules and with them came the first referees, or umpires as they were known, but they could only make a decision when asked by the players. The mind boggles, doesn't it?

I know many of the players in those early days were from public schools or the Army and were considered gentlemanly enough to call their own fouls but I doubt they had any better grasp of the complexities of football law than today's largely uneducated proponents, and to expect them to police themselves was clearly asking for trouble. So, gradually, the concept of a neutral official who would control matches using his own interpretation of the rules was developed and by the late 1800s the man with the whistle became central to the game of football.

According to the history of the Acme Thunderer, the most famous sporting whistle, which is still in worldwide use today, 125 years after it was invented, the first use of a whistle by a referee was in 1878 in a game between Nottingham Forest and Sheffield Norfolk. Prior to this, umpires had waved handkerchiefs to hold up play.

In 1891 the Football Association decided that the referee was to be the sole arbiter of fair play, thus ending the need for players to appeal to the official for a decision in their favour. Well, the road to hell is paved with good intentions. It might have worked back in the latter days of Queen Victoria's reign when people had a tendency to do as they were told without argument but, sadly, referees are no longer afforded such deference, more's the pity. Those original umpires, usually one from each participating club, were then banished to the touchlines, given a flag and told to help the ref out when they saw an infringement he had missed. Now that sounds like a novel idea. The final definition of officialdom was to introduce neutrality, thus ending any disputes over biased decisions. It did not help to make referees any more popular, of course.

The man in black has always been the fall guy, the first to be blamed for a losing side's shortcomings. In many ways it is a dirty, thankless job but someone has to do it. John Lewis, who was considered to be the best referee during the early period of football and officiated at three FA Cup Finals, in 1895, 1897 and 1898, later wrote, 'For myself, I would take no objection to hooting or groaning by the spectators at decisions with which they disagree. The referee should remember that football is a game that warms the blood of player and looker-on alike, and that unless they can give free vent to their delight or anger, as the case may be, the great crowds we now witness will dwindle rapidly away.'

Referees have to learn to live with it. If they get it wrong, they get slaughtered – by players, managers, media ... even their own hierarchy. George Flint knew the truth of that. And by and large they accept the terms of reference, stoically and in silence. But would it not be better for everyone's understanding and appreciation of the difficulties they face and the pressure they endure if, like the players and managers, they too were required to answer questions after games and explain exactly why they gave such a decision, or how they missed a crucial incident? We know they are only human but sometimes their immunity from such inquiries hinders their cause. They are an essential component of the sport and it is to their detriment that they are beyond such open examination of how they go about their work.

Above all things, referees crave respect. Without it they cannot perform their duties correctly, efficiently, confidently. That is especially true at grassroots level, where many young referees pursue their passion for the game but quickly lose heart when they are routinely abused, often physically, by players and spectators. It is a worrying trend and one the FA committed themselves to addressing with a campaign launched in 2010 to attract 8,000 new referees to the game. The only way they will do this is by education; by raising awareness of exactly what it is like to be a referee.

Players and spectators alike must be persuaded to appreciate the pressures the modern game places on referees. It will not make them any more popular but a little understanding can only help their cause. And the referees have to play their part too. There are times when they should be expected, perhaps even instructed, to face the music, expose their shortcomings to public examination, be prepared to come out and answer questions after a game, just as the managers and players do now. If they want respect, if they want their unique position in the game to be recognised and their worth to be valued, they should get up there and shout about it.

CHAPTER TWELVE

THE BEST OF
THE BEST

I love a good argument – politics, religion, movies, sex, drugs and rock 'n' roll – but especially football.

You can never win an argument about football and neither can you lose.

That's the beauty of an argument about football – it's all opinions. Put four people round a table in the pub, toss in the name of a player and you will get four different opinions: he's great, he's rubbish, he's good, he's not.

So here's an argument to get you going next time you drop into the Pig and Swill for a pint of Snotgoblin. Who would you put in your team of the 1970s?

I know my first XI and you might take the view that some of my choices are surprising ... but before I present the finest collection of Division One players from the 1970s, there is another argument to settle. It is a question with only two possible answers – yet a question almost impossible to answer. Who, back then, was the greatest footballing star of them all? Sadly, only one of them qualifies for my team, which is why this becomes a bonus argument – an appetite wetter for the main debate.

So was it the poor boy from the backstreets of Tres Coracoes, a cattle town in the southeast of Brazil, who rejoiced in the name of Edson Arantes de Nascimento, or the bad boy from the backstreets of the Cregagh in Belfast, who was christened George Best?

Pele or Bestie? South American genius or Irish will o' the wisp?

Pele was such a graceful player. Physical strength allied to a razor-sharp footballing brain. A player who could ride a tackle, sell a dummy, perfectly weight a pass, spot an opportunity unlike any other. For those not old enough to have seen him in his pomp, I can think of only one player of the modern era who has come anywhere near to Pele's majesty and that player was Zinedine Zidane, circa 1998.

Best was such an exciting player. Physical strength allied to an intuitive footballing brain. He relied on instinct and speed, limpet-like control and lion-hearted bravery. Indulgent Dads will always quote his memory when the young fans of today start bandying around names like Rooney, Giggs and Suarez. I can think of only two players of the modern era who come close to Bestie's brilliance ... but neither is quite in George's orbit.

One is Cristiano Ronaldo, a hugely talented player admittedly, with more tricks than Tommy Cooper. But he lacks Best's impish charm and humility and, more importantly ... well, for want of a better expression, he has been known to be perhaps slightly less than honest. He falls over at a touch lighter than butterfly wings, whinges like a politician caught in an expenses fiddle and tackles like Christopher Biggins.

You can watch any number of hours of George Best footage,

see him get clobbered by players of demonstrably inferior skill and he will always get up without a moan or rolling around in feigned agony. And you will see a player who always tried to stay on his feet while others were hacking at his ankles. The only dives Best was interested in came with neon lights, after-hours drinking and wall-to-wall crumpet.

The other aspirant to Best's mantle is Lionel Messi, of Argentina and Barcelona, who possesses many of the great man's qualities. To see him pick up a ball from deep, power past defenders with the ball tied by an invisible cord to his shiny gold boots, and then finish with the same natural calm is a reminder of Best in full flow. Messi is, right now, the most gifted player on the planet but, unlike Best, he does have weaknesses. Best was a terrific header of the ball, something you rarely see Messi involved in, and the Irishman was also prepared to roll his sleeves up and muck in defensively. He liked a tackle – an attribute I would not readily associate with either Messi or Ronaldo.

The son of a footballer known as Dodinho, Pele first displayed his precocious talent on the world stage in 1958 as a teenager in Sweden when Brazil lifted the old Jules Rimet trophy, the teenager scoring twice in a 5-2 win over the host nation in the final. By 1966 his reputation had already achieved the status of legend. He was the player to be feared and so the assassins lined up to take him out. Mauled by Hungary, crippled by Portugal, he was unable to influence his Brazilian team and they limped out of the competition at the group stage.

But if that was the nadir of Pele's World Cup career, just four years later in Mexico he took his admirable revenge as the fulcrum of the finest international team ever assembled.

Jairzinho, Carlos Alberto, Tostao, Gerson, Rivelino ... and Pele. He was at the height of his powers, a juggernaut in ballet shoes, Muhammad Ali crossed with Rudolf Nureyev. The dummy he sold hapless Uruguayan goalkeeper Ladislao Mazurkeiwicz became an iconic piece of soccer magic to stand alongside Cruyff's reverse flick and David Beckham's 50-yard goal. It left Kenneth Wolstenholme, the BBC's finest commentator, almost lost for words: 'Oh what ... what genius!'

Since then thousands of players have perfected the Cruyff shuffle and there have been a couple of Beckham-esque goals but I cannot recall anyone repeating Pele's stepover. Had he finished it by rolling the ball between the posts instead of just wide, it would stand in perpetuity alongside the greatest goals ever scored.

Not that Pele was over-impressed. He once told reporters, 'Listen, I scored a lot of goals in this World Cup that people don't remember. This play, every place I go people talk about it. If it was a goal, people might not have remembered it.'

And so to the 1970 World Cup final against Italy, no mean performers themselves, yet made to look as ordinary as a Sunday League pub side by the collective genius of Brazil and the individual majesty of King Pele.

He scored the first goal. Resorting to the *Acme Book of Soccer Clichés*, I can come up with no better way to describe it than to say Pele leaped like a salmon at the far post to head home Jairzinho's raking cross. Pele did not run onto the ball, he just jumped from a standing position, arched those bulging neck muscles and powered the header past startled Italian keeper Enrico Albertosi. Awesome.

'I have a special feeling for that goal because I scored it with my head,' he said. 'My father was a soccer player and once scored five goals in a game, all with his head. That was one record I was never able to break.'

The other champagne moment came with the final goal, the

brightest candle on Brazil's party cake. Jairzinho to Pele 25 yards out. With the ball at his feet, Pele waited. Bemused Italian defenders did not move, there was no incoming tackle; they stood off him because they dare not do anything else. Finally, without a backward glance, Pele laid it to his right, perfectly weighted, into the path of the galloping Carlos Alberto, who lashed it on the full, past Albertosi, then carried on running around the goal and into the history books. Brazil had won the Jules Rimet trophy for the third time and it would be theirs to take back to Rio. But how did Pele know Carlos Alberto was coming? Sixth sense was another of his innate attributes.

In a career that ran from his days in the Santos youth team of 1952 to his final appearance with New York Cosmos in 1977, he scored more than 1,000 goals. Number 1,000 – *O Milesimo* – came in a match against Vasco da Gama from a penalty kick at the Maracanã Stadium, Rio de Janeiro, in 1969. At senior level his tally was 470 goals in 412 games for Santos, 31 in 56 appearances for Cosmos and 77 goals from his 92 games for Brazil.

The only negative in the Pele story is that he never tested himself in the more challenging European leagues. Italy or Spain would have taken on the national debt to sign him and, had he been allowed to listen to overtures made at the time by Manchester United, just imagine the mouth-watering prospect of Pele, Best, Charlton and Law all lining up together. But such was his status in his homeland, the Brazilian government declared Pele 'an official national treasure' and ruled against any transfer out of the country.

Pele had to retire to escape. But that was in 1972, his 17th season at Santos, and when he made his comeback two years later, he was already 34 and no longer a wise investment for Europe's top clubs. Instead he led efforts to sell soccer to the

Americans, along with lesser known, ageing European and South American stars, in much the same way as David Beckham has done 30 years later.

Since he finalised his retirement, Pele has been voted Athlete of the Century, UNICEF Footballer of the Century and FIFA Player of the Century. It is a career path that differs more than slightly from that of George Best.

To be strictly accurate, Best's glory days were all but over by the start of the 1970s. His two league championship medals, plus that famous 1968 European Cup win, personified by his solo goal in extra time against Benfica at Wembley, and his selection as European Player of the Year all came in the second half of the 1960s.

Best was in his prime, able to juggle the demands of a top footballer with nightclub owner, womaniser, heavy drinker and teen idol. He was also the man some called 'the Fifth Beatle'. As the 1970s opened up, his football powers were just beginning to wane, along with his love affair with the game. More often than not, he began to put his natural talents to less creative uses. 'They say I slept with seven Miss Worlds,' he once said. 'I didn't. It was only four – I didn't turn up for the other three.'

But he was still capable of moments of extraordinary brilliance. 1 February 1970, an FA Cup Fifth-Round tie at Northampton Town. Manchester United won 8-2 and Best scored six of the goals: two with his head, one from a scramble, the other three by dazzling the goalkeeper and shooting into the empty net. When the sixth one went in, he stood by the goalpost and looked, almost sheepishly, towards his admiring team mates.

Hugh McIlvanney, in his own peerless style, captured the essence of Best better than most when he wrote, 'On the field, he was the incarnation of the game's most romantic possibilities.

THE BEST OF THE BEST

He appeared to regard gravity as an impertinent con trick unworthy of being taken seriously, gracefully riding tackles that looked capable of derailing a locomotive.'

If there was one moment from one match that crystalised every facet of George Best's outrageous talent and mischievous appeal, it came on 15 May 1971, at Windsor Park, Belfast, in an international match between Northern Ireland and England.

As England's greatest ever keeper Gordon Banks dropped the ball towards his left foot, ready to launch his kick into the Irish half, the lurking Best flicked out a boot and diverted it back over Banks' head. The two players scrambled for possession but Best was too quick. As Banks made a despairing dive, Best calmly headed into the empty net. At no point had he come into physical contact with Banks, who stood, bemused and humiliated, half-heartedly waving his arms in protest. To the disgust of the dancing Irish fans, the referee who, apparently, had not seen the incident, disallowed the goal due to ungentlemanly conduct.

And that leads to perhaps the only flaw in the case for naming George Best the greatest footballer ever. He never got the chance to perform on the international stage at the highest level. What World Cup stories we might be able to add to the saga had he been born in a terraced house in Salford instead of the Cregagh in Belfast.

With Bobby Moore behind him, Bobby Charlton at his shoulder and Martin Peters on his wavelength, England would have been so much more than they were under Alf Ramsey. With Best at his disposal, Ramsey might have fallen in love with wingers again. I know, it's a pointless argument, but don't you just love the fantasy?

By 1972 Best had staged his first, much-publicised walkout from Old Trafford, turning up on a Spanish beach to be photographed with his thumb inside the bikini briefs of a blonde he had just met.

He was only 27 when he left United at the beginning of 1974 (138 goals from 361 appearances) but to be honest, he was already burdened by booze, his influence diminished. It was the inevitable conclusion of the fatal flaw in Best's make-up. Northern Ireland international Harry Gregg put it like this: 'George Best had everything, but George couldn't carry the can of his greatness.'

Spells with Fulham, a clutch of American clubs, Hibernian in Scotland, Bournemouth and finally, Brisbane Lions merely emphasised the depth of his fall.

But time cannot erase the memories. He did things differently, instinctively. There was a goal against Spurs. The ball came to him and, faced with a crowd scene, George didn't blast it in hope, he lifted it serenely in expectation. Pat Jennings' face as it arced over his head and just under the bar was a picture. You could just sense the defenders acknowledging through gritted teeth they had been done by a master.

There was a goal against Sheffield United. He ran past defenders as team mates screamed for a pass. Defenders forced him wide, he couldn't score ... but, by God, he did.

You would be hard pressed to find anyone to decry Best's abilities. There is that famous quote by West Brom full-back Graham Williams, who apparently told George, 'Will you stand still for a minute so I can look at your face?'

'Why?' asked Best.

'Because all I've ever seen of you,' explained Williams, 'is your backside disappearing down the touchline.'

His great friend Sir Michael Parkinson once wrote this of Best: 'He wasn't handsome; he was beautiful – blue-eyed, black-haired and slim as a railing. He could have made a living on looks alone, but what set him apart and made him special were his gifts as a footballer. After watching him in action for the first time, I wrote that he had the physique of a toothpick, but the heart of a bull terrier. He was, and is, the best all-round player I ever saw.'

Oddly, not everyone shares that same high opinion of Pele. Luiz Felipe Scolari, who steered Brazil to World Cup triumph in 2002, is not one of his biggest admirers. He once said of the great man, 'I believe that Pele knows nothing about football. He has done nothing as a coach and his analysis always turns out to be wrong. If you want to win a title, you have to listen to Pele and then do the opposite.'

As Kenneth Wolstenholme said, Pele was a genius, but if it came down to buying a ticket to see one or the other, I would always plump for George the entertainer, a player and a man who, as Sinatra so eloquently put it, did it his way, despite being surrounded by people who thought they knew what was good for him, berated by headline writers, castigated by columnists. What they all forgot, or did not have the nous to understand was that George did not want their advice: he was living his own life to the full, intending to pack as much into it as the sands of time would allow. To paraphrase an oft-repeated homily, he was not to be confused with someone who gave a shit.

That wonderful story he first revealed on an edition of *Parkinson* succinctly captured the nonsense that surrounded George Best. A waiter delivering champagne to Best's hotel room saw thousands of pounds in casino winnings and a famous beauty queen, both arranged tastefully on the bed. Aghast at the evidence laid out before him, the waiter dolefully asked, 'Mr Best, where did it all go wrong?' Years later Best observed, 'Perhaps he saw something in me that I didn't.'

BEST, PELE AND A HALF-TIME BOVRIL

In 1999 George Best was voted 11th at the International Federation of Football History & Statistics European Player of the Century election and 16th in the World Player of the Century election. Fifteen players better than George Best? How did Marco van Basten or Gerd Müller get voted ahead of him, for instance? They knew better back home in Belfast, where they used to say, 'Maradona good, Pele better, George Best'.

So I ask the question again, Best or Pele? Well, I have thought of the perfect way to settle the argument: a litmus test for who was the greatest. With his calm elegance, style and natural feel for those samba rhythms Pele would be a sensation. I can see *Strictly Come Dancing* judge Bruno Tonioli's eyes rolling as, lips tightly pursed, he shoots an arm in the air and calls 'Ten!' But old snake hips Bestie would have brought a lascivious smirk to the face of Bruno's fellow judge Craig Revel Horwood – 'Fab-u-lous, darling!' – and head judge Len Goodman would not be able to resist the casting vote: 'For me, George was, without a doubt, the Best.'

Glad that's settled. Now let's get down to the business of picking my perfect team of the 1970s. To keep a sense of proportion, I am restricting my selection to players from the old First Division, which means I don't have to go for foreigners and argue the merits of Cruyff, Beckenbauer, Mueller et al. Johnny Foreigner might dominate the top level in the Noughties but back then it was still, largely, a home-grown competition.

Having already described Gordon Banks as the best England goalkeeper of them all, I ought to qualify that as being from the modern era as I have no idea how good the old Spurs and England keeper Ted Ditchburn was and I can only just remember Ron Springett of Sheffield Wednesday, who held the position before Banks. In truth, the goalkeeping position during the 1970s became something of a soap opera. Banks was Alf Ramsey's first choice. A stalwart of the side that won the World Cup in 1966, he was just as key to their hopes in 1970. He was expected to play in all England's games, no matter how deep into the tournament they progressed, and Peter Bonetti and Alex Stepney were seen merely as understudies.

That famous save from Pele, somehow lifting a downward header up and over the crossbar, has been described by many as the best in history and it was good enough to prompt Pele to include Banks in that same list of the 125 greatest players of all time.

Banks is not one to argue. He once told a reporter,

> That save from Pele's header was the best I ever made. I didn't have any idea how famous it would become – to start with, I didn't even realise I'd made it at all. I heard Pele shout 'goal' as he headed it, which was followed by a massive, almost deafening roar. Even though I'd got a hand to it, I thought he must have scored.
>
> Then I realised the crowd were cheering for me. I couldn't believe it. Bobby Moore came over and ruffled my hair – I like to tell people that he was having a go at me for not holding on to it! After all, our match against Brazil was still at 0-0 and we had a corner to defend. As I got to my feet I tried to look as nonchalant as possible, as if to say that I make that sort of save all the time. Not a day goes by when I don't get asked about it. That save is what I'll always be remembered for, even though I won the World Cup in 1966. I don't mind – I enjoy talking about it because that Brazil team is the

greatest to ever play the game. I've met Pele several times since that day and he always mentions that save and gives me an affectionate hug and a smile.

When England emerged from the group stages for a quarter-final showdown with the old enemy West Germany, the smart money was on Ramsey's side. They had a better balance than 1966 with the backbone of that team strengthened by the inclusion of Alan Mullery, Keith Newton and Terry Cooper. But on the eve of the quarter-final Banks went down with a stomach bug and Ramsey had to call up Chelsea's talented stopper, Peter Bonetti. England went 2-0 up and then Ramsey, thinking his side were safe and wanting to save talismanic but ageing Bobby Charlton for the semi-final, substituted the Manchester United star. The game opened up for Germany and that was when Bonetti was found wanting, his mistakes helping the Germans overhaul England for a famous 3-2 victory.

Conspiracy theories ran rampant. Banks had somehow been nobbled, was the outrageous claim. The player himself would have none of it but, with a fit Banks at the back, England would almost certainly have beaten the Germans and who knows, a second successive World Cup final might now be on the record books.

Although by then aged 33, Banks remained Alf's favourite, despite the growing claims of his natural successor, Peter Shilton. He showed no sign of losing his edge and would almost certainly have added to his 73 caps had a car accident on 22 October 1972 not cost him an eye. That was the end for Banks and the beginning of a ludicrous period of indecisive England management.

No wonder the national side failed to qualify for successive World Cups when the manager – and it was Ron Greenwood who was the main culprit – could not decide who was the better goalkeeper. Was it Shilton, or was it Ray Clemence of Liverpool? 'I don't know,' bumbled the inoffensive Greenwood, so he picked Shilton one match and Clemence the next.

It would have been tough on either one had the other been given the job permanently but those are the decisions that have to be made. Had Brian Clough got the England job instead of the mild-mannered West Ham man, can you imagine him perpetuating such a daft situation?

But I will pick neither. Had Banks not been injured in that car crash, he might have gone on for years. Peter Shilton would never have got near his remarkable tally of 125 caps – remarkable when you consider Clemence got 61 caps in the same era.

It has to be Banks, not just for *that* save but for being the best. Gordon Banks is my number-one goalkeeper.

At right-back comes one of the most consistent defenders ever seen in the top flight: Phil Neal, Northampton, Liverpool and England. I doubt there has ever been a full-back who could get up and down the line better. Seventy-six senior career goals emphasise the point.

When Bob Paisley took over the Anfield boot room from Bill Shankly, he inherited an ageing squad. First on his hit list was full-back Chris Lawler. Neal would be his replacement for the next 455 games, a total that included a remarkable run of 417 consecutive appearances during which he played a week after a flying elbow broke his cheekbone, and on another occasion wearing a boot one and a half sizes too big because of a broken toe.

He had a refreshing attitude that many of today's overpaid, pampered superstars would find hard to understand – 'I didn't miss a day's training in all those years I was there. I wouldn't ring in for a cold. Every day I had a smile on my face.'

Altogether he racked up a silver mountain of domestic and European honours with Liverpool and won 50 England caps at a time, it must be said, when England were no great shakes. But that was no fault of Phil Neal.

The other flank is a problem. There are a clutch of names to be thrown into the pot: Terry Cooper, his Leeds team mate Trevor Cherry, Colin Todd, Alec Lindsay, even Emlyn 'Crazy Horse' Hughes. But I will select the quiet man from Ipswich, Mick Mills – another player who suffered from Greenwood's shilly-shally style of management. One match he was right-back, the next left-back. It speaks volumes for his versatility that he was accomplished enough to handle both options.

Mills flourished under Bobby Robson's management at Ipswich and, as his team captain, shared in the triumph of taking that backwater club to an FA Cup final triumph over mighty Arsenal, and within spitting distance of a highly improbable First Division title.

Ironically, it would be Robson who would end Mills' international career, when he took over from Greenwood in 1982. But by then Mills had achieved just about everything a player from Ipswich Town could ever hope to achieve: more than 700 games for his club, 42 for his country and the honour of captaining them in the 1982 World Cup finals.

In the centre of defence the selection is straightforward and I will brook no dissension. Well, OK, you might argue the merits of Brian Labone – although I would not give him houseroom because of the brutal and premeditated tackle that effectively ended Joe Baker's career in a 1967 Forest-Everton cup tie – or Jack Charlton, Larry Lloyd and Jeff Blockley.

The most stylish centre-half of the 1970s, without question, was Derby County's Roy McFarland, and the story of how Brian

Clough and Peter Taylor persuaded him to move to the East Midlands when his hometown club Liverpool were on his trail has become part of the Clough legend.

Late one night they turned up at McFarland's terraced house in Liverpool, hauled him out of bed and, in front of his startled parents, talked into the wee small hours about the potential of Derby and what could be achieved if he came along for the ride. His Dad was convinced: 'If they want you that badly, son, I think you should sign.' At least it got Clough and Taylor out of the house.

But it proved to be a crucial piece of business. Building their team around McFarland, Derby won the first Division One title in their history and came close to a European cup final. 'He went on to become the best centre-half to play for England for many a year, arguably the best ever,' wrote Clough in his biography, *Walking On Water.* McFarland gets my number-five shirt.

And alongside him? Only one candidate – the incomparable Bobby Moore, gentleman, artist, inspiration. A total of 108 caps for England, 90 as captain, he was the bridge between the 1960s and 1970s. England captain when the World Cup was won in 1966, captain when they performed with such credit in 1970; more than 500 games for West Ham, an FA Cup winner's medal and the first footballer to become BBC Sports Personality of the Year. Yet, when he died of cancer in February 1993 at the age of 51, he was still plain Mr Moore, while some of his contemporaries wore the gilding of a knighthood. It doesn't seem fair.

Moore was the complete defender. He tackled in an unobtrusive way, could distribute the ball long and short, and had an innate sense of where he should be at any given time. Celtic and Scotland's Jock Stein came up with a wonderful assessment, once commenting, 'There should be a law against him. Bobby Moore knows what is happening 20 minutes before anyone else.'

Here's a couple of examples: the 1966 World Cup final. England are losing 1-0 as Moore strides forward. He is flattened by Wolfgang Overath but, thinking faster than most, he jumps up and places the ball, then floats it across to Geoff Hurst, who heads the equaliser. Then into the deepest recesses of injury time and England are clinging on to a 3-2 lead. The ball breaks to Moore on the edge of the England box. 'Belt it into row X,' plead the fans ... Moore looks up and delivers a 50-yard pass into the stride of Hurst, who shoots, his hat-trick; England win 4-2.

And it was not just the quality of that pass that encapsulated everything that was great about Bobby Moore. England, close to the point of exhaustion, were seconds away from winning the World Cup, the crowd was whistling for time and the natural instinct would have been to play it short, keep possession, take no chances, waste precious moments. Moore, whose clarity of thought was among his finest qualities, saw it differently. This was his view: 'It's always been in my manner to try to play, whereas others with another type of make-up might have just tried to hit the corner flag ball in that type of situation. The pass gave us the opportunity to get in behind them. It was the best way of finishing the game as it turned out.'

Fast forward four years: England v. Brazil in Mexico. Pele at his best, bearing down on the England penalty area. A sway, a drop of the shoulder, one defender to beat and he surely scores. Moore is the defender. He shoots out a boot and removes the ball from Pele's foot with the precision of a surgeon. At the end of the game, Pele wants Moore's shirt. Total respect. And remember, this is a player who went into that World Cup with scandal in his wake.

England were in Columbia for a warm-up game. Shopping in Bogotá for gifts with Bobby Charlton, Moore was accused of stealing a bracelet. The story blazed around the world, banner headlines. Moore was arrested, detained for four days; diplomatic pressure at the highest level ... he was released in time to rejoin England for the tournament, the case against him was dropped and, in the heat of Guadalajara, he played his heart out.

So for all those reasons and many others, Bobby Moore is my number-six and captain.

Now the debate gets even hotter. Who would you put in the centre of the best midfield of the 1970s? Well, I'm sorry to say, I cannot find a place for the galloping enthusiasm of Emlyn Hughes, nor Trevor Brooking, once famously described by Brian Clough as a player who 'floats like a butterfly ... and tackles like one'; not Gerry Francis, nor Ray 'the crab' Wilkins.

In my classic 4-4-2 formation I have gone for a best-of-Britain duo: Irish genius Johnny Giles and the destructive Liverpool colossus Graeme Souness. Souness had a reputation as a destroyer but he was also capable of sublime moments of skill and perception. There is a description of him somewhere as 'a bear of a player with the delicacy of a violinist'.

Intelligent and articulate, he could be a troublemaker. His first manager, Bill Nicholson, eventually flogged him for a song, finally tiring of the teenage Scotsman's constant assertion that he was the best midfield player at Tottenham. The Spurs engine room at the time consisted of Martin Peters, Alan Mullery and Steve Perryman.

Souness arrived at Anfield in 1978, via Middlesbrough, to complete a triumvirate of new Bob Paisley signings – Alan Hansen and Kenny Dalglish were the others – destined to restore Liverpool's dominance in domestic and European football. Four months after signing for a domestic record fee of £352,000, Souness was at Wembley to slide an inch-perfect pass for Dalglish to score the only goal of the 1978 European Cup final against Bruges. By the time he had finished, his status on Merseyside had reached iconic proportions: three European Cups, five League Championships, four League Cups, 54 Scotland caps.

He played his football with panache and steely resolve. The bubble hair and Zapata moustache might have been comical fashion statements but his steely resolve and liking for a tackle left no one in any doubt that he was not a player to be messed about. Indeed he was a player no one could take their eyes off. He ruled the park like Wellington: strutting disdainfully, directing, cajoling, browbeating. The assassin with a velvet touch, much in the same way as Roy Keane would become a generation later. To paraphrase Wellington's classic pre-Waterloo quote, 'I don't know what he does to the enemy but he scares the hell out of me.' Souness might not have been everyone's favourite – opposition fans would howl for his blood – but if I was picking this team for real, I would want him with me, not against me.

Irishman Johnny Giles, with the dark darting eyes beneath that crop of unruly hair, was another man whose canvas was painted in contrasting shades of light and dark; another footballer with something to say and the ability to get his message across. Although schooled at Old Trafford under Matt Busby, his character was developed by Don Revie at Leeds United. Giles bought into the Revie mantra of win at all costs. He could illuminate a match with a deft piece of control or an inch-perfect pass and then cloud it over with a slyness bordering on the ugly.

THE BEST OF THE BEST

He played in an era of hard men like Tommy Smith, Ron Harris, Peter Storey and his team mate Billy Bremner but, despite his diminutive stature, he could stand alongside players with such fearsome reputations and never take a backward step. Football was like that in the 1970s. Giles says, 'In those days there was a code among players whereby you'd never try to get someone carded. You could get stuck into each other during the match but at the end you'd shake hands. There was violence, and I'm not saying it was right, but at least no one ever tried to influence the referee – there was no diving or any of that rubbish.'

Although his best years were to come with Leeds in the early 1970s, who can remember him as a young inside forward at Manchester United, helping the Red Devils win the FA Cup at Wembley in 1963, his pass setting up David Herd for a goal against Leicester? He has been chosen as the Republic of Ireland's greatest ever player, a decision based on his 59 caps and, no doubt, his 300-plus games for Leeds, which brought plenty of domestic and European glory. But displaying a generosity of spirit that was never particularly evident in his playing days, he refers to others capable of challenging his standing in the Irish game: Keane, Paul McGrath, Mark Lawrenson and Liam Brady.

I would love to have found a place for Brady, another player of breathtaking vision and skill and, in the eyes of many Gooners, the best player they have produced. I still remember that goal he scored against Spurs, pouncing on little Jimmy Neighbour as he drew the ball clear of the penalty area. Brady dispossessed him with the dexterity of a Soho pickpocket and then, with the outside of his left foot, bent his shot inside the far post. John Motson on commentary: 'Look at that ... oh, look at that!'

But I want Best in my team, for reasons already explained, and on the other flank I want John Robertson of Nottingham Forest and Scotland. Surprised? Well, I will tell you this: if Robbo had played for United or Liverpool, he would have been up there among the legends of the game. This was the player who made the winning goal in one European Cup final and scored the winning goal in the next one. He was the product of Brian Clough and Peter Taylor. When Clough arrived at the City Ground in 1975, he found Robertson overweight, eating too many chips and smoking far too many fags. He rarely shaved, dressed like a tramp and shambled around the Second Division without a trace of ambition or desire.

But within a couple of seasons he had been transformed. He became Forest's get-out man. Give it to Robbo and he could hold it for as long as his team mates needed and then, with remarkable speed over the first five yards, make room for a cross that was invariably accurate. 'My word, how he could pick out a team mate!' wrote Clough. 'If you think David Beckham is fairly handy with his right foot, you should have seen the way Robbo crossed with his left.' And this final, characteristic Clough tribute: 'John Robertson was a very unattractive young man. If one day I felt a bit off-colour, I would sit next to him. I was bloody Errol Flynn compared but, give him a ball and a yard of grass, and he was an artist, the Picasso of our game.'

So Robbo on the left, Bestie on the right, Giles and Souness in the centre. With that lot doing the work, my mother-in-law could play centre-forward ... but actually pinning down the best number nine and ten is still a toughie.

One of them has to be Kevin Keegan. Compared to Pele and Best, he was a player of lesser ability, yet such was his drive and determination, his effervescence and passion, he made the most of what gifts he had, squeezing out every last drop of talent until he could give no more. Bill Shankly never did a better bit of business than spending £35,000 to take the 19-year-old miner's son from the satanic darkness of the Old Show Ground at Scunthorpe to the sunlit uplands of Anfield.

Then, by luck or sound judgement, he paired him with John Toshack to form the best double act since Tom had a profitable encounter with Jerry. It took him a mere 12 minutes to score the first of a century of goals for Liverpool and, from that day in 1971, with Keegan as their talisman, the Merseysiders began to establish a dynasty that would last for more than a decade, long after he had moved abroad. The Keegan years brought three First Division titles, two UEFA Cups, two FA Cups and the European Cup to Anfield.

Finally, my centre-forward. There are plenty of candidates but not one that screams at me. Perhaps it should be Allan Clarke, a goal poacher whose nickname of 'Sniffer' was totally apt. He was the friendly face of Leeds United, a prolific marksman and scorer of 10 international goals. Mick Channon was another player I admired. He always had a smile on his face, especially after scoring, as he wheeled away, his arm turning like a propellor. More than 40 games for England, 21 goals, his credentials stack up.

But I'm not sure he has the power for my line-up. With Best and Robertson pinging balls to the far post, I want an old-fashioned centre-forward in the tradition of a Lawton or a Lofthouse. That's why I have selected Tyneside hero Malcolm Macdonald. At club level he was dynamic, fearless, belligerent and, when in the mood, almost unstoppable. For seven consecutive seasons – five at St James's Park and two at Highbury following his big money move to Arsenal – he was his side's leading goal scorer.

He only played 14 times for England, yet his contribution to history is still remembered. On 16 April 1975, against Cyprus,

Supermac became the first player to score five goals in an international at Wembley and only the second to achieve such a feat for England. The long-forgotten Willie Hall of Spurs was the first in 1938. OK, it was only Cyprus, but it was a European Championship qualifier and England badly needed the goals. In the event it did not matter because Don Revie's side did not make it to the finals in Yugoslavia but Supermac had written his place in the record books and it is difficult to envisage anyone challenging it now that even the fall guys of international football are so well organised.

There it is then, my team of the 1970s: Banks, Neal, Mills, McFarland, Moore; Best, Souness, Giles, Robertson; Macdonald, Keegan. No place for Dalglish or Hansen, Tommy Smith or Colin Bell. No room for Trevor Francis, Alan Hudson or Rodney Marsh. It would make a heck of a sub's bench, though.

Already I hear the howls of derision. The arguments have started. Think you can do better? Well, let's get interactive. Email your choice to andysmart47@gmail.com and we might just feature it in the next edition.

CHAPTER THIRTEEN
JOHNNY FOREIGNERS

The foreign invasion of British football began as a trickle on 19 August 1978.

Until that day, the Football League had been a virtual closed shop, populated almost exclusively by players from the United Kingdom and Ireland. It's hard to believe that today, isn't it? Hard to believe that Arsenal once fielded a complete team of home-grown players; hard to believe commentators could pronounce the name of every Chelsea player without twisting their tongues; hard to believe that fans of Manchester United could chat with their heroes without recourse to a multi-lingual interpreter.

There had been the odd Johnny Foreigner who had tried his luck in England. Footballer writer Nick Harris established that the very first was a Canadian named Walter W. Bowman, way back in 1892. According to Harris, who revealed the truth in his 2003 book, *England, Their England*, Bowman first came to Britain with a Canadian touring team in 1888.

Bowman, nominally an inside right, caught the eye in a team that was praised for their 'clever and scientific' style of play.

The Canadians returned home but four years later Bowman was back, signing for Accrington, then in the First Division and, in so doing, became the first foreign player in the history of the Football League. Bowman moved on to Ardwick, the club that became Manchester City, playing alongside the legendary Billy Meredith.

Harris settled a long-running argument that had seen other candidates vie for the title of first foreigner. Spurs fans tried to claim the honour with a German-born player named Max Seeburg who was on their books in 1908–09, but Harris put them straight.

Down the years there have been the odd one or two who managed to get permission to ply their trade over here. Players like South African-born Italian Eddie Firmani, who was at Charlton in the late 1950s. A goal scorer of some quality, he also played for Sampdoria in Serie A, thus creating a unique record: the only player to score 100 goals in England and Italy.

And another pioneer, in more ways than one, was Albert Johanneson, who was not only one of the first foreign players in the Football League but also one of the first black players of note. He played for nine seasons with Leeds United and, when Don Revie included him in the 1965 FA Cup final team to face Liverpool, he became the first black player to be seen in the Wembley showpiece.

Bert Trautmann was another soccer immigrant who made his lasting reputation at Wembley. He had to travel a long, hard road to get there. Born in Germany, he became a paratrooper at the start of the Second World War, fighting for Hitler on the Eastern Front, where his bravery won him an Iron Cross (that particular trait would resurface many years later). He came to England as a prisoner of war and decided to stay there once peace was established, signing for Manchester City in 1949. The decision did not go down well with many of the Maine Road faithful, whose memories of the war were still raw. But Trautmann refused to buckle under the pressure; instead he became a City hero, hardly missing a game over the next 15 years and nearly 550 appearances.

But it was the 1956 FA Cup final against Birmingham City that earned him his place in the City hall of fame. With less than 20 minutes to go and his team leading 3-1, Trautmann dived at the feet of Blues' forward Peter Murphy to prevent a near-certain goal. He was injured in the process but played on and was able to climb the 39 steps to the Royal Box to collect his medal. Only later was it discovered that he had played those final minutes with a broken neck.

Until the late 1970s such foreigners were a rare breed but then a couple of significant events occurred. In 1978 the European Community decided there should be no restrictions placed on the number of players moving from one EC country to another. The Football League was forced to change its position and lift what amounted to a ban on foreign players, not just from Europe, although they did insist no more than two could play in the same team at any one time. This alerted one or two of football's more enlightened men to the possibilities of importing overseas talent ... the 1978 World Cup in Argentina revealed just what was out there.

The host nation, which believed that it rather than Brazil was the spiritual home of South American football, had been desperate to win the trophy since it was inaugurated in 1930, having lost that first final held in Montevideo to South American rivals Uruguay 4-2. The arrival of the 1978 World Cup tournament in Argentina provided them with their best opportunity.

FIFA had taken the decision to award the tournament to Argentina more than a decade earlier, long before a bunch of self-serving generals had taken an interest in snuffing out the democratically elected, totally corrupt government with their own form of corruption.

Despite wide protest from organisations such as Amnesty International about the political situation, FIFA's leaders Joao Havelange and Sepp Blatter predictably stuck with their decision, much to the delight of General Jorge Videla and his cohorts, who saw it as a way of winning over a few hearts and minds in the beleaguered country, which had been ravaged by kidnappings and thousands of assassinations, including the unsolved murder of Omar Actis, head of the World Cup Organising Committee, and a dissenting voice about the cost to Argentina of hosting the tournament.

There was some disquiet in Europe about legitimising such a regime and some concerns about safety for the competing teams, with many European footballers expressing their worries. Dutch master Johan Cruyff was, perhaps, the biggest star to stay at home, although many years later he would refute allegations that he had deliberately boycotted the event. However, after the government and rebel Monteneros had agreed a truce in the interests of the nation's passion for football, the tournament went ahead, but more than three decades later, the memory of Argentina 1978 remains tainted with serious suggestions of financial ineffieciency, among other things.

Chain-smoking Argentinian coach Cesar Menotti was an outspoken opponent of his country's rulers but he was allowed to stay in the job. The Generals realised *El Flaco* ('the skinny one') was their best chance of achieving victory. Menotti had at his disposal a squad of prodigious talent, good enough to leave a young and emerging starlet named Diego Maradona out of his final 22.

England weren't there, of course, but Scotland, under the eccentric management of Ally MacLeod, travelled on a tidal wave of predictably misplaced optimism, with perhaps the most gifted squad ever assembled before the Tartan Army, led by Kenny Dalglish, Martin Buchan, Archie Gemmill, Joe Jordan, Don Masson, Bruce Rioch, John Robertson and Rangers mercurial winger Willie Johnston, who would make his own indelible mark on World Cup history.

Scotland were grouped with Peru, Iran and Holland, and were expected to progress with some comfort to the second phase. When Joe Jordan gave them an early lead against the little-fancied South Americans in their first group match, everything seemed to be going according to plan. Then the Scots pressed the self-destruct button. A chunky old schemer named Teofilo Cubillas ran them ragged, laying on an equaliser before half-time and scoring two more, one a collectors' item blasted in from fully 30 yards.

Scotland's misery deepened when Willie Johnston later failed a drugs test and was sent home in shame, a year's ban from international football chained to his ankle. And then it got worse, thanks to the Iranians. They were the whipping boys of the group, beaten out of sight by Peru and Holland. But somehow they foiled the Scots, who once again fell apart after taking the lead with a dodgy own goal. The abiding memory of Scotland's campaign is Ally MacLeod holding his head in his hands as Iran scored their humiliating equaliser.

Scotland could still qualify if they could beat the talented Dutch by three clear goals. In the face of such a seemingly impossible challenge at last they showed a glimpse of their capabilities. Although they quickly went one down to a Rob

Rensenbrink penalty, Dalglish inspired the fight-back with an equaliser from Jordan's assist. Gemmill then gave them the lead with a penalty before producing one of the great World Cup goals, jinking past three Dutch defenders before shooting low into the net. Even English fans were willing Scotland to pull off the miracle but it was not to be. Johnny Rep fired in a late goal from way out and at 3-2, there was no way through for the Scots.

Eight teams from the four qualifying groups went through to a second round of matches to decide who would contest the final. Argentina qualified in less than impressive style, having lost to Italy before narrowly beating Hungary and France. And here the waters started to get a little murky. Places in the final came down to two matches: Brazil v. Poland and Argentina v. Peru. There seemed to be more than a little accommodation for the home nation when Brazil's game was played in advance of Argentina's, allowing them the luxury of knowing exactly what they had to do to reach the final. In the event, they needed to beat Peru by four clear goals. They managed this with a couple of goals to spare, raising suspicions that Peru, and especially their Argentinian-born goalkeeper Quiroga, hadn't given their all. Still, it ensured the final FIFA almost certainly wanted: Argentina v. Holland, South America v. Europe.

The final was a thrilling, if somewhat disquieting encounter, presaged by some outrageous gamesmanship by the Argentinians, who kept their opponents waiting on the pitch for five minutes while 80,000 impassioned Argentina fans threw torn newspapers and toilet rolls into the air, creating a ticker-tape snowstorm of litter and one of the most hostile, intimidating atmospheres world football has ever experienced. Argentine left-back Alberto Tarantini later said, 'I think the best way to describe it is watching the looks on the Dutch faces as they walked onto the pitch. That says it all.'

Confirmation came from Holland's Johnny Rep, who said, 'It was not a good atmosphere. It was too hot. All the *militaire*. It was too heavy. It was *kokend*, boiling.'

But that was the Argentinian way, according to Tarantini: 'There's no other place in the world where they live and breathe football like here. I was talking to some English journalists a while ago and they told me watching football in Argentina is like going to the theatre. It's different here. Argentinians live for football, and the support we got from the people showed that. To see everyone shouting, crying, kneeling down. I don't think we were the only ones to lift the Cup, the millions who were cheering us on did so too.'

When the Argentine team eventually emerged from the players tunnel, they immediately began a protracted protest about a plaster cast protecting Dutchman Rene van de Kerkhof's injured wrist – something he had worn without comment during the entire tournament.

Although the poorly refereed final was littered with free kicks, it did produce some sublime moments. Star on the night was Argentina's number 10, Mario Kempes. Every inch the rock star of the Pampas, he gave them a half-time lead, stretching to push the ball past Dutch keeper Jan Jongbloed and release another cascade of paper from the terraces. The Argentinians held the lead until the 81st minute when, finally, Holland took one of many chances, Dick Nanninga's flying header pulling them level. And in the dying seconds of normal time, history was almost changed by Rensenbrink's shot, which cannoned back off the post. The ill fortune was to condemn the talented Dutchmen to their second successive World Cup final defeat.

BEST, PELE AND A HALF-TIME BOVRIL

In extra time Kempes danced through the Dutch defence and, although Jongbloed half-stopped his shot, it somehow bobbled into the net. Then Kempes, of Valencia, the only European-based Argentinian at that time, set up Daniel Bertoni for the clincher.

The style and panache of the Argentinians had certainly caught the eye, particularly Kempes, who was already spoken for with Valencia, and little Osvaldo Ardiles – known as Pitón (python) because of his dribbling skills – who pulled all the strings in midfield, despite being hampered by injuries including a broken toe and swollen ankle. No one was in any doubt that he would be top of the shopping list for the big guns of Serie A and La Liga, traditional playground for the best South American talent.

So you could almost hear the gasps of amazement just two weeks after the final when sports journalists assembled at White Hart Lane for a hurriedly called press conference and were told, in broad Yorkshire tones by beaming manager Keith Burkinshaw, that it was Spurs who had signed Ardiles, along with another World Cup squad member Ricardo Villa, for the bargain price of £700,000.

So how had Tottenham, newly promoted after a season in Division Two, trumped the biggest clubs in the northern hemisphere? It was Sheffield United boss Harry Haslam who brokered the deal through his considerable contacts in Argentina. Although his club couldn't afford Ardiles, he offered to smooth the way for Burkinshaw and Spurs, even flying out to Buenos Aires with the Tottenham boss to clinch the deal.

Ardiles who, presumably, could have waited for Milan or Real Madrid to come calling, signed without hesitation ... and then suggested his mate Ricky Villa wouldn't mind the gig either. Less than half an hour later Osvaldo Cesar Ardiles of Huracán and Racing Club's Ricardo Julio Villa were Tottenham players.

The headlines that followed were written big and bold, capturing the astonishment of the football world that this famous old English club had pulled off such an audacious transfer coup, a sapient comment in the *Guardian* crystallising the momentous nature of the business: 'It was as if the janitor had gone to buy a tin of paint and come back with a Velásquez.'

Would you believe, I never found the inspiration for a line so good in all the years I was covering Mansfield Town? It gave Tottenham's opening fixture of the 1978–79 season, at the home of Division One champions Nottingham Forest, just a smidgeon of extra appeal and more than 41,000 people were on Trentside for the occasion.

It was the sort of day exclusively reserved for the opening of a new football season ... hot enough to fry an egg on Yul Brynner's head. The appearance of Ardiles and Villa had generated a fever of anticipation, interest and curiosity, and when the Latin double act trotted out in the white shirts of Tottenham, they began a cultural revolution in British football that today has totally transformed the game we watch.

They were an odd couple: artist and artisan, rapier and cutlass, mosquito and bumblebee. Ardiles, his razor-neat haircut slapped down with grease like a tango dancer in a Buenos Aires speakeasy, was a slight figure; so precise, so sharp, he might have been mistaken for a Savile Row tailor. His movements around the pitch were explicit and calculated, his passes thoughtfully conceived.

Villa was more the archetypal Latin idol: swarthy and handsome, his long, dark hair flowing around strong features hidden behind a full beard, something rarely seen among footballers and only successfully carried off by George Best before him.

Ardiles and Villa – the meerkat and the grizzly.

'We were the first foreigners in England,' Ardiles recalled. 'We knew nothing about Spurs and the country when we arrived. I knew of some players like Kevin Keegan and the 1966 World Cup team but that was it. Coming here was quite a shock, especially the food.'

And Villa's memories ran along similar lines. 'Keith [Burkinshaw] wanted to buy two Argentinian World Cup players, but the big names, like [the captain, Daniel] Passarella, were not available. I played for Racing, Ossie for Huracán, poor clubs which needed the money, so we came here. We didn't know much about English football. We knew about Manchester United because they had played against Estudiantes de la Plata in 1968, and we knew a little about Liverpool but I'd never heard anything about "Tottingham".'

That trip to Nottingham provided the South Americans with a sobering introduction to English football in the late 1970s. Rival fans were battering each other on the streets of the city hours before the kick-off! A local police chief admitted they had been taken by surprise by the number of Spurs fans who had travelled north, attracted by the Argentinian factor. 'We didn't expect whole packs of idiots to be descending on the area of the ground and rampaging around three and a half hours before a ball was kicked,' Superintendent John Yarnell told reporters in the aftermath of an outbreak of violence that led to 43 arrests, fairly spread between proud citizens of Nottingham and London, and more than 50 casualties. Welcome to England, señors!

In the midst of all this mayhem, Forest and Spurs played out an entertaining 1-1 draw. Seen through the eyes of local reporter John Lawson, it was Villa who caught the eye. Lawson wrote: 'Ardiles was content to do the simple things while Villa, who allies a surprising level of skill to his powerful running, made more of an impact.

'His big moment came in the 26th minute when, with the Reds' defence in disarray, he swooped on a low cross from Ian Moores, side-stepped Peter Shilton and coolly planted the ball past two Forest defenders on the line.'

Interestingly, after the game Forest's management duo of Brian Clough and Peter Taylor made the astute assessment that had it been an English striker, he would have bottled the opportunity when faced with the looming presence of Shilton. And there was no doubt that Clough, renowned for pulling the odd transfer rabbit out of the hat during his days at Derby and Forest, had made a mental note of Tottenham's decision to bring Ardiles and Villa over to England. 'Of course we would like to buy a top foreign player,' he said, before adding, 'But he would have to be right for us.'

Like the vast majority of Division One managers, Clough was to keep a watchful eye on the progress of the South Americans and mischievously hinted maybe the deal had been done without due thought to the long term: 'I only hope for their sake Keith Burkinshaw, Bobby Robson, Harry Haslam and any other manager on the point of signing a player from abroad has done his homework.'

In the event, it was Ardiles who thrived to become a 'Tottingham' giant while Villa, who had been a bit-part player in Menotti's World Cup squad, was often on the fringe of things at White Hart Lane. 'I adapted a lot quicker than Ricky,' recalled Ardiles. 'I moved around a lot. He was a lazy bastard, waiting for players to give him the ball. And they wouldn't. I said to our captain, Steve Perryman, "Just give the ball to Ricky!" The first time Steve passed to him, Ricky tried to beat his man, lost the ball and the opponents counter-attacked and almost scored. Steve turned to me and said, "See! That's why I don't give the ball to Ricky!"'

Villa again: 'The money was good and the club was brilliant to me but I couldn't read the papers, couldn't watch television and, even though Ossie was here, I missed Argentina. Now I realise I was lucky. And I have to recognise that I am a little part of the history of English football.'

In their five years with Spurs, Ardiles would play nearly twice as many games as his compatriot, 221 against 133, but Villa still managed to claim his place among the club's greats, thanks largely to his remarkable FA Cup final solo goal in the 1981 replay against Manchester City, just days after slouching off the Wembley pitch when he was substituted.

One other First Division manager was bold enough to take a punt on one of Menotti's World Cup winners. Much-travelled Jim Smith, who was in charge of Birmingham City at the time, liked the look of Argentina's teak-hard full-back Alberto Tarantini, a rampaging defender with a Kevin Keegan bubble perm and fiery temperament. Nicknamed '*Conejo*' (rabbit) because of his prominent front teeth, he looked to be an even bigger bargain than the Spurs duo, arriving for a fee of around £275,000.

But it didn't work. Tarantini completed only 23 games for the Blues and managed to distinguish himself on just two occasions, once when he flattened Manchester United's Brian Greenhoff with all the subtlety of a Soho bouncer and then when he launched himself into the St Andrew's crowd, in response to some ill-chosen insult, years before Eric Cantona turned it into an art form. Tarantini also scored one top-flight goal in England ... against Bristol City. It was a far cry from the River Plate stadium and the World Cup final. After a season in the Midlands, he returned to Argentina but did come back to Europe, finishing his career in Switzerland with St Gallen. Thirty years down the line opinion about Tarantini is still divided. Jim

Smith says he was one of the most talented players he ever signed. Most other people include him in the top-20 worst foreign players to come to England.

Ardiles, Villa and Tarantini, as World Cup winners, quite rightly arrived in the full glare of media attention but the foreign invaders were also making a quieter landing in East Anglia, where Bobby Robson continued to go about his work at Ipswich Town without too much fuss but with the maximum effect.

That same year, 1978, he bought a stylish midfield player named Arnold Johannes Hyacinthus Mühren from FC Twente for £150,000, the first Dutchman to play in England since the well-known Gerrit Keizer turned out for Arsenal in the 1930s.

Recalling those groundbreaking days, Mühren said, 'I loved Robson. He was such a sweet guy, like a father. My first game was against Liverpool. They hailed me as some sort of demi-God and I had to play against Terry McDermott. Everything was kick and rush and I hardly touched the ball. I only had to run after McDermott, who asked me after the match, "Enjoy yourself?" I said, "No, not really." He said, "Me neither."'

It wasn't what Mühren wanted and things had to change, quickly. It came on the training ground – 'We had to do a circuit, dribbling the ball past a couple of poles ... I saw that most players couldn't do it! They stumbled and lost the ball. I took the ball and almost glided past those poles. The fans went wild. After that session, I talked to Robson. I told him, "Let them give me the ball." After that, things changed and we started to play real football.'

Robson, ever astute and willing to embrace innovation, liked what he saw and, when Mühren tipped him the wink about a pal from his FC Twente days named Frans Thijssen, the manager quickly reunited them at Portman Road. 'We had quite a team,' said Mühren. 'Eric Gates, Alan Brazil, John Wark, Terry Butcher … We really changed English football.'

They would help Robson's Ipswich to win the UEFA Cup in 1981, Thijssen scoring goals in both legs of the final against AZ Alkmaar, and Mühren would go on to collect two FA Cup winners medals with Manchester United in the 1980s.

Robson was happy to concede his part in the foreign influence: 'Yes, well, I helped to start all that. I brought two players to Ipswich – Arnold Mühren and Frans Thijssen – who you couldn't find in England. Mühren was a wonderful passer, great vision. Thijssen was a fantastic dribbler. I sold [Brian] Talbot for £450,000, bought Mühren for £150,000, Thijssen for £200,000, both better players than Talbot, and put £50,000 in the bank.'

The days of multi-culturalism in the dressing room had begun, although to be honest, it was the impetus of television money that led that trickle to become a flood. As late as 1992 there were still only 11 players from outside the home nations who were plying their trade in the Premier League and to be fair, they were all of some standing and most of them representative of the traditional footballing nations of Europe: Peter Schmeichel (Denmark), Man United; Andrei Kanchelskis (Russia), Man United; Jan Stejskal (Czechoslovakia), QPR; Roland Nilsson (Sweden), Sheffield Wednesday; Michael Vonk (Holland), Man City; John Jensen (Denmark), Arsenal; Anders Limpar (Sweden), Arsenal; Hans Segers (Holland), Wimbledon; Tony Dorigo (Australia), Leeds; Eric Cantona (France), Leeds; Gunnar Halle (Norway), Oldham.

How different it is today. There is now hardly a football-playing country in the world that has not contributed at least one player to the Premier League among the 260-plus foreign nationals spread around the division's 20 teams.

JOHNNY FOREIGNERS

Don't get me wrong, I love to watch players of the class and ability of Sergio Aguero, Robin Van Persie and Juan Mata but I am less moved by the likes of a Kenyan named Victor Wanyama, a Malian named Modibo Maïga or Haris Vuckic from Slovenia, and numerous other international journeymen who, likely as not, are keeping good, young home-grown players from making progress. The discussion point is whether the English game is better for the proliferation of overseas players or whether it has so heavily subjugated the progress of young, homegrown talent that we are losing a generation of potential England players.

Sir Trevor Brooking, the FA's director of development, is among those who believe it is harming the national side: 'If you look at Italy when they won the last World Cup, I think they had over 70 per cent of their league made up of domestic players. Spain, France, Holland, they're all up there too. Germany aren't much better than us but we're the lowest.

'The more that goes down, and the pool of choice reduces, we must come under pressure. In ten years' time you don't want us just being pleased to qualify for tournaments.'

Well, that situation is closer than Sir Trevor envisaged and the foreign malaise is not lost on beleaguered England manager Roy Hodgson, who regularly has to patch up his depleted squads with players largely untried at the highest level, often because they cannot get past the foreigners at club level. Hodgson said, 'Quite a few of the games I go to do not have any English players so one has to be very careful these days when talking about the Premier League and talking about the Englishness of it because more than two-thirds of the players in the League are not English. We have one of the lowest number of home-grown players to choose from in all the leagues, which, if you are national team manager, is not a great advantage, to be frank.'

BEST, PELE AND A HALF-TIME BOVRIL

At some point in the future you would think that football will butt up against the real world and be forced to revert to finding and nurturing home-bred talent instead of throwing cash around for quick-fix foreigners that bring too little to the table. Bobby Robson, who admitted to playing his part in the foreign invasion, said not long before his untimely death, 'We need to keep the door open for more English players to play in the Premiership. We've got to find better young players, better coaches, good facilities, maximise our time and produce some good English players over the next few years.'

It will have to be a voluntary move. European law has enshrined the right of any worker, not just in football, to seek employment anywhere among the member nations. They will keep coming so long as demanding, impatient club chairmen keep dangling obscene amounts of money in their eyes. But does it do anything for English football? I wonder, deep down, if Arsenal supporters of a certain age get the same buzz out of roaring on the current crop of largely foreign players as they did back in the days when Bertie Mee's class of 1971 was winning the double. If put to the vote, would they choose a team made up of a new breed of Charlie Georges, George Grahams, Geordie Armstrongs, Peter Storeys and Bob Wilsons over the Flaminis and Rosickys? Is it really all down to winning and who cares where he was born as long as he scores for the men in red shirts?

In the summer of 2013 Tottenham Hotspur spent more than £100 million to try and gatecrash the exclusive cartel at the top of the Premiership. I confess names like Erik Lamela and Vlad Chiriches meant little to me – I suppose if Spurs become a Champions League fixture, win a cup or two, it will have all been worth it. But I'm afraid it doesn't work for me. I love watching the very best foreign talent – indeed I would pay good money to watch the best foreign talent. But they should be the gild on the lily. I can't get emotional about players in the same way as I did years ago. It wasn't like that back in the 1970s when my team, your team, belonged to the community; when my team, your team, had as good a chance as the next. That was the decade when Forest and Derby won titles, West Brom and QPR almost won titles; Sunderland and Southampton won cups.

But that is firmly in the past. It all happened in the 1970s – and that was football's last great decade.

THE HONOURS
BOARD

1969–70

	Played	Won	Drawn	Lost	For	Against	Points
Everton	42	29	8	5	72	34	66
Leeds Utd	42	21	15	6	84	49	57
Chelsea	42	21	13	8	70	50	55
Derby County	42	22	9	11	64	37	53
Liverpool	42	20	11	11	65	42	51
Coventry City	42	19	11	12	58	48	49
Newcastle Utd	42	17	13	12	57	35	47
Manchester Utd	42	14	17	11	66	61	45
Stoke City	42	15	15	12	56	52	45
Manchester City	42	16	11	15	55	48	43
Tottenham Hotspur	42	17	9	16	54	55	43
Arsenal	42	12	18	12	51	49	42
Wolves	42	12	16	14	55	57	40
Burnley	42	12	15	15	56	61	39

Nottingham Forest	42	10	18	14	50	71	38
West Brom	42	14	9	19	58	66	37
West Ham Utd	42	12	12	18	51	60	36
Ipswich Town	42	10	11	21	40	63	31
Southampton	42	6	17	19	46	67	29
Crystal Palace	42	6	15	21	34	68	27
Sunderland	42	6	14	22	30	68	26
Sheffield Wed	42	8	9	25	40	71	25

DIVISION TWO

PROMOTED: Huddersfield, Blackpool
RELEGATED: Aston Villa, Preston North End

DIVISION THREE

PROMOTED: Orient, Luton Town
RELEGATED: Bournemouth, Southport, Barrow,
Stockport City

DIVISION FOUR

PROMOTED: Chesterfield, Wrexham, Swansea, Port Vale
RELEGATED: Bradford Park Avenue

FA CUP: Chelsea 2, Leeds Utd 1 (after replay)
LEAGUE CUP: Manchester City 2, West Bromwich Albion 1

EUROPEAN CUP: Feyenoord 2, Celtic 1
INTER-CITY FAIRS CUP: Arsenal 4, Anderlecht 3
EUROPEAN CUP WINNERS CUP: Manchester City 2,
Gornik Zabrze 1

FOOTBALLER OF THE YEAR: Billy Bremner

THE HONOURS BOARD
1970–71

	Played	Won	Drawn	Lost	For	Against	Points
Arsenal	42	29	7	6	71	29	65
Leeds Utd	42	27	10	5	72	30	64
Tottenham Hotspur	42	19	14	9	54	33	52
Wolves	42	22	8	12	64	54	52
Liverpool	42	17	17	8	42	24	51
Chelsea	42	18	15	9	52	42	51
Southampton	42	17	12	13	56	44	46
Manchester Utd	42	16	11	15	65	66	43
Derby County	42	16	10	16	56	54	42
Coventry City	42	16	10	16	37	38	42
Manchester City	42	12	17	13	47	42	41
Newcastle Utd	42	14	13	15	44	46	41
Stoke City	42	12	13	17	44	48	37
Everton	42	12	13	17	54	60	37
Huddersfield Town	42	11	14	17	40	49	36
Nottingham Forest	42	14	8	20	42	61	36
West Brom	42	10	15	17	58	75	35
Crystal Palace	42	12	11	19	39	57	35
Ipswich Town	42	12	10	20	42	48	34
West Ham Utd	42	10	14	18	47	60	34
Burnley	42	7	13	22	29	63	27
Blackpool	42	4	15	23	34	66	23

DIVISION TWO
PROMOTED: Leicester City, Sheffield Utd
RELEGATED: Blackburn Rovers, Bolton Wanderers

273

DIVISION THREE

PROMOTED: Preston North End, Fulham
RELEGATED: Reading, Bury, Doncaster Rovers, Gillingham

DIVISION FOUR

PROMOTED: Notts County, Bournemouth, Oldham
Athletic, York City
RELEGATION: All clubs re-elected

FA CUP: Arsenal 2, Liverpool 1
LEAGUE CUP: Tottenham Hotspur 2, Aston Villa 0

EUROPEAN CUP: Ajax 2, Panathinaikos 0
INTER-CITY FAIRS CUP: Leeds 3, Juventus 3 (Leeds won
on away goals)
EUROPEAN CUP WINNERS CUP: Chelsea 2, Real Madrid
1 (after replay)

FOOTBALL WRITERS PLAYER OF THE YEAR: Frank
McLintock

1971–72

	Played	Won	Drawn	Lost	For	Against	Points
Arsenal	42	29	7	6	71	29	65
Leeds Utd	42	27	10	5	72	30	64
Tottenham Hotspur	42	19	14	9	54	33	52
Wolves	42	22	8	12	64	54	52
Liverpool	42	17	17	8	42	24	51
Chelsea	42	18	15	9	52	42	51

THE HONOURS BOARD

Southampton	42	17	12	13	56	44	46
Manchester Utd	42	16	11	15	65	66	43
Derby County	42	16	10	16	56	54	42
Coventry City	42	16	10	16	37	38	42
Manchester City	42	12	17	13	47	42	41
Newcastle Utd	42	14	13	15	44	46	41
Stoke City	42	12	13	17	44	48	37
Everton	42	12	13	17	54	60	37
Huddersfield Town	42	11	14	17	40	49	36
Nottingham Forest	42	14	8	20	42	61	36
West Brom	42	10	15	17	58	75	35
Crystal Palace	42	12	11	19	39	57	35
Ipswich Town	42	12	10	20	42	48	34
West Ham Utd	42	10	14	18	47	60	34
Burnley	42	7	13	22	29	63	27
Blackpool	42	4	15	23	34	66	23

DIVISON TWO
PROMOTED: Sheffield Utd, Cardiff City
RELEGATED: Blackburn Rovers, Bolton Wanderers

DIVISION THREE
PROMOTED: Preston North End, Fulham
RELEGATED: Reading, Bury, Doncaster, Gillingham

DIVISION FOUR
PROMOTED: Notts County, Bournemouth, Oldham
Athletic, York City
RELEGATED: All clubs re-elected

BEST, PELE AND A HALF-TIME BOVRIL

FA CUP: Arsenal 2, Liverpool 1

FOOTBALL LEAGUE CUP: Stoke City 2, Chelsea 1

EUROPEAN CUP: Ajax 2, Inter Milan 0

UEFA CUP: Tottenham Hotspur 3, Wolverhampton Wanderers 2

EUROPEAN CUP WINNERS CUP: Rangers 3, Dynamo Moscow 2

FOOTBALLER OF THE YEAR: Gordon Banks

1972–73

	Played	Won	Drawn	Lost	For	Against	Points
Liverpool	42	25	10	7	72	42	60
Arsenal	42	23	11	8	57	43	57
Leeds Utd	42	21	11	10	71	45	53
Ipswich Town	42	17	14	11	55	45	48
Wolves	42	18	11	13	66	54	47
West Ham Utd	42	17	12	13	67	53	46
Derby County	42	19	8	15	56	54	46
Tottenham Hotspur	42	16	13	13	58	48	45
Newcastle Utd	42	16	13	13	60	51	45
Birmingham City	42	15	12	15	53	54	42
Manchester City	42	15	11	16	57	60	41
Chelsea	42	13	14	15	49	51	40
Southampton	42	11	18	13	47	52	40
Sheffield Utd	42	15	10	17	51	59	40
Stoke City	42	14	10	18	61	56	38
Leicester City	42	10	17	15	40	46	37

Everton	42	13	11	18	41	49	37
Manchester Utd	42	12	13	17	44	60	37
Coventry City	42	13	9	20	40	55	35
Norwich City	42	11	10	21	36	63	32
Crystal Palace	42	9	12	21	41	58	30
West Brom	42	9	10	23	38	62	28

DIVISON TWO
PROMOTED: Burnley, QPR
RELEGATED: Huddersfield Town, Brighton

DIVISION THREE
PROMOTED: Bolton Wanderers, Notts County
RELEGATED: Swansea, Scunthorpe

DIVISION FOUR
PROMOTED: Southport, Hereford Utd
RELEGATED: All teams re-elected

FA CUP: Sunderland 1, Leeds Utd 0
FOOTBALL LEAGUE CUP: Tottenham Hotspur 1,
Norwich City 0

EUROPEAN CUP: Ajax 1, Juventus 0
UEFA CUP: Liverpool 3, Borussia Mönchengladbach 2
EUROPEAN CUP WINNERS CUP: AC Milan 1,
Leeds United 0

FOOTBALLER OF THE YEAR: Pat Jennings

BEST, PELE AND A HALF-TIME BOVRIL
1973–74

	Played	Won	Drawn	Lost	For	Against	Points
Leeds Utd	42	24	14	4	66	31	62
Liverpool	42	22	13	7	52	31	57
Derby County	42	17	14	11	52	42	48
Ipswich Town	42	18	11	13	67	58	47
Stoke City	42	15	16	11	54	42	46
Burnley	42	16	14	12	56	53	46
Everton	42	16	12	14	50	48	44
QPR	42	13	17	12	56	52	43
Leicester City	42	13	16	13	51	41	42
Arsenal	42	14	14	14	49	51	42
Tottenham Hotspur	42	14	14	14	45	50	42
Wolves	42	13	15	14	49	49	41
Sheffield Utd	42	14	12	16	44	49	40
Manchester City	42	14	12	16	39	46	40
Newcastle Utd	42	13	12	17	49	48	38
Coventry City	42	14	10	18	43	54	38
Chelsea	42	12	13	17	56	60	37
West Ham Utd	42	11	15	16	55	60	37
Birmingham City	42	12	13	17	52	64	37
Southampton	42	11	14	17	47	68	36
Manchester Utd	42	10	12	20	38	48	32
Norwich City	42	7	15	20	37	62	29

DIVISION TWO

PROMOTED: Middlesbrough, Luton, Carlisle
RELEGATED: Crystal Palace, Preston North End, Swindon Town

THE HONOURS BOARD

DIVISION THREE

PROMOTED: Oldham, Bristol Rovers, York City
RELEGATED: Cambridge, Shrewsbury Town, Southport,
Rochdale

DIVISION FOUR

PROMOTED: Peterborough Utd , Gillingham, Colchester
Utd, Bury
RELEGATED: All teams re-elected

FA CUP: Liverpool 3, Newcastle Utd 0
LEAGUE CUP: Wolverhampton W 2, Manchester City 1

EUROPEAN CUP: Bayern Munich 4, Atlético de Madrid 0
UEFA CUP: Feyenoord 4, Tottenham Hotspur 2
EUROPEAN CUP WINNERS CUP: FC Magdeburg 2,
AC Milan 0

FOOTBALLER OF THE YEAR: Ian Callaghan

1974–75

	Played	Won	Drawn	Lost	For	Against	Points
Derby County	42	21	11	10	67	49	53
Liverpool	42	20	11	11	60	39	51
Ipswich Town	42	23	5	14	66	44	51
Everton	42	16	18	8	56	42	50
Stoke City	42	17	15	10	64	48	49
Sheffield Utd	42	18	13	11	58	51	49
Middlesbrough	42	18	12	12	54	40	48

Manchester City	42	18	10	14	54	54	46
Leeds Utd	42	16	13	13	57	49	45
Burnley	42	17	11	14	68	67	45
QPR	42	16	10	16	54	54	42
Wolves	42	14	11	17	57	54	39
West Ham Utd	42	13	13	16	58	59	39
Coventry City	42	12	15	15	51	62	39
Newcastle Utd	42	15	9	18	59	72	39
Arsenal	42	13	11	18	47	49	37
Birmingham City	42	14	9	19	53	61	37
Leicester City	42	12	12	18	46	60	36
Tottenham Hotspur	42	13	8	21	52	63	34
Luton Town	42	11	11	20	47	65	33
Chelsea	42	9	15	18	42	72	33
Carlisle Utd	42	12	5	25	43	59	29

DIVISION TWO
PROMOTED: Manchester Utd, Aston Villa
RELEGATED: Millwall, Cardiff City, Sheffield Wed

DIVISION THREE
PROMOTED: Blackburn Rovers, Plymouth Athletic,
Charlton Athletic
RELEGATED: Bournemouth, Watford, Tranmere Rovers,
Huddersfield Town

DIVISION FOUR
PROMOTED: Mansfield Town, Shrewsbury Town,
Rotherham Utd, Chester City
RELEGATED: All clubs re-elected

THE HONOURS BOARD

FA CUP: West Ham Utd 2, Fulham 0
FOOTBALL LEAGUE CUP: Aston Villa 1, Norwich City 0

EUROPEAN CUP: Bayern Munich 2, Leeds Utd 0
UEFA CUP: Borussia Mönchengladbach 5, FC Twente 1
EUROPEAN CUP WINNERS CUP: Dinamo Kiev 3,
Ferencvaros 0

FOOTBALLER OF THE YEAR: Alan Mullery

1975–76

	Played	Won	Drawn	Lost	For	Against	Points
Liverpool	42	23	14	5	66	31	60
QPR	42	24	11	7	67	33	59
Manchester Utd	42	23	10	9	68	42	56
Derby County	42	21	11	10	75	58	53
Leeds Utd	42	21	9	12	65	46	51
Ipswich Town	42	16	14	12	54	48	46
Leicester City	42	13	19	10	48	51	45
Manchester City	42	16	11	15	64	46	43
Tottenham Hotspur	42	14	15	13	63	63	43
Norwich City	42	16	10	16	58	58	42
Everton	42	15	12	15	60	66	42
Stoke City	42	15	11	16	48	50	41
Middlesbrough	42	15	10	17	46	45	40
Coventry City	42	13	14	15	47	57	40
Newcastle Utd	42	15	9	18	71	62	39
Aston Villa	42	11	17	14	51	59	39
Arsenal	42	13	10	19	47	53	36

West Ham Utd	42	13	10	19	48	71	36
Birmingham City	42	13	7	22	57	75	33
Wolves	42	10	10	22	51	68	30
Burnley	42	9	10	23	43	66	28
Sheffield Utd	42	6	10	26	33	82	22

DIVISION TWO

PROMOTED: Sunderland, Bristol City, West Bromwich Albion
RELEGATED: Oxford Utd, York City, Portsmouth

DIVISION THREE

PROMOTED: Hereford Utd, Cardiff City, Millwall
RELEGATED: Aldershot, Colchester Utd, Southend Utd, Halifax Town

DIVISION FOUR

PROMOTED: Lincoln City, Northampton Town, Reading, Tranmere Rovers
RELEGATED: All teams were re-elected

FA CUP: Southampton 1, Manchester Utd 0
FOOTBALL LEAGUE CUP: Manchester City 2, Newcastle Utd 0

EUROPEAN CUP: Bayern Munich 1, St Etienne 0
UEFA CUP: Liverpool 4, Bruges 3
EUROPEAN CUP WINNERS CUP: Anderlecht 4, West Ham Utd 2

FOOTBALLER OF THE YEAR: Kevin Keegan

THE HONOURS BOARD
1976–77

	Played	Won	Drawn	Lost	For	Against	Points
Liverpool	42	23	11	8	62	33	57
Manchester City	42	21	14	7	60	34	56
Ipswich Town	42	22	8	12	66	39	52
Aston Villa	42	22	7	13	76	50	51
Newcastle Utd	42	18	13	11	64	49	49
Manchester Utd	42	18	11	13	71	62	47
WBA	42	16	13	13	62	56	45
Arsenal	42	16	11	15	64	59	43
Everton	42	14	14	14	62	64	42
Leeds Utd	42	15	12	15	48	51	42
Leicester City	42	12	18	12	47	60	42
Middlesbrough	42	14	13	15	40	45	41
Birmingham City	42	13	12	17	63	61	38
QPR	42	13	12	17	47	52	38
Derby County	42	9	19	14	50	55	37
Norwich City	42	14	9	19	47	64	37
West Ham Utd	42	11	14	17	46	65	36
Bristol City	42	11	13	18	38	48	35
Coventry City	42	10	15	17	48	59	35
Sunderland	42	11	12	19	46	54	34
Stoke City	42	10	14	18	28	51	34
Tottenham Hotspur	42	12	9	21	48	72	33

DIVISION TWO

PROMOTED: Wolverhampton Wanderers, Chelsea, Nottingham Forest

RELEGATED: Carlisle Utd, Plymouth Argyle, Hereford Utd

DIVISION THREE
PROMOTED: Mansfield Town, Brighton & Hove Albion, Crystal Palace
RELEGATED: Reading, Northampton Town, Grimsby Town, York City

DIVISION FOUR
PROMOTED: Cambridge City, Exeter City, Colchester Utd, Bradford City
RELEGATED: Workington Town

FA CUP: Manchester Utd 2, Liverpool 1
FOOTBALL LEAGUE CUP: Aston Villa 3, Everton 2

EUROPEAN CUP: Liverpool 3, Borussia Mönchengladbach 1
UEFA CUP: Juventus 1, Atletico Bilbao 0
EUROPEAN CUP WINNERS CUP: Hamburg 2, Anderlecht 0

FOOTBALLER OF THE YEAR: Emlyn Hughes

1977–78

	Played	Won	Drawn	Lost	For	Against	Points
Nottingham Forest	42	25	14	3	69	24	64
Liverpool	42	24	9	9	65	34	57
Everton	42	22	11	9	76	45	55
Manchester City	42	20	12	10	74	51	52

THE HONOURS BOARD

Arsenal	42	21	10	11	60	37	52
WBA	42	18	14	10	62	53	50
Coventry City	42	18	12	12	75	62	48
Aston Villa	42	18	10	14	57	42	46
Leeds Utd	42	18	10	14	63	53	46
Manchester Utd	42	16	10	16	67	63	42
Birmingham City	42	16	9	17	55	60	41
Derby County	42	14	13	15	54	59	41
Norwich City	42	11	18	13	52	66	40
Middlesbrough	42	12	15	15	42	54	39
Wolves	42	12	12	18	51	64	36
Chelsea	42	11	14	17	46	69	36
Bristol City	42	11	13	18	49	53	35
Ipswich Town	42	11	13	18	47	61	35
QPR	42	9	15	18	47	64	33
West Ham Utd	42	12	8	22	52	69	32
Newcastle Utd	42	6	10	26	42	78	22
Leicester City	42	5	12	25	26	70	22

DIVISION TWO

PROMOTED: Bolton Wandererers, Southampton, Tottenham Hotspur

RELEGATED: Blackpool, Mansfield Town, Hull City

DIVISION THREE

PROMOTED: Wrexham, Cambridge Utd, Preston North End

RELEGATED: Port Vale, Bradford City, Hereford Utd, Portsmouth

DIVISON FOUR

PROMOTED: Watford, Southend Utd, Swansea City, Brentford

RELEGATED: Southport

FA CUP: Ipswich Town 1, Arsenal 0
FOOTBALL LEAGUE CUP: Nottingham Forest 1, Liverpool 0 (after replay)

EUROPEAN CUP: Liverpool 1, Bruges 0
UEFA CUP: Eindhoven 3, Bastia 0
EUROPEAN CUP WINNERS CUP: Anderlecht 4, Vienna 0

FOOTBALLER OF THE YEAR: Kenny Burns

1978–79

	Played	Won	Drawn	Lost	For	Against	Points
Liverpool	42	30	8	4	85	16	68
Nottingham Forest	42	21	18	3	61	26	60
WBA	42	24	11	7	72	35	59
Everton	42	17	17	8	52	40	51
Leeds Utd	42	18	14	10	70	52	50
Ipswich Town	42	20	9	13	63	49	49
Arsenal	42	17	14	11	61	48	48
Aston Villa	42	15	16	11	59	49	46
Manchester Utd	42	15	15	12	60	63	45
Coventry City	42	14	16	12	58	68	44
Tottenham Hotspur	42	13	15	14	48	61	41
Middlesbrough	42	15	10	17	57	50	40

Bristol City	42	15	10	17	47	51	40
Southampton	42	12	16	14	47	53	40
Manchester City	42	13	13	16	58	56	39
Norwich City	42	7	23	12	51	57	37
Bolton Wanderers	42	12	11	19	54	75	35
Wolves	42	13	8	21	44	68	34
Derby County	42	10	11	21	44	71	31
QPR	42	6	13	23	45	73	25
Birmingham City	42	6	10	26	37	64	22
Chelsea	42	5	10	27	44	92	20

DIVISION TWO

PROMOTED: Crystal Palace, Bright & Hove Albion, Stoke City

RELEGATED: Sheffield Utd, Millwall, Blackburn Rovers

DIVISION THREE

PROMOTED: Shrewsbury Town, Watford, Swansea City

RELEGATED: Peterborough Utd, Walsall, Tranmere Rovers, Lincoln City

DIVISON FOUR

PROMOTED: Reading, Grimsby Town, Wimbledon, Barnsley

FA CUP: Arsenal 3, Manchester Utd 2

FOOTBALL LEAGUE CUP: Nottingham Forest 3, Southampton 2

EUROPEAN CUP: Nottingham Forest 1, Malmo 0

UEFA CUP: Borussia Mönchengladbach 2, Red Star Belgrade 1

EUROPEAN CUP WINNERS CUP: Barcelona 4,
Dusseldorf 3

FOOTBALLER OF THE YEAR: Kenny Dalglish

IN MY OPINION

That was then and this is now. Basically, football is still the same game once the whistle blows. There has been a little evolution: three points for a win, longer shorts, multi-coloured boots, the snood, a rounder ball, green pitches in winter, more cheats, better actors, silly rules, even dafter goal celebrations ... but it is still basically the same beautiful game with the capacity to excite and enrage, shock and amaze, provoke and seduce in equal measure.

However, at some point in the last 40 years football walked up to the crossroads and made its pact with the Devil. It sold its soul to television in return for a pot of gold. The game is no longer in the hands of those for whom its spectacle, its history, its tradition means everything. Now money means everything. It's as simple as that. Every decision that is made, every change to the way things used to be, is done for money. FIFA, UEFA, the FA, whoever, they have abrogated their responsibilities to make the playing of the game fairer, faster, cleaner, better; to make the administration more transparent, honest and user friendly.

Foreign investors, some with dubious antecedents, are allowed into English football and, in a few notable instances, walk away, leaving an unholy mess in their wake.

Billions of pounds are pouring into the game from broadcasters, sponsors and obscenely wealthy plutocrats who see English clubs as the latest must-have possession. Yet football in England is teetering on the edge of financial meltdown. Our greatest clubs carry the equivalent of third-world debts while their employees walk away with all the profits.

For the vast majority of people in the Western world the end of the noughties brought misery and despair. Thousands lost their jobs, millions lost their savings; pensions plummeted. Businesses went bust, shops were boarded up, redundancies and bankruptcies reached record levels.

But football was operating in a parallel world. For instance, at the start of the 2009–10 season Real Madrid spent in the region of £250,000,000 on a few talented players: Ronaldo, Kaka, Benzema and Xavi Alonso. Manchester City did their best to catch up, spending around £150,000,000 on Robinho, Emmanuel Adebayor, Kolo Toure et al. The pace of spending hasn't slackened. Countries like Spain, and England, might be ensnared in a prolonged economic recession, which is impacting on the everyday lives of the majority of their populations, but their football clubs still find the money to spend £85 million on a Gareth Bale.

How can football sustain that level of profligacy? The simple answer is that it can't and that is being proved by the number of clubs being lined up in front of a firing squad of winding-up orders and administration threats. The writing was written large on the South Coast, where proud Portsmouth have been reduced to paupers at the banquet just a few years after winning the FA Cup

– years that saw them accumulate around £95 million in transfer income. The richest league in the world allowed it to happen.

In March 2010, the football world stood by and watched Chester City, a club founded in 1885, go to the wall. Does anyone believe Chester will be the last?

Football is now so divorced from the real world, it has lost touch with the people it was originally designed to amuse. The dads and sons who turn up on a Saturday afternoon to cheer on their favourites are now so inconsequential to football's grand plan that they might as well not be there. In fact, the people in power would sooner have them at home, sitting in front of a television screen, soaking up the advertisements for Nike and Renault, Coca-Cola and Carling.

And in return for this reckless investment, can we honestly say the football is better than it was 40 years ago? Faster and fitter, for sure – certainly too fast for a man with a whistle to handle, unaided. Why are we still waiting for the football authorities to dig their heads out of the sand and embrace the new technology being exploited to positive and dramatic effect in virtually every other sport? Football is the world game, watched and loved by countless millions of fans, yet instead of illuminating the path ahead it still shuffles along in the dark, continually racked by controversy and poor decision-making.

The Premier League is fast coming to resemble the top flight in Scotland: an annual shoot-out between a chosen few, sustainable only through the ridiculously inflated egos of their cash-sodden owners. Yet, attendances at league games are on the increase, football has never been more popular. For me, some of the magic has gone. That is exemplified by the demise of the FA Cup. Young football fans, and players alike, are being led away from the FA Cup, educated in the belief that it doesn't matter.

The sight of row upon row of empty seats at ties in the latter stages of the competition almost defies belief.

The competition's slump in popularity is not helped by the influx of foreign players who have little knowledge of the tradition and appeal of the cup and, too often, it shows.

But all those doubters, or those living in ignorance, should take note: when you get two sides up for the cup, particularly if one is Premier, the other Championship, in front of a packed crowd, there is nothing like it. The excitement level can blow your socks off. Just ask the fans of Oldham Athletic after they had dumped Liverpool in the 2013 competition. The tie at Boundary Park had thrills and spills, thud and blunder, controversy and hyperbole. In short, it was everything the FA Cup should be, and could be again, if the authorities and the top-end clubs would give back some of the prestige and unique sense of achievement that it deserves. But sadly, I can't see that happening. Instead of addressing such issues, the authorities are more interested in ideas, or gimmicks, designed solely to generate income for the top clubs.

While they are dreaming up schemes like a 39th Premier League game on foreign soil, or play-offs for the final Champions League game, perhaps they would do well to heed those wise words of Len Shipman, which appear at the beginning of this book:

> The roots of football in this country are almost certain to founder for want of nourishment if the smaller club is not to be allowed to live. The League could disintegrate at the very time it is enjoying its greatest success. Wise counsel, based on wider considerations than self-interest, must prevail.

THAT WAS THE SEVENTIES, THAT WAS

Football may, for most people, be at the centre of their particular universe but in the greater scheme of things it has to take its place in the cosmos and so, purely in keeping with the nostalgic premise of this book, this almanac of events, people and issues that shaped and defined the 1970s is designed to provide a sense of perspective where football is concerned.

1970

What Jim Lovell really said was 'Houston, we have had a problem' but Hollywood has never let the facts interfere with a good story and in the great pantheon of rewritten movie history, the omission of one word hardly amounts to a hill of beans. It was on 11 April 1970 that *Apollo 13* blasted off the tarmac at Cape Kennedy, intending to carry its three astronauts to the moon and the third lunar landing, at a cost of $4 billion. But along the way something went wrong. *Apollo 13* suddenly found itself floating in the outer space equivalent of no man's land and short of power.

Astronauts Lovell, mission commander; Jack Swigert, command module pilot; and lunar-module pilot Fred W. Haise defied shortage of fuel, loss of heat and diminishing water to nurse their craft back to earth, little realising one day their story would earn £300 million at the box office.

Was there a bigger story in 1970? Actually, there were several. It was a hot year for headlines and it all depends on your perspective as to which one had the biggest impact. For me, it came on 10 April when Paul McCartney sat in front of a battery of microphones and camera flashes to announce to the world that The Beatles were no more. It was bad enough saying farewell to the 1960s and all the pleasures it had brought but to see the band leaders, the vanguard of peace and love, the pioneers of pop, kick it all into touch was a savage blow.

So what does that say about my sense of priorities that I put it higher on my list than Concorde's first supersonic flight, the deaths of four protesting students at Kent University, Ohio, the end of Great Britain's rule in Rhodesia, or Dana winning the Eurovision Song Contest with 'All Kinds Of Everything'? The simple truth is that at the time I was more interested in sport and music than world affairs. Come to think of it, those parameters probably still apply.

1970 was Brazil's World Cup year, the brilliance of Pele, Jairzinho and captain Carlos Alberto live on in the memory. Smokin' Joe Frazier bludgeoned his way to the world heavyweight crown inside five rounds against hapless Jimmy Ellis; former champ Sonny Liston suffered the ultimate knockout, at the age of 38, and to this day no one knows if the fatal blow was self-inflicted or a mob hit.

Tragically, his wasn't the only sporting death of the year. In those far-off days before safety became the paramount issue, when you could actually see the drivers' faces and not just a multi-coloured blob of fibreglass, 1970 proved to be one of the blackest of years in Formula 1. New Zealander Bruce McLaren, whose name at least lives on, was killed at Goodwood and German-born Austrian Jochen Rindt died horrifically at the wheel of his Lotus 72 during practice for the Italian Grand Prix at Monza, having already secured enough points to take the world championship.

Tony Jacklin became the first British golfer in nearly 50 years to win the US Open, in the year after he became the first Brit in 18 years to win The Open Championship. Jacklin's victory at Hazeltine was remarkable, finishing seven shots clear of Dave Hill, and he was the only player under par. He won $30,000, compared to the $1.4 million Justin Rose trousered last year. Jacklin, of course, was the man who years later finally broke the American hold on the Ryder Cup, leading Europe to successive victories including their first in the United States. It does beg the question: why has Tony Jacklin never been knighted for his prodigious services to golf? Incidentally, that was also the year Jack Nicklaus defeated Doug Sanders, 'the peacock of the fairways', after Sanders missed a 3ft putt on the 18th at St Andrew's for the title.

Sanders eventually retired with that sad crown of the best player of his era never to win a major and many years later he was asked if he ever thought about that putt to win the Open. 'Don't think about it much,' replied Sanders. 'No more than three, four times a day.'

A horse called Nijinsky II had the best four legs in the business, winning all manner of races, including the English Triple Crown and the Irish Derby. In snooker it was the year of

Dracula (or Ray Reardon, to be more formal), the Welshman taking the first of his six world titles by beating old-timer John Pulman by the not inconsequential score of 37 frames to 33. And you thought today's lot were boring!

We are also talking about a different era in tennis ... the Australians were really quite good at it, back then. In fact, the statuesque Margaret Court was unbeatable, taking the Grand Slam of the Australian, French, Wimbledon and US Opens. And she was able to take to the floor for the traditional Wimbledon Championships opening dance with another Aussie, John Newcombe.

Musically, it wasn't a good year. For a start, Rolf Harris was everywhere with his Stylophone. As well as The Beatles calling time, so did Simon and Garfunkel, Diana Ross and the Supremes, The Monkees and the Bonzo Dog Doo Dah Band.

You might just remember this. George C. Scott produced a titanic performance in the title role of war movie *Patton* but the grumpy persona of the snarling World War Two American general seemed to have stuck because when they called out Scott's name at the Oscars, he wasn't there. Apparently, he was at home watching ice hockey on TV and later commented, 'The whole thing is a goddamn meat parade! I don't want any part of it.' Still, it all helped at the box office as the movie became the fourth-biggest grossing picture of the year.

And top of the tickets that year? *Love Story*.

1971

Graeme MacKenzie took the new ball for Australia and bowled a sharp delivery to Yorkshire's Geoff Boycott. The scene was the Melbourne Cricket Ground, the date 5 January 1971, and the occasion? The very first One Day International.

THAT WAS THE SEVENTIES, THAT WAS

It was a hastily arranged affair to appease a large final-day crowd after the Test match had been aborted due to rain. In the event, 46,000 enthusiastic, curious cricket fans piled into the ground to share the novel experience. What they saw encapsulated the future for one-day cricket.

England were rubbish, Australia won at a canter, despite the fact that English counties had been playing limited overs stuff for a decade.

Australian captain Bill Lawry won the toss and elected to field. England managed a paltry 190 from their 40 eight-ball overs, John Edrich top scoring with 82. It was all too easy for the Aussies. Ian Chappell led their run chase with 60 and they knocked off the target with more than six overs to spare.

The idea caught on, although no one was quite sure about the format, and in 1975 England hosted the World Cup. The winners were the West Indies. It would take the intervention of a mega-rich media tycoon named Kerry Packer later in the decade to exploit limited overs potential with his pyjama game, but on that day in January 1971, 46,000 can say they witnessed the first tentative steps of a revolution.

There were other revolutions to talk about during that year: Idi Amin took over Uganda; the British government took over a bankrupt Rolls-Royce; Britain switched to decimal currency and IRA terrorists exploded a bomb in London's Post Office Tower.

The year had started badly. Long before Heysel and Hillsborough, events at Ibrox Park in Glasgow at the end of the 'Old Firm' derby had illustrated, graphically and tragically, the potential for disaster whenever huge crowds are accumulated in confined spaces.

Ask people today who remember those events and they will, likely as not, trot out the popular version, handed down the years by a kind of Chinese whispers, that with the game near its end and Celtic winning 1-0, Rangers fans began to stream down the exit stairs, only to turn back when Colin Stein scored a late equaliser. But an Inquiry into the disaster ruled that out. Everyone was moving in the same direction, it concluded, and it was the collapse of steel barriers, giving way under the crush of so many fans, which caused the pile-up and the deaths of 66 fans. Ibrox today is a much safer environment for watching football but the scars remain, the memories never fade, the names are forever etched in Glasgow's history. Rangers' captain on the day was John Greig: 'From a personal point of view, it's something I'll never forget. It's always at the back of my mind when I take people around the new stadium we have rebuilt that it has been built in memory for those unfortunate supporters and their families.'

People don't forget but the tide of life continues to ebb and flow and the world of sport had one or two other important stories to tell in the year of 1971. The biggest was played out in Madison Square Garden, New York, when undefeated heavyweight champion of the world Smokin' Joe Frazier met undefeated challenger, and bitter rival, Muhammed Ali. It was Ali's first fight in three years. When he last went in the ring, he had been Cassius Clay, world champ, but his refusal to answer the Vietnam draft cost him his title and his living. Reinstated on appeal, he fought twice to earn the right to challenge Frazier, dubbed 'the black Marciano'.

In front of the glitterati, which included Frank Sinatra, Woody Allen and Burt Lancaster, the two warriors slugged themselves to a standstill. It was a merciless, mesmerising battle: Frazier the puncher, bobbing and weaving around Ali's rapier-like jabs. It was close to the end, but when Frazier dumped Ali on the seat of his pants in the 15th round, he just about clinched a points verdict. It was the first of three ground-shaking encounters and we will catch up with the sequels as the decade unfolds.

Elsewhere Eddy Merckx won the third of his five successive Tour de France titles, Jack Nicklaus won another major (US Masters) and it was Australia Day again at Wimbledon with John Newcombe this time sharing the singles glory with Evonne Goolagong. It was also the year a 16-year-old named Chris Evert competed for the first time at the US Open, losing in the semi-final to eventual winner Billie Jean King.

Scotland's Jackie Stewart took the F1 championship but the sport was in mourning again, this time for Mexican racer Pedro Rodriguez, who was killed while competing in a sports-car race in Germany, nine years after his brother Ricardo had died in the Mexican GP.

The French Connection swept the top awards at the Oscars in a year that also had *Fiddler On The Roof* earning the most money and *A Clockwork Orange* the biggest controversy. Director Stanley Kubrick finally brought Anthony Burgess's apocalyptic story to the screen with Malcolm McDowell leading his gang of Droogs – a definite improvement on original plans to feature The Rolling Stones.

1971 was the year Mick Jagger married Bianca Peres Moreno de Macias and went into tax exile in France, Jim Morrison took his last bath and either side of the Atlantic, something was stirring. In London a singer named Farookh Bulsara was completing a promising line-up of Imperial College students. He would become Freddie Mercury and they were Queen. In California a five-piece country-rock band was about to start their meteoric rise to fame, fortune and all the other trappings of rock and roll, under the performing name of The Eagles.

And now for something completely different. The Monty Python team were at the peak of their popularity, trying to flog dead parrots, singing about Spam and gay Lumberjacks, and creating that classic Upper-Class Twit of the Year obstacle race. Memory suggests there was quite a bit of decent television to enjoy in 1971. Was it a case of little is more, or were we so easily pleased?

The Liver Birds was the top sit-com, Brucie's Bonus could always guarantee *The Generation Game* was worth watching, and who could forget The Phantom Raspberry Blower of Old London Town, created by the brilliant Ronnie Barker and Ronnie Corbett, although, to be accurate, the raspberry was actually blown by David Jason? But my favourite TV memory of 1971 has to be the first showing of Steven Spielberg's breakthrough movie in which businessman Dennis Weaver is chased along sand-blown desert roads by a sinister truck that seems to have a life of its own. Called *Duel*, it has become something of a cult classic.

1972

Bernard Manning used to tell this joke about going to Newcastle with George Best to launch a ship. 'Never happened,' said Bernard. 'George wouldn't let go of the frigging bottle!' Then there was one about going to Old Trafford for a match and an officious-looking doorman sees him and says, 'Straight through, Mr Manning.' Behind Bernard came Seb Coe and the doorman tells him he will have to use the entrance on the other side of the ground. 'Don't you know who I am?' he replies. 'I'm Seb Coe.' 'Well,' says the doorman, 'it won't take you long then, will it?'

Manning was a stalwart of the hit TV show *The Comedians*, which was first aired in 1972 with a line-up that included Russ

Abbot, Lennie Bennett, Jim Bowen, Duggie Brown, Frank Carson, Colin Crompton, Stu Francis, Ken Goodwin, Tom O'Connor and Mike Reid. The show finished its life in 1994 when Les Dennis was the lead act.

It was quite a year for pioneering television. The first series of highbrow quiz show *Mastermind* was aired and proved an instant hit, helped enormously by the intimidating atmosphere in which contestants sat in a darkened room under a harsh spotlight, to be interrogated by stern host Magnus 'I've started so I'll finish' Magnusson. I was hardly surprised to discover that director Bill Wright drew on wartime memories of the Gestapo to create the inquisition.

An irritatingly clever detective also walked into our lives in 1972 when actor Peter Falk created Lt Columbo. Falk lost an eye through disease at the age of three and for a time it seemed likely to hamper his acting career.

He once failed a screen test at Columbia Pictures and was told by studio boss Harry Cohn that 'for the same price I can get an actor with two eyes'. But *Columbo* gave Falk everlasting fame as, over the decades, he brought some of the most famous guest stars in Hollywood to justice, among them Leonard Nimoy, Patrick McGoohan, William Shatner and Dick Van Dyke. But here's a piece of trivia for the next time you are in the pub – who was the only star of *Columbo* to 'get away with it'? Answer: Janet Leigh in an episode called 'The Forgotten Lady'.

It can't be described as a great year for music, however, not with Donny Osmond's 'Puppy Love' and The New Seekers attempting to teach the world to sing. And it was also the year rhythm and blues pioneer Chuck Berry had his only Number One hit. The genius behind songs like 'Johnny B. Goode', 'Memphis Tennessee' and 'Sweet Little Sixteen' hit the top spot with a daft novelty song called 'My Ding-A-Ling', helped in no small way by TV clean-up campaigner Mary Whitehouse calling for it to be banned.

A new phrase, which has since been exploited by writers the world over – and may even be found within the pages of this tome – was heard for the first time. 'I'm gonna make him an offer he can't refuse,' mumbled Marlon Brando in top-grossing film of the year, *The Godfather*. Brando, who hit the mark again in 1972 with a promotional film for the butter industry called *Last Tango In Paris*, won the Best Actor Oscar for his portrayal of cuddly old Vito Corleone but he didn't turn up to collect it, sending a Native-American woman named Sacheen Littlefeather in his place, to make a point about the way her race had been treated by the film industry.

Personally, I would have given it to that banjo player in *Deliverance*. The sequence where he plays 'Duellin' Banjos' while a grizzled old hillbilly does a tap dance in the dust remains one of spookiest moments in the movies. And on the subject of eerie moments, in January 1972 a Japanese soldier named Shoichi Yokoi was found hiding in a cave on the Pacific island of Guam. He had been there for 28 years, having gone on the run after American troops had liberated the island in 1944, still believing his country to be at war with the world.

That war was long since passed but on the streets of Northern Ireland the Troubles were just beginning. 30 January has passed into history as Bloody Sunday, the day 13 unarmed civil-rights marchers were shot and killed when men of the 1st Battalion The Parachute Regiment opened fire. The whys and wherefores of that tragic incident are still being analysed and debated to this day but it would set the tone for a year of global terrorism, culminating in the massacre of 11 Israeli athletes at the Munich

Olympic Games by Arab terrorists calling themselves Black September, an atrocity followed by millions on television.

In competition, Munich gave us Mark Spitz and his seven swimming golds, the charm of gymnast Olga Korbut and a grand total of four British gold medals, led by smiling pentathlete Mary Peters.

But the year's greatest sporting drama was played out in the final minutes, over the last two holes of the 1972 Open Golf Championship at Muirfield. Scunthorpe-born Tony Jacklin, the player who had reignited interest in the sport in Britain by winning the 1969 Open and 1970 US Open, was tied for the lead with wisecracking Tex-Mex character Lee Trevino as they came to the par-five 17th. Trevino hit his fourth shot way over the green onto a steeply sloping bank and immediately indulged in a spot of angry club throwing. Jacklin fired his third to the green and had an 18ft putt for a birdie: the Open was within his grasp. But, not for the first time that day, Trevino stunned Jacklin and the gallery. Believing he had blown his chance, he nonchalantly slapped the ball onto the green and then watched in amazement as it curled towards the flag and quietly slipped into the hole. A shattered Jacklin raced his putt three feet past the hole, missed the next and, in that brief episode in time, relinquished his chance of a second Open. He would never come that close again.

Trevino's post-match view didn't help. 'I had already told Jacklin, "Take it on out, baby. I'm cooked, I'm done – stick a fork in me."' Jacklin has never forgotten the blow to his heart – 'I've watched film of what happened again and again and I wince every time I see it.'

Now I didn't remember this. Ask me who won Wimbledon in Jubilee year 1977 and the answer is straight there, easy, Virginia Wade. Ask me who won the 1972 Australian Women's Open and I wouldn't have had a clue but it is the same answer: Virginia Wade. Wade also won the 1968 US Open and, at the time of writing, remains the last British woman to win any Grand Slam singles title.

The lady should be made a dame.

1973

It has to be said that 1973 wasn't exactly a great time to be a politician – either in the UK or across the pond.

The scandal in Britain came about, basically, because certain prominent MPs couldn't keep it in their trousers, while Americans came to the conclusion that they had a president who couldn't lie straight in bed.

Antony Lambton was a Harrow-educated Tory MP who had worked his way up to the position of a junior Minister for Defence when his predilection for the services of Mayfair prostitutes was exposed. Lambton, a viscount by inheritance – his brother shot himself – but who insisted on being known simply as Lord Lambton, was forced to resign from Harold Macmillan's government when a photograph of him in bed with two call girls, while smoking marijuana, was made public. Well, might as well be hung for a sheep as a lamb!

There were fears that, as a defence minister, national security might have been compromised, just as it had 10 years earlier during the Profumo affair but an Inquiry decided there was nothing much to worry about. When later interviewed by Robin Day, Lambton brazenly claimed he had often used 'whores for sex' because 'people sometimes like variety. It's as simple as that.'

President Richard Nixon was caught with his proverbial pants down over the Watergate scandal when he was implicated in a cover-up conspiracy after a break-in at the Democratic Party

HQ. As some of his aides were invited to experience the American penal system's equivalent of porridge, Nixon, politically isolated, faced the threat of impeachment.

This was also the year that 16-year-old John Paul Getty III hit the headlines when he was kidnapped, in Rome, with a $17 million ransom placed on his head. It all got a bit messy when his dad, JPG II, asked grandad JPG I for the cash and the old man said 'no' ... until the kidnappers sent the family JPG III's ear in the post! Even then filthy-rich Getty Sr didn't want to pay up and finally got his grandson back for a knockdown $2 million, arguing, had he just paid up, all his grandchildren would have been at risk. Sadly, young John Paul never quite recovered from the ordeal, falling into a chasm of alcohol and drug addiction.

And just to complete this round-up of gloom and despair, 1973 was also the year of the Yom Kippur War, which resulted in a 20-day Israeli victory; the oil crisis as OPEC hit back at the Americans for helping Israel's war effort; and the IRA bombing of Whitehall and the Old Bailey.

Time for some light relief ... so how about a glimpse of Nora Batty's wrinkled stockings, seen for the first time in *Last Of The Summer Wine*? Even dafter, Michael Crawford doing his 'ooh, Betty' bit in *Some Mothers Do 'Ave 'Em*. Smuttier was *Are You Being Served?* with Mrs Slocombe and her ubiquitous pussy.

Roger Moore raised an eyebrow for the first time as James Bond in *Live And Let Die* and there was much turning of heads in the classic shocker *The Exorcist*, especially when it shot to the top of the box-office list for the year. Amazing what a bit of foul language and green vomit can do for putting bums on seats! But I tend to agree, for once, with the Oscars jury, which chose *The Sting* as Best Picture, with Paul Newman and Robert Redford at their finest.

BEST, PELE AND A HALF-TIME BOVRIL

Having been a teenager through the 1960s and, by now, happily married with child number one due, 1973 was probably my last year of musical dedication. I could put up with Sweet's 'Blockbuster' and a bit of Slade – but Donny Osmond, Peters & Lee and David Cassidy? I finally came to the desperate conclusion that the days of The Grateful Dead, Pretty Things and MC5's 'Kick Out The Jams, Motherfucker!' were well and truly over. '*Quelle domage*', as Del Boy would say ... only not for a few years yet.

Now, I don't know the first thing about horse racing. I can name you a few horses, a few jockeys, but I couldn't tell you who won what, where and when, except for one: three times Grand National champion and the nation's favourite pony, Red Rum, who did it for the first time in April 1973. It was one of the great Aintree races with Crisp, the mount of Richard Pitman, looking for all the world like the winner until the last fence, which he clobbered good and hard, lost his rhythm and, in the final couple of strides, lost the race as Brian Fletcher urged old Rummy across the line. It was the start of the Red Rum legend.

Elsewhere in sport, Ray Illingworth relinquished the captaincy of the England Test team after a thrashing by the West Indies, and F1 ace Jackie Stewart retired after his fellow Tyrrell team driver François Cevert was killed in practice for the US Grand Prix. It was not the only motor-racing tragedy of the year. Roger Williamson crashed during the Dutch GP at Zandvoort and was trapped in his blazing car. Despite the efforts of fellow racer David Purley, dramatically witnessed by a huge TV audience, nothing could be done to rescue the stricken young Brit.

Champions that year included George Foreman, who took the heavyweight title off Joe Frazier; American golfer Tom Weiskopf, who won the Open, his only major triumph; a Czech named Jan

Kodes took advantage of the Wimbledon tennis row over professionalism, which led to a boycott of leading players and Ray Readon beat Eddie Charlton 38-32 in snooker.

There is one final sporting postscript to 1973 that is worthy of mention. In American football a certain OJ Simpson became the first player in NFL history to rush for more than 2,000 yards in a single season and was voted Male Athlete of the Year. Now, whatever happened to him?

1974

Since a long-forgotten lady named Lys Assia won the first Eurovision Song Contest for Switzerland in 1956, it is probably fair to say that only two international, everlasting careers have been directly launched by the show – *Riverdance* in 1994 and, 20 years earlier, the phenomenon that was Abba. How could any red-blooded male forget the sight of Agnetha Fältskog in those skin-tight, shimmering blue pantaloons, tottering on high-heeled spandex boots, while Benny Andersson strummed away on a guitar that had more points than a compass? 'Waterloo' won by a country mile (Australian Olivia Newton-John finished fourth for GB with 'Long Live Love').

From there Abba's rise was stratospheric and 40 years on the cash cow shows no signs of ageing. At times it was cheesy, always ultra-commercial, but there is no denying Benny and Bjorn Ulvaeus did pen some of the best pop songs of all time and, along with Lennon and McCartney and the Bee Gees, must be rated as some of the most influential songwriters of the modern era.

And it wasn't only Abba making significant musical moves in 1974. Within a few weeks of each other the Ramones and Van Halen debuted, Mick Taylor left the Rolling Stones, Peter Gabriel left Genesis, and Fleetwood Mac adopted the line-up that would carry them towards the all-conquering *Rumours* album when Lindsay Buckingham and Stevie Nicks were added to the staff. On the sales front, 'Kung Fu Fighting' by Craig Douglas was as big as any that year.

Moviegoers were appalled and amused in equal measure by Mel Brooks' provocative comedy *Blazing Saddles*, which was way ahead of its time yet so politically incorrect there is no way its sledgehammer approach to racism and flatulence would be allowed today. *Carry On Cowboy* without the subtlety or, as Brookes himself was heard to say, 'It rose below vulgarity.' It was just pipped by a few million dollars in the box-office stakes by *Towering Inferno*, arguably the best of the 1970s fondness for disaster movies – *Earthquake* was another big hitter in 1974 – winning three Oscars out of eight nominations.

We met a selection of unforgettable TV characters that year, including Mr 'Lah-de-Da' Gunner Graham, Bombardier 'Gloria' Graham and little 'Lofty' Sugden in *It Ain't Half Hot Mum*; and Norman Stanley Fletcher in Ronnie Barker's magnificent prison sit-com, *Porridge*. But it was also the end for Monty Python as a TV show, although there were even finer moments to come on the big screen.

Broadcast on 5 December, the swansong ran under the collective title of *Party Political Broadcast* and included memorable sketches including 'The Most Awful Family in Britain', 'Appeal on Behalf of Extremely Rich People' and 'The Man Who Finishes Other People's Sentences'.

There was something of a phenomenon in Hollywood, a sequel arguably better than the original. That is the popular conception of *The Godfather II* in which Robert De Niro picked up the role of young Vito Corleone and turned it into an Oscar-winning vehicle, to go with Best Picture, Best Director, Best

Script Page Turner ... you name it, this movie probably won it. Personally, I thought *Chinatown* knocked it into a cocked hat, but what do I know?

In real life, there was just as much drama, topped by the resignation of Richard Nixon over the Watergate Scandal and his alleged part in it. He sloped out of office, proclaiming he wasn't a crook, and a year later, that nice Mr Gerald Ford, who had taken over Nixon's White House throne, gave him a pardon.

Newspaper heiress Patty Hearst grabbed headlines around the world when she was kidnapped by the Symbionese Liberation Army – in truth, a bunch of well-heeled, middle-class, All-American kids who fancied a spot of rebellion under the clarion cry, 'Death to the fascist insect that preys upon the life of the people'. Exactly! Later in the year young Patty reappeared, although now known as 'Tania' and brandishing a rifle as the SLA pulled a bank heist. Revolution comes with a price tag, you know. Anyway, to cut a long story short, the FBI gunned down half a dozen SLA members before capturing Hearst, who was later tried, sentenced to seven years' hard labour for bank robbery, released after 21 months and, years later, pardoned by that nice Mr Clinton.

Mixed-up Ian Ball got the royal brush-off when he tried to kidnap feisty Princess Anne at gunpoint and discovered she was having none of it. Naff orf!

And just to remind you that there is nothing new under the sun, the global recession was deepening, the oil crisis was causing shortages at the pumps and Britain was gripped by a series of strikes. Plenty for the voters to think about ... and they had to make their minds up twice in a single year after the first election brought about a hung parliament. Harold Wilson won the rematch with Edward Heath and Liberal leader Jeremy Thorpe on the losing side.

Muhammad Ali continued to be the most talked about, best-loved and most recognisable sportsman on the planet, adding to his legend with an extraordinary victory over world heavyweight title-holder George Foreman in the 'Rumble in the Jungle' in Kinshasa, Zaire. Ali adopted a calculating tactic, soaking up Foreman's incessant attacks for round after round until the champion was, to put it bluntly, knackered. Come the 8th and only 20 seconds to the bell, Ali suddenly exploded off the ropes with a flurry of brutal punches: a left, a right, another left. The champ is down; he doesn't look like beating the count. Eight, nine, ten … you're out, sucker! Ali is champion again.

1974 was also the last hurrah for the greatest cricketer the world has ever seen, one Sir Garfield St Aubrun Sobers, who played his final Test match for the West Indies, against England in Port of Spain, Trinidad. He would have wanted to sign off with a win but he was thwarted by that quintessential Englishman Tony Greig – I know, sarcasm is the lowest form of wit, but that South African accent did used to grate, especially in the Home Counties. In the event, Greigy returned match figures of 13 for 156 to guide England to victory and level the series. As for Sir Garry, he finished his career with more than 8,000 Test runs, 235 Test wickets and 109 catches.

Another stellar sporting icon recorded his final triumph. He was Gary Player. Fifteen years after he won his first Open Championship and his first major, the South African golfer won his ninth and last major, fittingly in the Open Championship, at Lytham St Anne's.

Red Rum won his second Grand National, Emerson Fittipaldi took the F1 championship and Eddy Merckx won his fifth and final Tour de France.

It was outside a fish and chip shop in a Nottinghamshire mining village that the vicious killer Donald Neilson's reign of terror came to a close. You will remember him better by his media soubriquet, 'The Black Panther'. Neilson had killed four people by the time he was captured on a cold December day in 1975.

He had shot dead sub-postmasters Donald Skepper, Derek Astin and Sidney Grayland during his merciless crime spree in Yorkshire, Lancashire and the West Midlands but the atrocity that catapulted him to the top of the wanted list was the kidnap and subsequent murder of teenage heiress Lesley Whittle.

Two Notts police constables stopped their panda car for a routine check on a man walking along the road and suddenly came face to face with a double-barrelled shotgun. Neilson climbed into the police car and forced the officers to drive off. As they reached the little mining village of Rainworth, the officers made a grab for the gun, which went off in the struggle. The car stopped outside a chippie and customers raced to help overpower the killer. Neilson is now serving a life sentence for his crimes.

So, too, is Peter Sutcliffe, aka The Yorkshire Ripper, who began his violence against women on a June night in Keighley, attacking a woman with a hammer and leaving her for dead. He would continue the attacks for the next six years, on 13 defenceless victims, before being caught by a similar piece of routine policing.

The IRA campaign of violence showed no signs of easing. London was hit by four bombing incidents, the highest profile being an explosion at the Hilton Hotel, which claimed two lives, and they also targeted Ross McWhirter, co-founder of *The Guinness Book of Records*, and a high-profile critic of the Irish struggle, having offered a £50,000 reward for the capture of the bombers.

Down in the town of Alberquerque, New Mexico, the roots of a monster were being planted. A former college student developed a version of the programming language BASIC for the first microcomputer – the MITS Altair. From that small beginning, along with his friend Paul Allen, he created a company now known as Microsoft. He is, of course, Bill Gates.

On 30 April the city of Saigon fell to the communist army of North Vietnam, leading to a mass evacuation of American and South Vietnamese personnel and the symbolic film of the last helicopter rising from the American embassy roof as Vietcong tanks rumbled through the streets of the city. It was also the year Maggie Thatcher pushed Edward Heath out of the Conservative leadership; a UK referendum backed our membership of the EU, and the Birmingham Six were jailed for crimes it was later proved they didn't commit.

Financially, if you think we have had it bad the last couple of years, cast your mind back to 1975, when spiralling inflation hit 24.2 per cent and the price of petrol increased by nearly 70 per cent to 72p a gallon. That's a gallon, mind – we still hadn't succumbed to the litre, back then. The average house price was around £11,700 – which equates to about £70,000 today. And just to put all the 21st-century monetary doom and gloom into some sort of perspective, spare a thought for New Yorkers. Their city was about to go bankrupt until President Gerald Ford loaned them a bit of cash to tide them over ... around $3 billion.

The big musical notes in the year of the curly perm came with the Bee Gees' hit singles 'Nights On Broadway', which had Barry Gibb singing falsetto for the first time, followed by the disco single 'Jive Talkin''. The Bee Gees had found the new sound they were looking for – history was beckoning. And Freddie Mercury put pen to paper and from somewhere drew the surreal musical picture he called 'Bohemian Rhapsody'. Although nearly six minutes long, Mercury's friend DJ Kenny Everett gave it radio air time and it shot to Number One, where it stayed for a record nine weeks.

It was a year of real contrast in the charts: from the sublime David Bowie's 'Space Oddity' and 10cc's 'I'm Not In Love' to the ridiculous, topped by Windsor Davies and Don Estelle from *It Ain't Half Hot Mum*, singing 'Whispering Grass' and Billy Connolly's Tammy Wynette spoof 'D.I.V.O.R.C.E.'.

The year also saw the first concert by the Sex Pistols, the birth of Motörhead and the Boomtown Rats, along with the demise of The Faces. And if you had enough cash, and a dashboard the size of a 747, you might have listened to the latest sounds on an eight-track autocharger.

It was the music that got you in the year's big movie. Suddenly, we all had a best mate who thought it was a real hoot to creep up behind you, going 'der-der ... der-der'. Right, *very* funny! *Jaws* set box-office records that wouldn't be beaten until the dawn of *Star Wars* and established Stephen Spielberg as the *wunderkind* of Hollywood directors. The story goes that Charlton Heston desperately wanted the part of police chief Brody, which went to Roy Schieider. After he was turned down Heston had a go at Spielberg and vowed never to work with him. I bet Spielberg was gutted!

It didn't make as much money as *Jaws* but cult status has been afforded *The Rocky Horror Picture Show*. As Frank-N-Furter suggests, 'Give yourself over to absolute pleasure'.

Speaking of pleasure, TV introduced us to Farty Towels ... sorry *Fawlty Towers*, and its array of suitably manic characters led by John Cleese's brilliant creation Basil Fawlty. Whenever I hear him tell that deaf old battleaxe, 'What did you expect to see out of a

Torquay hotel bedroom window? Sydney Opera House, perhaps? The Hanging Gardens of Babylon?' I cannot resist a chuckle.

Muhammed Ali and Joe Frazier renewed their rivalry for the third and final time in the Phillippines, where Ali won a TKO but only after both fighters had knocked seven bells out of each other in what many claim was the finest heavyweight title fight in history. Well, Ali would say that, wouldn't he?

Arthur Ashe became the first black tennis player to win the Wimbledon Men's Singles title – nearly 30 years after American Althea Gibson had claimed the same honour for the Women's. And on 30 December 1975 at Cypress Cliffs, California, Earl and Kultida Woods became the proud parents of a bouncing baby boy they named Eldrick but who will forever be known simply as Tiger.

1976

Phew, it was a scorcher! Week after week of record temperatures topping 30ºC, sunburned bodies and tinder-dry grass, forest fires and melting tar, happy holiday memories.

How was your luck? Better than mine, I hope ... and certainly better than celebrated hermit, multi-millionaire and hypochondriac Howard Hughes, who checked out for the final time on a plane trip to hospital having spent the last decade of his life locked behind the penthouse doors of various hotels around the world. So few people had seen Hughes, they had to check his fingerprints to make sure it was really him. The aviation pioneer and intimate friend of Hollywood stars such as Lana Turner and Jane Russell left an estate worth a measly $2 billion.

It was lights out as well for Ulrike Meinhof, co-leader of the notorious urban-terrorist gang, the Red Army Faction, who hanged herself in her German prison cell, thus saving the authorities from a task they were perhaps looking forward to, considering she had spent the previous few years bombing and robbing her way across the country.

Infinitely less palatable was the death of Dora Bloch, a 74-year-old British passenger on an Air France jet hijacked by Palestinian terrorists and flown to Uganda. While ailing Mrs Bloch was being treated in a Kampala hospital, Israeli Special Forces assaulted the aircraft, killed the terrorists and freed the rest of the passengers. In his fury, Ugandan president Idi Amin sent a murder squad to drag Mrs Bloch from her bed and murder her. The Israelis called the mission 'Operation Thunderball' but it has since become known as the Entebbe Raid.

Early in 1976 that remarkable Anglo-French triumph called Concorde flew commercially for the first time, covering the 3,500-mile trip to Bahrain in 4 hours, 15 minutes. The Americans weren't impressed and banned Concorde until 1977 on environmental grounds, even forcing HM The Queen to cross the Atlantic on the Royal Yacht instead, when she attended the USA's bicentennial celebrations. But really it was just that they were so annoyed because they couldn't come up with anything supersonic of their own.

And so to sport, which was also packed with drama, politics, triumph and tragedy in fairly equal measures. It started with the Olympic Games – scheduled for Montreal but on the brink of cancellation because Canada refused to recognise independent Taiwan in favour of the People's Republic of China. This prompted a bunch of African nations to withdraw but the Games went ahead, allowing names like Nadia Comaneci, Alberto Juantorena and Sugar Ray Leonard to become sporting legends. There was also a little bit of history when show jumper Princess Anne became the only female competitor not required to take a sex test.

In cricket, England came up against the West Indies at Old Trafford. The Windies opened their gentle attack with Andy Roberts, Wayne Daniel and Michael Holding, a chap they called 'Whispering Death'. Less than 30 overs later, England were back in the hutch with just 71 on the board. It was James Hunt's year in F1, taking the title in his McLaren, but not a good season for Niki Lauda and Ferrari. The Austrian driver was horrifically burned in a crash at the Nürburgring – a race he had wanted cancelled because of his safety fears. And finally, an ice-cool Swede with the personality of a raw potato but the talent of a tennis god won the first of five consecutive Wimbledon titles. Hard to believe Björn Borg and Abba share a national identity.

Speaking of Abba, they had more hits in 1976 than you could shake a stick at: 'Mamma Mia', 'Dancing Queen', 'Fernando' – not even the Wurzels, who topped the charts with 'Combine Harvester', could match that. Remember the best of the rest? Showaddywaddy ('Under The Moon Of Love'), Demis Roussos ('Forever and Ever'), Brotherhood of Man, who won Eurovision with 'Save Your Kisses For Me'. Still, it wasn't all bad. The Sex Pistols were snapped up by EMI and suddenly yellow Mohican haircuts and noses stapled with paper clips became fashion essentials. Later in the year they politely told TV presenter Bill Grundy where to stick it, getting him sacked and ensuring their everlasting notoriety. The Eagles released 'Hotel California' and in Ireland a band called Feedback (now U2) was formed.

The *Rocky* franchise began with Sly Stallone's inspirational story about stumblebum fighter Rocky Balboa's climb to the top of the boxing world, which pulled in an impressive three Oscars, and there was also that remarkable dialogue from *Taxi Driver* Travis Bickle: 'You talkin' to me? You talkin' to me? You talkin' to me? Then who the hell else are you talking ... you talking to me? Well, I'm the only one here. Who the fuck do you think you're talking to?' De Niro was never better.

Now, I'm not sure how it happened but the must-watch TV show of the year featured a bunch of felt-faced puppets with oddly whining voices who became ridiculously popular and achieved a fair degree of celebrity. Even the notoriously grumpy Bob Dylan agreed to be a guest of The Muppets and who could ever forget Michael Parkinson trying to get it on with a dummy named Miss Piggy? Other televisual delights in 1976 were *Starsky & Hutch*, who spawned a global epidemic of horrendous granny-knit cardigans, *The Rise and Fall of Reginald Perrin* and *When The Boat Comes In*.

And finally, back to the news and one of those daft stories about Australian painter and clairvoyant John Nash who sold his home, packed up his belongings and left the city of Adelaide behind because he was convinced it was about to be obliterated. According to a Reuters report, 'The biggest wave seen on the beachfront at Glenelg was a six-inch high ripple on the surf'.

1977

Think back to 16 August 1977 and I bet you know exactly where you were when you heard the news. Elvis Presley was dead, the King of Rock 'n' Roll was no more – he had succumbed to an addiction to prescription pills and artery-blocking junk food at the age of 42. It was one of those singular moments in time that no one ever forgets. JFK, John Lennon, Princess Diana and Elvis – the big four.

Presley was found dead on his bathroom floor. Not down in the jungle room with the guys who became known as the Memphis Mafia, nor in his bed. It was an undignified end for the man who had influenced a generation and whose legacy is as strong today as it ever was. Everyone one knows the story but is it the full story? Following Elvis's death, his father Vernon demanded that the autopsy report be sealed for 50 years. We will have to wait until the year 2027 to discover the truth.

There was another major news story from 1977 – the collision between two Boeing 747 'jumbo' jets on the runway at the old Tenerife North airport. A KLM flight with 248 passengers was coming into land at the fog-bound airport, just as a Pan Am jet carrying 396 people was taxiing along the same runway. The landing gear of KLM 4805 ripped into the roof of Pan Am 1736, destroying both aircraft in a catastrophic inferno of burning aviation fuel. When the smoke cleared, only 61 people had been rescued alive. And a Boeing 747 was in the news again later in the year when it piggy-backed the first Space Shuttle towards free flight.

Double killer Gary Gilmore faced execution by a Utah firing squad with the final words 'Let's do it' and was then immortalised, first by Norman Mailer in his award-winning book, *The Executioner's Song*, and then by actor Tommy Lee Jones when the story was transferred to the big screen. Several months later, American justice would also catch up with David Berkowitz, a New York killer who became known as the 'Son of Sam'.

On the home front, the Troubles in Northern Ireland continued to dominate headlines, the disappearance and apparent murder of SAS officer Robert Nairac being one of the major stories of the year.

It was left to HM The Queen to try and lift the gloom as she embarked on a marathon national tour to mark her Silver Jubilee, an event celebrated by several sports, most notably tennis, with Virginia Wade appropriately winning the Jubilee Women's Singles title at Wimbledon; and England stuffed the Aussies 3-0 to seize the Ashes. That wasn't the only significant outcome of the series, however. For the third Test played at Trent Bridge, England, already one up in the series, brought a prodigious young all-rounder named Ian Botham into their XI. The 21-year-old took 5 for 74 to begin a career-long personal crusade against the Aussies.

But Botham hadn't made the trip Down Under in March 1977 for the Centenary Test match to be played at the Melbourne Cricket Ground where, 100 years earlier, Australia had won the first Test match by 45 runs. It turned out to be a remarkable occasion: Australia were shot out for 138, England made just 95. Australia then posted a score of 419, leaving England with a victory target of 452. Nottinghamshire's Derek Randall led the charge with 174, one of the best innings by an English batsmen Down Under. Randall had to face a fearsome barrage of bouncers from the deadly duo of Dennis Lillee and Jeff Thomson and at one point, after ducking under yet another head-high bumper, he doffed his cap to Lillee. Sadly, Randall's heroics weren't enough, England finishing 45 runs short – bizarrely, the exact figure by which they had lost in 1877.

The United States once again thrashed Great Britain and Ireland in the Ryder Cup, leading Jack Nicklaus to come up with the idea of including European players in the GB&I side, to save the biennial event from dying of boredom. It proved to be a double-edged sword. The Ryder Cup is now one of the biggest sporting spectacles in the world but the US, having lost only three times in the previous 50 years, are playing catch-up.

Niki Lauda completed a remarkable comeback from his injuries to clinch the 1977 F1 title but, once again, the sport claimed a life, with Welshman Tom Pryce dying at the wheel of his Shadow car when he collided with a track marshal at Kyalami in South Africa.

It was a blockbuster year at the box office with the first *Star Wars* movie hitting the silver screen, making the career of Harrison Ford, who can perhaps count himself a little fortunate as Kurt Russell, Nick Nolte, Christopher Walken, Jack Nicholson, Al Pacino, Chevy Chase, Steve Martin and Bill Murray were also considered for the role of Han Solo. And the Bee Gees struck paydirt with *Saturday Night Fever*, prompting Barry Gibb to comment, 'It changed our lives. We're very proud that music created so long ago is still appreciated and treated as current. But we still just don't get it!'

Then there was that other bunch of nice young lads who came up with a song with which to mark the Queen's Silver Jubilee – and immediately earned themselves a place in the rock 'n' roll hall of shame. The Sex Pistols released the single 'God Save The Queen', which the BBC banned because of its 'treasonous sentiments', taken from their equally controversial album, *Never Mind The Bollocks*.

Paul McCartney penned a far gentler and more acceptable ditty for the year's biggest single, the monotone called 'Mull Of Kintyre', and Fleetwood Mac produced far and away the best collection of songs in 1977 with their timeless album, *Rumours*.

In telly land, Wolfie's anthem 'Power To The People' helped to make Robert Lindsay's *Citizen Smith* the best sit-com of the year.

1978

Here is a question for trivia buffs: what nationality was the first man not from the USA or the USSR to go into space? The answer fooled me as well. I was thinking maybe a German, on the grounds that they have known a thing or two about rockets since way back. Canadian? Brit? Ten points if you guessed it was Czech cosmonaut Vladimír Remek. A useless bit of knowledge admittedly but you never know when it might crop up in the pub quiz.

Louise Brown is another good pub-quiz question. She became the world's first test-tube baby when she was born on 25 July in a hospital in Manchester. She weighed in at a fragile 5lb 12oz but her survival also gave birth (!) to the fertility revolution that has helped millions of couples ever since. As for Louise, she is now happily married with a family of her own. All say 'aah!'

And can you remember the name of that chap who was murdered in the centre of London, stabbed with a poison-tipped umbrella? All very Ian Fleming, but chillingly true. His name was Georgi Markov, a Bulgarian writer who fled his Stalinist homeland and then made a number of anti-government broadcasts from the West. It is assumed he was murdered by the Bulgarian Secret Police with a bit of help from the KGB. Markov's killer was never caught, unlike another of those dubiously celebrated American monsters Ted Bundy, trapped after killing an estimated 35 people in a five-year lust for blood. He was executed in 1989.

The most notorious crime in Britain happened on a September afternoon when paperboy Carl Bridgewater arrived at a remote farmhouse in Staffordshire to deliver a newspaper to an elderly couple, who on that particular day weren't at home. As was his normal practice, Carl let himself into the house and, apparently, disturbed a burglary. The 13-year-old was callously shot in the head. As the result of an investigation by the now discredited West Midlands Crime Squad, four men were arrested and later convicted of the dreadful crime. It would take the legal system 17 years to come to the conclusion that the Bridgewater Four – Michael Hickey, Vincent Hickey, Jimmy Robinson and Patrick Molloy – didn't do it. The Hickey cousins and Robinson were immediately set free but it was too late for Molloy, who had died in prison in 1981. And the real killer of Carl Bridgewater has never been caught.

1978 was the year of the superhero (or heroine). I fell in love with an Amazonian goddess named Linda Carter. No, not the Linda Carter who was once runner-up in the Miss ICI Noxious Gas Division beauty competition, the good-looking one with a figure like the *Venus de Milo* but with arms, of course, and legs all the way up to her rather shapely chin. The fact that she usually wore a scanty red, white and blue costume with rather fetching gold trim and went around bashing the bad guys just made Wonder Woman all the more alluring.

She was the perfect counter-balance to that other legendary hero of DC Comics, Superman, who came to the big screen in 1978 in the capable hands of Christopher Reeve. *Grease* gave us that nagging 'Summer Nights' song, which wasn't too bad in the movie but, a hundred karaokes later, should be laid to rest; and Alan Parker confirmed his directorial talent with the harrowing *Midnight Express*. But it was *The Deer Hunter* that proved to be the year's dominant movie, picking up awards and nominations by the dozen. Thankfully, Maggie Smith struck a blow for the Brits when collecting the Best Supporting Actress award at the Oscars for her part in *Coming Home*.

TV also introduced us to three young actors who would go on to do rather well for themselves: Todd Carty, Susan Tully and Michelle Gayle were all seen for the first time in school drama *Grange Hill*, long before they made their performing homes in the BBC soap *EastEnders*. You might also remember that 1978 was the year *Top Gear* went national but have you any idea who the first presenter was? Would you believe Angela Rippon? I know Jeremy Clarkson looks old enough to have been there from the beginning but he is a relative Johnny-Come-Lately, joining the show in 1988.

On to *Dallas*, with Larry Hagman magnificent as the totally amoral JR Ewing, leading a cast of the most disturbed characters you could see outside Prime Minister's Question Time. Wealth, sex, intrigue and power struggles ... yes, it really was Westminster with padded shoulders! Remember JR's long-suffering wife S'wellen played by the gorgeous Linda Gray; Ken Kercheval as the scheming Cliff Barnes, who could never quite get the better of wily old JR? And my favourite, pretty little Charlene Tilton as Lucy Ewing, who will live long in the memory, thanks to presenter Terry Wogan's wickedly affectionate nickname for her ... the Poison Dwarf. Not nice, Tel!

In the music world a phenomenon was born on the US TV show *Saturday Night Live* when a band called The Blues Brothers made their first appearance. It was the brainchild of comedians Dan Akroyd and John Belushi, an idea dreamed up for a TV sketch which begat a best-selling album, a cult movie and, certainly in the UK, a highly lucrative cottage industry for tribute acts. And in a similar way, a song written and originally recorded by country artiste Don Schlitz took Kenny Rogers to Number One and into the movies, with five films and a TV series all spinning off the success of *The Gambler*. However, it was sayonara to The Sex Pistols, torn apart by bassist Sid Vicious and his tempestuous relationship with groupie Nancy Spungin. In October of the same year Nancy was found dead, stabbed with a knife owned by Vicious. He confessed to the murder but never stood trial, dying from a drugs overdose in January 1979.

Best-selling single of the year was the Bee Gees' 'Stayin' Alive', with The Village People's 'YMCA' running them close.

Muhammed Ali celebrated his 36th birthday in 1978 and once again he confounded everyone by rewriting the record books. Early in the year he gave a near-supine display against up-and-coming fighter Leon Spinks, who was contesting only the eighth bout of his pro career. But Spinks was not the brightest: he made several poor career decisions, which saw his title taken away from him before he agreed to a rematch with Ali for the WBA crown. Ali took the upstart apart and thus became the first man to win the heavyweight title three times.

There was yet another death in motorsport, with the likeable Swede Ronnie Peterson succumbing to injuries he received in a huge pile-up at the start of the Italian Grand Prix at Monza.

1979

The early-morning California sun was warming the pastel blue sky when 16-year-old Brenda Spencer opened fire. It was a Monday ... and Brenda didn't like Mondays. They got her down, made her feel blue. So on this particular Monday morning in January 1979 she took a treasured birthday gift from her father – a .22 semi-automatic rifle (complete with 500 rounds of ammunition) – and, from her home, she shot at people in and around Cleveland Elementary School, San Carlos, which was just across the road. She felt better afterwards.

Two adults lay dead, eight children aged between six and eleven, and a police officer were injured and, briefly, Brenda Spencer was famous. Thirty years on, her name is virtually forgotten but her savage, mindless villainy is immortalised in the Boomtown Rats' classic hit 'I Don't Like Mondays', which topped the UK chart in July 1979. Rats' vocalist Bob Geldof was in the southern city of

Atlanta when the airwaves suddenly burst alive with the shocking news – 'I wrote it in Atlanta about 20 minutes after I was doing a college interview and they were playing tracks and the telex machine was coming through with the news and I was just reading it, as the machine disgorged this stuff.'

Somehow a journalist had been able to get a call through to little Miss Spencer, gun in hand, and asked her if she was trying to kill anyone in particular. Then he asked her why she was doing it ... and out came the stunningly banal yet chilling statement, 'Because I don't like Mondays.' Geldof couldn't shake the line from his head and slowly the lyrics emerged. Brenda Spencer was eventually convicted of murdering the school principal and its caretaker, wounding eight children and a police officer. She is currently serving two twenty-five-to-life sentences. All her appeals for parole have been turned down.

While Bob and the Rats were maintaining their climb from raw punk to everyday pop, a new influence was emerging with groups like Madness, The Specials and Bad Manners, who had plundered an original Jamaican genre called Ska and given it a commercial makeover to produce hits like 'One Step Beyond' and 'Too Much Too Young'. And two decades later Ska lives on, with Madness in particular still skanking like good 'uns.

Eurovision also came up with a bit of a phenomenon when the final was held in Israel. Not noted as one of the great cradles of modern music, it comes as a bit of a surprise to discover that Israel had won in 1978 with the memorable 'A-Ba-Ni-Bi' and then hung on to the title 12 months later with a song called 'Hallelujah' by Gail Atari – no computer jokes, please – and her backing group, Milk and Honey. The phenomenon is that 'Hallelujah' was later translated into 82 different languages, earning it a place in *The Guinness Book of Records*, and has been voted by contest fans as the best Eurovision song ever. And I always thought it was Lulu's 'Boom Bang A Bang!' The year started with Village People at Number One with 'YMCA' and ended, surprisingly, with Pink Floyd's 'Another Brick In The Wall' as the Christmas chart-topper.

On 4 May the face of British politics changed dramatically and entered one of the most significant periods in recent history when the Conservatives ousted Jim Callaghan's Labour government and Grantham grocer's daughter Margaret Hilda Thatcher became the first female prime minister in history, walking through the door of Number 10 with those oft-repeated words, 'Where there is discord, may we bring harmony. Where there is error, may we bring truth. Where there is doubt, may we bring faith. And where there is despair, may we bring hope.'

Only a few weeks earlier Airey Neave, one of her closest political allies and a World War Two hero who had famously escaped from Colditiz Castle, was blown up by Irish dissidents in the car park of the Houses of Parliament. It was a portent of the violence that would mark Mrs Thatcher's tenure. Later in the year Lord Louis Mountbatten was assassinated when an IRA bomb destroyed his pleasure boat near his Irish holiday home, on the same day that 18 British soldiers were killed at Warrenpoint, County Down. The year ended with crisis in the Middle East when more than 50 US Embassy staff in Tehran were taken hostage at the start of a 444-day ordeal.

In the movies John Hurt was seen having a touch of tummy trouble in the sci-fi shocker *Alien*, Dustin Hoffman and Meryl Steep had a memorable courtroom battle over custody of their son in *Kramer vs. Kramer*, which proceeded to sweep up an armful of Oscars and Golden Globes, and a new kid appeared on the block, riding a junk machine across a post-apocalyptic landscape, hunting down the greasy bastards that killed his wife. The *Mad Max* franchise was born and Mel Gibson was en route for the stratosphere.

TV came up with its own cult hero but of a much gentler nature. *Worzel Gummidge*, starring Jon Pertwee as the wart-faced, cake-eating scarecrow, came to life in 1979, as did two other classic comedies: *To The Manor Born* and *Minder*, starring Dennis Waterman, who had just transfered from *The Sweeney*. The first episode was called 'Gunfight at the OK Laundrette'. Catherine Bach flashed the best pair of legs since Betty Grable in *The Dukes of Hazzard* but it was the final curtain for *Fawlty Towers*. After only two series and just 12 episodes the team bowed out with the brilliant instalment titled 'Basil The Rat'.

BIBLIOGRAPHY

Biting Talk: My Autobiography, Norman Hunter, Hodder and Stoughton Ltd (2004)

Bob Paisley: Manager of the Millennium, John Keith, Robson Books Ltd (1999)

The Bumper Book of Football, Hunter P Davies, Quercus (2007)

Charlie George – My Story, Charlie George, Century (2005)

Cloughie: Walking On Water: My Life, Brian Clough, Headline (2005)

Colin Bell – Reluctant Hero: The Autobiography of a Manchester City and England Legend, Colin Bell (with Ian Cheeseman), Mainstream Publishing (2006)

Daily Telegraph Football Chronicle, Norman Barrett, Ebury Press (1996)

The Doc: My Story – Hallowed be Thy Game, Tommy Docherty, Headline (2007)

England! England! The Complete Who's Who of Players Since 1946, Dean Hayes, The History Press Ltd (2004)

England – The Official F.A. History, Niall Edworthy, Virgin Books (1997)

England, Their England: The Definitive Story of Foreign Footballers in the English Game, Nick Harris, Pitch Publishing (2004)

The England Managers: The Impossible Job, Brian Scovell, NPI Media Group (2006)

The Football Hall of Fame: The Ultimate Guide to the Greatest Footballing Legends of All Time, Robert Galvin & The National Football Museum, Portico (2011)

Guinness Record of the World Cup: 1930–1994, Jack Rollin, Guinness Publishing (1994)

The Guinness Football Encyclopedia, Graham Hart (ed), Guinness World Records Limited (1995)

Hooligans Vol. 2: M–Z of Britain's Hooligan Gangs v. 2, Nick Lowles and Andy Nicholls, Milo Books (2007)

The Mavericks: English Football When Flair Wore Flares, Rob Steen, Mainstream Publishing (1995)

One Hump Or Two? The Frank Worthington Story, Frank Worthington (with Steve Wells and Nick Cooper), Polar Print Group Ltd (1994)

Provided You Don't Kiss Me: 20 Years with Brian Clough, Duncan Hamilton, Harper Perennial (2008)

Rothmans Football League Club Guide, 1975–76, Leslie Vernon and Jack Rollin (eds), Queen Anne (1975)

Shanks: The Authorised Biography of Bill Shankly, Dave Bowler, Orion (2013)

Three Lions On The Shirt: Playing for England: 100 Years of Playing for England, Dave Bowler, Orion (2000)

True Grit, Frank McLintock, Headline (2006)

The Umbro Book of Football Quotations, Peter Ball and Phil Shaw (eds), Stanley Paul (1993)

The Unforgiven: The Story of Don Revie's Leeds United, Rob Bagchi and Paul Rogerson, Aurum Press Ltd (2009)

ACKNOWLEDGEMENTS

I would love to say this was all my own work but anyone who has toiled over a book like this knows that can never be the truth. There are so many people who have been involved at some step of the way that I am sure to miss out a name or two. If it is you, I apologise, but that doesn't mean I am not grateful. No one deserves more thanks than Duncan Hamilton, who didn't just unlock the door for me to achieve a lifelong ambition, he held it wide open and led me through, step by step. On the other side of that door, which Ian Johnson helped me step through, was John Blake Publishing, who took me on; special thanks to Chris Mitchell at John Blake for his patience and guidance. I must say a big thank you to Graham Glen and Malcolm Pheby, former editors of the *Nottingham Evening Post*, who gave me unfettered access to the photographic archives, and to Carolyn Maginnis, one-time stalwart of the library who patiently helped me sort them out. Brian Saunders provided much-needed enlightenment on the world of referees, and the input and encouragement of David Lowe, who has been down this road before, counted for a lot. The most important people should be left to the last so I will now say a huge thank you to my family who give me so much. As for the book, my son Jonathan came up with his appropriate memories and a whole lot more besides; my daughter Emma gave me the benefit of her considerable experience of the literary world; and my wife Jean was there for the dark moments, of which there were many.

INDEX

INDEX

Hennessey, Terry 119, 161
Herd, David 249
Hereford United FC 34, 59–63, 70
Heynckes, Jupp 101, 108
Hibbitt, Terry 60, 61
Hidegkuti, Nandor 177–8
Hill, Gordon 50, 187, 223, 226
Hill, Jimmy 221
Hindley, Peter 126
Hinton, Alan 119
Hoddle, Glenn 160
Hodgson, Roy 160, 267
Hoeness, Uli 147
Holland national side 25–6, 257, 258–60
Hollins, John 38, 40, 183
Holmes, Nick 47
hooliganism 7, 135–52, 262
    politicians vow to stamp out 151
    'symptom of ill health' 152
    and terrace 'poets' 137
Hooligans 2 (Lowles, Nicholls) 136
Houseman, Peter 39
Houston, Stewart 185, 205
Howard, Pat 144
Howe, Don 78, 80, 86, 190
Howell, Denis 141, 151
Huddersfield Town FC 90, 94, 218, 224
Hudson, Alan 4, 41, 52, 160, 171, 252
Hughes, Emlyn 9, 20, 25, 31, 44, 49, 50,
    99–100, 101, 108, 109, 121, 244, 247
Hull City FC 138, 218
Humble, Wilf 197
Hungary national side 258
Hunt, Ernie 222
Hunt, Roger 95, 96, 97, 98
Hunter, Norman 19, 20, 21, 39, 58, 59, 161,
    179
Hurst, Geoff 16, 17, 20, 30, 201, 220, 246
Hutchinson, Ian 39, 41

Ibrox 297–8
IFK Göteborg FC 147
Ince, Paul 211
Inter Milan 97
Ipswich Town FC 12, 34, 66, 173, 188,
    190–1, 266
    FA Cup win of 51–4, 191
Italy national side 25, 31, 212, 258

Jackson, Tommy 72, 126
Jago, Gordon 22, 168, 169
Jairzinho 18, 233, 234–5, 294
James, Leighton 65
Jennings, Eric 40
Jennings, Pat 53, 55, 84, 150, 238
Jensen, John 266
Johanneson, Albert 199, 200, 254
John, Elton 4, 87, 210
Johns, Hugh 19, 20
Johnson, David 49
Johnson, Terry 67, 68, 69
Johnston, Willie 257
Jones, Joey 49, 50, 107
Jones, Mick 39, 41, 57, 179
Jones, Roger 68
Jongbloed, Jan 259, 260
Jordan, Joe 54, 55, 257, 258
Juventus FC 5, 25, 122

Kaká 290
Kanchelskis, Andrei 266
Keane, Roy 248, 249
Keegan, Kevin 5, 9, 25, 30, 31, 44–5, 49, 50,
    99–100, 101–2, 106, 108, 108–9, 121,
    132, 148, 196, 250–1
    on Paisley 105
    Revie alienates 24
Keizer, Gerrit 265
Kellett, Les 37
Kelly, Eddie 81, 83, 85
Kempes, Mario 259, 260
Kendall, Howard 196
Kennedy, Ray 49, 76, 80, 82, 86, 107
Kettering Town FC 64
Kew, Gordon 144, 145, 219
Kialunda, Julian 80–1
Kick Racism out of Football 212
    see also black players; racism
Kidd, Brian 186
Kidd, George 37
Kirkland, Jack 123
Kirkpatrick, Roger 219
Kirton, Glen 28–9
Kitabdjian, Michel 147
Klondyke Kate 37
Kneib, Wolfgang 108
Kreitlin, Rudolf 14
Kwango, Johnny 37

INDEX